Twayne's Theatrical Arts Series

Warren French
EDITOR

Nicholas Ray

Nicholas Ray
Ray directing Ida Lupino in *On Dangerous Ground*
credit: American Academy of Motion Picture Arts and Sciences

Nicholas Ray

JOHN FRANCIS KREIDL

BOSTON

Twayne Publishers

1977

Published by Twayne Publishers,
A Division of G. K. Hall & Co.
Copyright © 1977 by G. K. Hall & Co.
All Rights Reserved
First Printing

Library of Congress Cataloging in Publication Data

Kreidl, John.
  Nicholas Ray.
  (Twayne's theatrical arts series)
  Bibliography: p. 219–20.
  Filmography: p. 221–28.
  Includes index.
  1. Ray, Nicholas, 1911–   2. Rebel without a
cause. [Motion picture] I. Title.
PN1998.A3R347   791.43'0233'0924   77-23514
ISBN 0-8057-9250-3

MANUFACTURED IN THE UNITED STATES OF AMERICA

Contents

About the Author

John Francis Kreidl's involvement with film dates from childhood attendance at screenings arranged by the film club founded by his father, Dr. Norbert Kreidl, who developed the glass used for the CinemaScope lens, James Card, now curator of the Eastman Museum's Film and Archival Branch, and Vachel Lindsay Blair, a newsreel cameraman, all of whom are early influences on his film career. Mr. Kreidl made his first short film, a one hour 16mm black and white narrative film, *Gunfight at Copper Creek* while an undergraduate at Swarthmore College. Mr. Kreidl graduated from the University of Rochester with a B.S. in chemistry and while a graduate student in Vienna, he made his second movie. *Tom Dooley in Vienna* was a serious experimental film in 8mm with sound starring Hungarian actress Eva von Wornay, Austrian actor Gerhard Poechsteiner and himself. The film was shot so the final sequence was visually post-synchronized with the Kingston Trio version of the song, "Tom Dooley."

Since 1963, Mr. Kreidl has studied film both formally and contextually. He has not specialized in either American or European cinema but has continued to study and write about both. In 1974 and 1975, he attended Harvard University for a special course in cinematic analysis taught by Professor Vladimir Petric and since 1975 has been Professor Petric's research assistant.

Mr. Kreidl has published over one hundred articles, essays, interviews, translations, and film reviews in both scholarly and popular media. The June 1977 issue of *Academic Film Quarterly* will include one of his essays. He is the author of two forthcoming Twayne Theater Arts series volumes on Alain Resnais and Jean-Luc Godard and has co-authored, with Professor Petric, a forthcoming study of the Soviet pioneer of the documentary and self-referential film, Dziga Vertov. Mr. Kreidl also holds two U.S. patents in chemistry and has recently applied for a process patent on a method for producing perfect CinemaScopic aspect ratio frame enlargements.

Editor's Preface

This first detailed critical study in English of Nick Ray should be viewed as both a trail-blazing tribute to a too much overlooked artist and as part of a collaborative publishing venture that seeks to provide—to use a cinematic term—a "montage" of creative achievement in the distinctively twentieth-century art of film and in the other theatrical arts. Eventually this overall design should enable serious students of public spectacle to perceive the achievements of those who have worked through the performing arts to shape our international culture, both as individual masters and in their relationship to the breathtakingly rapid growth of these arts throughout the world.

Long an admirer and student of Nicholas Ray's work, John Francis Kreidl properly focuses this book on *Rebel Without a Cause* as the climax of Ray's artistic career and as the film that emblemizes the confused sensibility of the United States during a period of crisis. Kreidl shows how Ray, through all his earlier ventures, was moving toward *Rebel* and his unique collaboration with James Dean. Then, following the film from its inception to its international reception, Kreidl shows how the team of Ray and Dean worked together to create a mythological film that remains one of those most often viewed by restless young people. Had Dean lived to work with Ray on other films, this book might tell a much different story; but after Dean's sudden death, Ray could never hit upon the right combination to make a second masterful film—nor could young America find a new idol to replace the still-revered James Dean.

Rebel Without a Cause remains not just the isolated peak at the center of Ray's career, but the emblematic revelation of American hysteria at the midpoint of those aimless years of disenchantment between the end of World War II and the inauguration of President John F. Kennedy. During those years the United States itself was a "rebel without a cause"—reaching the limits of nearly two centuries of incessant expansion (except for the moon and stars), while the restless, immature energies that had made this expansion possible still seethed beneath the surface and boiled over into "chickie runs" everywhere from small-town drag-strips to unstable international borders. As John Kreidl points out, *Rebel Without a Cause* remains uniquely valuable in its embodiment of the 1950s, and it well repays the close structural analysis made of it here.

WARREN FRENCH

Preface

One of the prime theses of this book is that Ray deserves credit for pushing (or helping to push) the American cinema from the crude second generational stage he inherited (and Hollywood inherited) from D. W. Griffith to a more advanced form that would be later perfected in Europe as an ontological cinema, a cinema of experience and not just psychologism or narrative, a true third generation, in the never-too-systematic evolution of the cinema medium. In practical terms, this meant he helped film to move from a stage of incarnating heroes (such as in his early film, *Knock on Any Door*) and making B-grade color films *(The Flying Leathernecks)*, toward a supremely confident mise-en-scéne style that could bring forth nuances no matter what the topic of the film *(Rebel Without a Cause* and *Party Girl)*. For this reason a study of Nick Ray's films should make a good subject for a university course particularly because of its relevance to five areas of filmic/sociological interest.

First, those who are interested in the technical and creative evolution of American cinema as entertainment will find that Nick Ray's twenty films are as good an example of the cumulative and continuing development of Hollywood cinema as the work of either Howard Hawks or John Ford. From 1945 to 1960, the American cinema evolved into a serious art medium and became a world power in the arts. Ray did more than the above two gentlemen to see that the American cinema did progress, for he did not confine himself to presenting filmed variations on the same old fictive themes but was also very aware that the cinema required its own unique language and methodology. He advanced filmic discourse by his use of cutting in CinemaScope and by employing acting and dialogue in new ways. Indeed Ray did more than any other American director, including Elia Kazan, to adapt Method Acting to the iconography of the cinema. However, none of these technical innovations was employed purely for its own sake. Ray, by his incessant interest in social confrontation and in America's nervous system, rather than in its Hollywoodized myths and in its autohyped, intellectualized, "egg-headistic," self-righteous concept of itself, and, in particular, by his understanding of young people both in and out of film, ("no one could direct young people as well as Nick Ray"—Alan Pakula) made his own personal progress in his chosen medium. So plastic was the period during which he directed such epics as *Rebel Without a Cause*, his best-known film, that many of his cinematic innovations and pro-youth attitudes went undetected! We now know better, and in this book I hope to correct the critical neglect of Nick Ray as an artist uniquely in touch with his time.

Secondly, Ray was a pioneer who, nevertheless, could work within a system. "Film is an eclectic and a collective art," he was fond of saying. His unique rebel-with-a-system approach deserves socio-historical study for its own sake, and this can be done through his films. His battles with studios eventually drove him away from Hollywood forever, but, as his co-worker Robert Wagner, Natalie Wood's husband, observed that "Ray seemed to do his best work when rebelling against the studio as a sort of father figure.

By reason of his neurosis, Ray was able to span a gap between an older and a younger generation. He liked the power of being a Hollywood director; but, he always openly sided with youth. He maintained the creative power of a member of the older generation, while, at the same time, being in total sympathy with the younger one. This led to such curious and powerful films as *Rebel Without a Cause* (1955) and *Johnny Guitar* (1953), adult-crafted but very youth-oriented films in their own, unique, far-seeing ways.

Thirdly, Ray should interest those who are concerned with the development of the technical palette of any art form, in this case, the cinema. Since roughly half of his twenty-odd films are in CinemaScope, his pioneering of that medium (which has contributed to the fact that the *average* aspect ratio of the present day movie is 1:1.85 and not the academy ratio of 1:1.33) deserves the same kind of art historical study, surely, as the lighting techniques of Karl Freund and F. W. Murnau, or Reuben Mamoulian's pioneering of three-color Technicolor, or Peter Bogdanovich's use of 45 rpm records as verbal lietmotifs in *The Last Picture Show*. What Ray accomplished here is unfortunately taken for granted today, and he has gotten none of the credit he deserved for raising the CinemaScope film form from an oddity to an art form. In short, Ray developed a new way of seeing in "Scope" that was envisaged by only a very few others, notably Anthony Mann in the U.S. and, later, Truffaut, Godard, and Antonioni in Europe.

Fourthly, Ray is important for his special influence on the French New Wave film directors, particularly François Truffaut (when you see Truffaut's *Adele H,* you also see Ray's *Johnny Guitar*) and Eric Rohmer (Jean-Marie Maurice Sherer), who first spoke of the *moral tale* in conjunction with Ray's *Rebel Without a Cause* and its purity of purpose. From Ray's cinema to France and back again, via the New Wave, is very reminiscent of our own rock 'n' roll going to England and coming back again via the Beatles. As Ray himself said, "America has only ever had two cultural exports, movies and jazz!"

And finally, there is Ray as Americana. Ray, in a way he himself could not have foreseen (but now something completely realized by "nostalgia buffs"), was so much of an archetypal creator and incarnator of the American 1950s, that his cinema created pop sociology and now deserves pop sociological consideration on all levels, including on the lowbrow, mass culture level that launched his protege, James Byron Dean, as America's teen-ager off the screens of *Rebel Without a Cause.* Those who watch the TV show, "Happy Days," (currently one of the most popular shows in the U.S.) probably don't realize that, in his *Rebel Without a Cause,* Ray invented the characters we see there, many times over. James Dean, at the beginning of the story of *Rebel,* is what Richie Cunningham (of "Happy Days") is. Fonzie is what all teen-agers in 1955 respected (though most wouldn't have wanted to have been him) and was represented in *Rebel* by the character called Crunch.

Ray also represents Americana in a deeper sense. Let me explain.

I have always thought of Nick Ray, and his fellow directors, Orson Welles, and Joseph Losey as being upper-middle-class Midwestern Americans, who, through their good characters, faith in themselves, and intelligence, functioned *like* upper-class Americans—like an aristocracy of character—along with all that implies, whereas William Randolph Hearst ("Citizen Kane") to me represents the upper-class American who is only upper class because of money— who behaves like a plastic, wishy-washy, upper-middle-class citizen, a Mr. Magoo, not unlike the caricature of the California father played by Jim Backus in Ray's *Rebel Without a Cause*. This similarity is the only real point of connection between the themes of the films of these Midwestern contemporaries.

As directors, they had quite different goals, though all of them are aesthetic formalists and not fiction filmmakers in the straight Hollywood mold, nor documentarists. In addition, all three were difficult and fussy about their product. It would be an injustice to all three of these bold men to lump them any closer together. In fact, it is their vastly diverse aims and the relative differences in their popular success that make a fascinating story. Welles had the magical touch; Losey, the austere, cramped touch; Ray, the popular touch. While Ray's films were either popular or remained unknown, Welles' were terribly controversial, and Losey's little known. None of the three attracted pseudo-intellectual followers. None ever won an Academy Award. In terms of commercial success, it was, not surprisingly, Ray's films that did best at the box office in proportion to their cost. The public responded to his accessibility more than they ever did to Welles' best magic or Losey's most sincere psychological studies. Finally, and this is where Ray departs the most from his peers, Ray was a notorious eclectic, an unrepentant eclectic in the best sense—not confined to any single, imitative style—twenty years before it was fashionable to be one.

Something else Ray, Welles, and Losey had in common—but this is definitely only an outgrowth of their being aesthetic formalists: they all began their careers with a strong first film, Welles with *Citizen Kane* in 1941, Losey with *The Boy with Green Hair* in 1948, and Ray with *They Live by Night* (made in 1947, released in Great Britain in 1948 and in the United States in 1949). One could say—both from "reading" their earlier films and listening to their statements—that all three kept faith with the individual during a period when America merged into the global mass. It is interesting to speculate how Ray's career might have differed had he been part of a movement rather than a loner.

But they separated quite soon. In fact, the three separated geographically. Welles went to New York and then to Hollywood; Losey went East to Dartmouth and on to England; Ray went to Chicago. Losey became an Eastern intellectual and finally a quasi-Englishman; Welles became a citizen of the world; Ray remained, even though he lived in Hollywood for ten years and travelled widely, the man whose contact with the Midwest remained strongest. This later was to help bring him together with a similar personality—James Dean.

Frank Lloyd Wright, under whom Ray studied, once proclaimed: "Early in life I had to choose between honest arrogance and hypocritical humility. I chose honest arrogance and have seen no reason to change." Though Ray's personal behavior is not to be equated with Wright's grandiose, Florentine temperament, he did display the same Midwestern iconoclasm, the same belief in independent thought, the same belief in the individual—all beliefs which would later cause Ray to be revolted by Senator Joseph McCarthy (also, ironically from Wisconsin) and to revolt against him.

Ray, like Wright, must have made a similar choice about arrogance; but on the several occasions that I have observed Ray with other people, I did notice a much milder man who seemed, however, to want to be bitchier than he was and more like Wright and other super-iconoclasts. Ray is not without his own brand of arrogance, but it is more that of the craftsman or the ship's captain than that of the temperamentalist. One of Ray's self-defining statements in *I'm a Stranger Here Myself*, the documentary film made about him, shows the former kind of arrogance: "And finally, there is the director. Everything ends with me."

Unlike Orson Welles, who is still trying to make his *one* successful film after *Citizen Kane*, Ray almost made his successful film several times over, with *Rebel Without A Cause* coming closer than any other to being a classic. His *They Live by Night* and *Knock on Any Door* rivaled Henry Hathaway's *The Kiss of Death* as among the best *film noirs* by cult standards and also as good entertainment. But these were early versions of *Rebel*.

Nick Ray, as a filmmaker, has to be honored for being a man who was effective in his time, the period between 1947 and 1962—perhaps the most peculiar, unpredictable period in American film history. These fifteen years spanned the time from his making *They Live by Night* to his walking off the *55 Days at Peking* project.

It is important to note two things about the accident of time in Ray's career. First, he quit (just in time) before film criticism switched from daily newspaper style to cultist style. He retired from the scene, therefore, before he would have been "discovered" as an articulate interview subject and a "fascinating person" to spin articles around. (It was at this time that a character in Bernardo Bertolucci's *Before the Revolution*, in a bar sequence, suddenly, glowingly refers to the magnificence of a Nick Ray 360-degree pan shot in *Johnny Guitar*. But this type of homage was yet to come in American "criticism.") Second, the historical period during which Ray's films were made was not "the 50s"—the early 1950s belong to 1940–55 as a period and the late 1950s to 1955–63, thus Ray's cinema traversed two fundamentally different periods in the nation's film history and in its social development. *Rebel Without a Cause* was the median film, both chronologically and emotionally, in Ray's career and probably its psychological high-water mark. *Rebel* suggested, in a visionary way, what the next period might demand, more sincerity and involvement from our youth, a reason why this film stands alone in both Ray's development and in American film history.

It is hoped that the above information will help the reader to see why this book, the first full-length critical study of Nick Ray to include all of his films, was written.

Finally, the approach to Ray's cinema that I have taken is biocritical, rather than structural. I have concentrated on showing Ray's intentions and relating the results of his films to his intentions, something that is closer to an author analysis than an attempt to read his films independently of their authorship. I like to call this approach a Husserlian analysis of the synthetic intentionality, one perceived through cross-analysis of the resultant film with the director's *known* intentionalities. This method works fine with Nick Ray as he is not metonymic, but, of course, can not be used where little or fallacious biographical material exists (say, as in the case of Italian director, Michelangelo Antonioni.

In the case of *Rebel Without a Cause*, I have departed from the above approach by adding a specialized chapter on the relationship of Ray's narrative to image, and also sections on the cinematic conversion of nonfilmic dialogue to filmic-like dialogue, as this was one of Ray's special talents. The narrative/image analysis and the dialogue analysis are evaluative; the rest of the book attempts to maintain more distance from evaluation, in order to allow Nick Ray's approach to speak for itself.

It is hoped that Nick Ray will emerge as a somewhat gruffer, less romantic personality than the idealistic tone of his films indicates, and that the reader will appreciate some of the struggle that gave his filmmaking that optimistic but never false ring that makes it vibrant even today.

Acknowledgments

I would like to thank the following people who helped me: David Helpern Jr., who gave me vital information, and whose film, *I'm a Stranger Here Myself* helped spark the rediscovery of Ray; Boyd Norcross, Jr. for the frame enlargements; Vladimir Petric, for discouraging thematic analysis; Leonard Roseman for suggesting that we permanently bury James Dean, and for his help on the *Rebel* chapters; Nick Browne, for discussions on narrative and structure; Ed Mark, for screening *CinemaScope* Westerns in *CinemaScope*. I would also like to thank Walter Hitesman, who more than any one, helped me escape the laudatory-uncritical climate of the late 60s, and helped me to refuse to write this book any other way than the way I did. Thanks go, as well, to Warner Bros. for letting me see the shooting script of *Rebel*. Picture credits include Warner Bros. Republic Films, The Museum of Modern Art Film Stills Archive and The American Academy of Motion Picture Arts and Sciences, and Thomas Consilvio. Finally, this book is dedicated to Nick Ray, who should have written this book himself, but who never did.

Chronology

1911   Nicholas Ray born Raymond Nicholas Kienzle in LaCrosse, Wisconsin, on August 7.

1929   Wins scholarship to the University of Chicago; studies under Frank Lloyd Wright in workshop-seminar group.

1930   Marries for the first time and was later divorced. (The name of Mr. Ray's first wife is not generally known and Mr. Ray has not been forthcoming on the subject.)

1931   Son Tony born.

1935–   Involved in Theater of Action as an actor; meets John
1937   Houseman and Elia Kazan.

1937   Travels around the Rocky Mountains; studies American folklore, meets singer Woodie Guthrie.

1938   Loses sight of right eye in accident that makes him 4-F during World War II.

1942   Named by John Houseman to radio section of U.S. Office of War Information.

1944   Goes with Elia Kazan to Hollywood as assistant director on *A Tree Grows in Brooklyn*.

1947   Directs first film, *They Live by Night* (not released in U.S.A. until 1949).

1948   Marries actress Gloria Hallward Grahame and directs her in *A Woman's Secret*.

1949   Directs *Knock on Any Door*.

1950   Directs *In a Lonely Place* with Humphrey Bogart and Gloria Grahame. Secretly separates from Grahame during filming. Directs *Born to Be Bad*.

1951   Directs *On Dangerous Ground* and *The Flying Leathernecks* (the latter for Howard Hughes).

1952   Directs *The Lusty Men*.

1953   Regards himself as "greylisted" and goes to Spain to direct
        Joan Crawford in *Johnny Guitar.*

1954   *Johnny Guitar* released in U.S.A. in May; gets office at
        Warner Brothers studio and meets James Dean.

1955   Directs *Rebel Without a Cause, Run for Cover,* and *Hot
        Blood;* heartbroken at accidental death of James Dean.

1956   Directs *Bigger Than Life.* Visits Paris and begins having
        heavy contact with *Cahiers du Cinema* cinéastes.

1957   Directs *The True Story of Jesse James,* but refuses to edit
        film; increasingly dissatisfied with Hollywood, despite high
        salaries, he goes abroad to direct *Bitter Victory.*

1958   Back in U.S.A. to direct *Wind Across the Everglades* and
        Party Girl; works with an Italian company on *The Savage
        Innocents.*

1959   Researches *King of Kings* project in Europe.

1961   *King of Kings* released in U.S.A.

1962   Directs and acts in *55 Days at Peking,* his last Hollywood-
        style epic, but doesn't complete it. Second unit director An-
        drew Marston finishes it when Ray walks off set to begin
        six-year "European exile."

1962–   Based in Paris, but travels extensively, contemplating un-
1968   fulfilled projects.

1967   In Zagreb, Yugoslavia, to direct *The Doctors and the Devil;*
        designs set, but never finishes film, which is completed by
        Italian director Baldi; spends time with Claude Chabrol
        in Paris.

1968   Returns to Chicago to try to make film about violence at
        Democratic National Convention in house rented for pur-
        pose by Marcel Ophuls; some footage appears in Ophuls'
        America Revisited (1972).

1971–   Hired to teach advanced seminar in practical filmmaking at
1973   Harpur College (State University of New York, Bingham-
        ton); attempts to complete film variously titled "Gun Under
        My Pillow" and "You Can't Go Home Again," but never
        does.

1974   Attends Cannes Festival; subject of a documentary film by
        David Helpern, Jr., *I'm a Stranger Here Myself.*

1975   Screens incomplete "You Can't Go Home Again" in New
        York City (where he continues to live) to poor reception; also
        appears in segment of a pornographic film playing a janitor
        having erotic fantasy.

1

The Man from Wisconsin

NICK RAY WAS BORN Raymond Nicholas Kienzle in LaCrosse, Wisconsin, on August 7, 1911. LaCrosse, on the Mississippi River, is heartland America, closer to Minneapolis than Chicago, yet close enough to the Windy City for one to gravitate there naturally if one were looking to make one's mark and yet not willing to lose one's regional identity. Joseph Losey, another film director of note, was born in LaCrosse two years before Ray; and both men's parents are buried in the cemetery there. But Losey chose Dartmouth and the East and eventually England, whereas Ray chose Chicago, so that their paths became unalterably separated. Two other area colleagues were to be two of the four major influences on Ray: George Orson Welles, born in Kenosha, Wisconsin, in 1915; and Frank Lloyd Wright, born in 1869, some forty miles from LaCrosse in Richland Center. (The two major influences from elsewhere—Elia Kazan and John Houseman—we will encounter later.)

At the age of sixteen, Ray let go with a burst of precocity and fired off a radio script to the University of Chicago. This won him a scholarship there during the great days of Robert Hutchins. Later, he studied architecture there under Frank Lloyd Wright; and from Wright he absorbed—or already paralleled him in believing—a statement that later would help make *Rebel Without a Cause*. "The real American spirit," Wright pontificated, "capable of judging an issue on its own merits, lies in the West and Midwest, where breadth of view, independent thought, and a tendency to take common sense into the realm of art, as in life, are more characteristic. It is alone in an atmosphere of this nature that the Gothic spirit of building [by organic craftsmanship working from within to without] can be revived."[1]

Ray was eighteen when the Depression began. As with many Americans, it changed the course of his life. In the early 1930s he

23

took a trip around America, married, had a son named Tony, and decided to become involved in theater as an actor/designer/director. He was in the Theater of Action, a travelling collective road company, and the functioning of this group was to remain an ideal of his, a model of how a film community should work. In 1935 he acted in a play that was Elia Kazan's first directorial effort at the Group Theater, *The Young Go First*. At this time, Ray also met Clifford Odets and other Group Theater people who were to figure later in his life. He knew Kazan, Losey, Harold Clurman, and probably was at least acquainted with everyone who functioned in playwriting in the group, although, strangely, Ray is not mentioned in Clurman's book on the Group Theater. He later joined John Houseman's Phoenix Theater Company in New York City when Orson Welles' Mercury Theater also became a reality in 1938 (Ray never, as far as we know, actually worked for Welles). He travelled throughout the United States, studying folklore, music (he knew Woodie Guthrie), and living for a time in the Rocky Mountains.

As radio drama was then as big as television is now, Ray next made inroads in this area. By 1941, at age thirty, he had shown promise not only as an actor and set designer, but also as a radio playwright and as an overall director of stage and radio productions. His eclectic background—a combination of the training of Fritz Lang and Orson Welles—was to prove invaluable to him in a Hollywood that afforded no such training ground.

After Pearl Harbor, Ray became a War Information Radio Program Director, thanks to John Houseman, who was made chief of the foreign service of the United States Office of War Information. If there had been any chance of Ray's being drafted in World War II, it was dispelled because he had lost the use of his right eye in a bizarre accident late in the 1930s. (The black eyepatch he wore was thus not quite the affectation of a Hollywood director.) In 1943 Ray wrote and directed a Broadway play, *Back Where I Came From*. He also directed and did the stage production for *Lute Song*, which also had a successful New York run. In 1944 Elia Kazan, by then a successfully established New York theater director, was offered the opportunity to direct films; and he took Ray along to Hollywood as his assistant director on the film version of *A Tree Grows in Brooklyn*.

On the Twentieth Century-Fox lot Ray kept a diary for himself and Kazan, in which he noted comments on how to make and deal with cinema. It was filled with such remarks as "don't overdirect" and "The hero should not be written better than you or I. You must recognize him as a fellow human. Then, under special circumstances, he becomes better than I." (Ray seems to have applied this statement to many of his films, notably *Rebel Without a Cause*.) Kazan's comment on Ray's notes was that "Nick liked that kind of generalization on aesthetics. A lot of them were influenced by [director Louis] Lighton and others were thoughts or things I said."[2]

Ray, back in New York, next directed Alfred Drake in *Beggar's Holiday*. John Houseman moved to CBS (which had pioneered television in 1940), and Ray adapted the enormously successful radio play, *Sorry, Wrong Number* for TV. Houseman paved the way for the next step in Ray's career. Having received a commission from Dore Schary, the executive producer at RKO studios, to produce *They Live By Night*, a *film-noir*-like vehicle based on Edward Anderson's novel *Thieves Like Us*, Houseman nobly agreed to produce only if Ray would be the film's director and be responsible for the screenplay. So, in 1947, at the age of thirty-six, Nick Ray began his Hollywood career as a director.

That same year he married aspiring film actress, Gloria Grahame Hallward, who had dropped her last name professionally and begun a lackadaisical career under her mother's maiden name. It was the second marriage for both.

2

Ray's Dark, Humanistic Cinema: 1947–1951

NICK RAY'S FIRST FILM, *They Live By Night* came about as a result of Dore Schary's wanting to try to make a series of low-budget films with new directors. Schary was to be personally responsible for the inauguration of Edward Dmytryk's *Crossfire* (1947) and Joseph Losey's *The Boy With The Green Hair* (1948). Ray's film, originally called *The Twisted Road,* was completed in August, 1947 and scheduled for 1948 release. In May, 1948, Howard Hughes took over control of RKO. Schary left the following month, and Hughes tabled release of *The Twisted Road* in the United States. It was released in England in late 1948 as *They Live By Night,* and in the United States in October, 1949, after Ray's second film, *A Woman's Secret* (1948) and Ray's third and quite successful film, *Knock on Any Door* (1949), with the result that the public became acquainted with Ray's second and third films as if they were his first and second. Such accidents of release dates often have strange positive or negative effects on the careers and reputations of directors; but in Ray's case it seems to have worked to his benefit as the simultaneous appearance of *They Live By Night* and *Knock on Any Door* gave him the immediate reputation of being skilled in showing both sensitivity (Farley Granger and Cathy O'Donnell as the Romeo and Juliet-like couple in *They Live By Night*) and toughness (the unrepentant bitterness of John Derek as Nick Romano in *Knock on Any Door.*)

They Live By Night was based on Edward Anderson's novel *Thieves Like Us.* Even though Ray's film and Robert Altman's later *Thieves Like Us* are based on the same story, they bear no resemblance to each other: Ray is seemingly more interested in the tragic love story and in the difference between the "good" and "bad" members of the gang; Altman, in concentrating on the sociology of the Depression South, a *Nashville*-like, regional study of ruralism and poverty, and on pictographic qualities that would show the

27

Gloria Grahame and Nick Ray on the set of *In A Lonely Place.*
credit: American Academy of Motion Picture Arts and Sciences

background and space in which the characters operated. One sees why *Bonnie and Clyde* (1967) was a milestone movie. Before that film was made, one could, as Ray did, excerpt a story out of the bigger story; after *Bonnie and Clyde*, one had to compete with and transcend it by making the film explain its characters. *They Live By Night* was a genre film, but one made in a *small*-scale way that does no harm to the genre of the "on the run" film, sub-genre: the Depression South. *Bonnie and Clyde* killed the genre by trying to make the story *bigger* than life, mythic, and impressionistic. *They Live By Night* holds up well, as it is Expressionistic, honest, and under Ray's control. In its concentration on the love story aspect of a gang, the film doesn't try for too much. Later on, in *The True Story of Jesse James*, Ray would tackle this genre again and stumble a bit.

Nick Ray's twelve years of theater experience taught him direction of actors and acting, but his only film experience before directing *They Live By Night* was as Elia Kazan's assistant director on *A Tree Grows in Brooklyn* (1944). (At this time, most Hollywood "A" films were still based on novels; theatrical experience for a director was thus not without use. But it did not, *per se*, prepare him for Hollywood film direction.)

As mentioned earlier, Ray not only assisted Kazan, but kept the log book full of comments on film craft for him. These comments were relevant to the direction and shooting of any motion picture, and a copy of the log, if it still exists, would be invaluable to any study of Nick Ray. In it, Ray noted such comments as Kazan's having said: "Don't direct a natural."[1] (This would become Nick's credo when dealing with James Dean.)

Considering Elia Kazan's influence on Nick Ray, what is so surprising about *They Live By Night* is not only that it shows such a mature style for a first film, but that it shows so little Kazan influence. After all, it is quite natural for an assistant director's first film away from the director he assisted to show some of the "master's" influence. Finally, with this film, Ray began his "off-centeredness," a critics' term that implied he never did anything one could easily peg. It was inevitable that critics would see *They Live By Night* much more as a typical *film noir* than as a heroic-tragic love story. (Would *Romeo and Juliet* be considered a *film noir?*)

Why Ray's early films are not *films noirs* needs a little explaining. *Film noir*, as used to describe certain American films, is an analog to the French literary term, *roman noir*, meaning "dark novel," Gothic novel. *Roman noir*, like *roman policier*, the police novel, were, to the French, sub-genres of literary specificity and familiarity. One didn't read such a genre book to find the unexpected. So, with the term *film noir*, the French took the liberty of creating a film genre by literary analogy. The French term suggests such films will be predictable and conform to some kind of synchronic topology. That topology would be some kind of mood, a sense of being in a dark world.

Unfortunately, American critics turned the term into a catchall. They turned a precise film term into an imprecise one, and created confusion. No longer is it possible even to try to distinguish and differentiate a *film noir* from an urban drama like *Force of Evil* (1948). How does one differentiate between films that are only shot at night, and daytime films that have a dark mood? Should we call the former *films soir* and the latter *films gris?* I would prefer to keep to a very strict interpretation of *film noir*, and limit the term to the 1940s films of Alfred Hitchcock, Robert Siodmak, Fritz Lang, Billy Wilder, and Orson Welles mentioned in the chapter on "Black Cinema" in Charles Higham and Joel Greenberg's *Hollywood In The Forties.*

All this is to argue that to see Nicholas Ray as starting out his film career as a bitter maker of the hopeless, hapless *film noir* is to lose all perspective of who he was and what he wanted his cinema to achieve. Ray's partially nocturnal urban dramas (more dramatic in structure than melodramatic in content) and his nocturnally "on the run" *They Live By Night*, his Bogart-Grahame (in place of Bacall) psychodrama in *In a Lonely Place* are all films of a unique kind. They are films of an aestheticized, architecturally invented place, peopled with highly realistic characters. (Look ahead to the imaginary high school full of real people in *Rebel*.) Ray, in his early films, did no *noirs*, but maintained a kind of tension—much as Italian neo-realism did in a much more forceful and socially conscious way—between an aesthetically imposed framework coming from the director, and a real following through of the characters' lives, giving them all the detail, authenticity, and credibility that is associated with documentary or street-location shooting. That is not to say that Ray could ever shoot *Mean Streets* without giving it his touch, but that he was opposed to the typical Hollywood melodramatic plots of the early 1940s.

Ray's early films were those of a Midwestern cosmopolitan person. (*Knock on Any Door* versus Abraham Polonsky's *Force of Evil* is the difference between Chicago and New York, as *Party Girl* versus *Scarface* is the distance between Ray's memory of Chicago and Hollywood's concept of it.) Yes. Ray created *Welts* (German— "worlds")—those old standbys of Expressionist filmmakers of the 1920s; but in these *Welts*, highly modern 1950s youth, restless Nick Romanos, and reformist Jim Starks roamed, guided not by Ray's hand so much as by his camera.

Ray's early films were all urban dramas depicting dark humanism: in them we find care, hope, naïve optimism, a sense of humanism seen through the perspectives of neurotics who feel crippled by it all, and we see that through the character development of his screen characters, or through his own personal slogans that he has his characters articulate, Ray insists that we try to confront life and improve it. Nick Romano in *Knock on Any Door* is on the bitter side as he does not have the background to make heads or tails of the postwar American society; Bogart and Grahame do not suffer the "you didn't love him enough" of Nick, but, in *In a Lonely Place*, they show the more sophisticated person's side of the same coin: marriage can't work smoothly as a panacea in a society loaded with malaises. Farley Granger and Cathy O'Donnell are the innocent side of America, Romeo and Juliet when they are young. Bogart and Grahame are the knowing side of America when it reaches middle age. In each case, these films strive toward a resolution, no matter how painful, rather than move rigidly toward a foregone conclusion, as in a classic *film noir*. (The identity of this genre is further discussed in A. M. Karimi's *Toward a Definition of American Film Noir (1941–1949)* (1976).

A *Woman's Secret* (1948) and Gloria Grahame

Ray's least known film is *A Woman's Secret* (1948). (It is one of the rare Hollywood feature films, for example, that was never reviewed in the *New York Times*.) RKO saw it as a vehicle for Gloria Grahame, then Ray's second wife. Her marriage to Ray lasted only two more years and they separated during the filming of *In a Lonely Place*. Ray praised Gloria for not spilling the beans on their separation, to the studio, for it would have meant his dismissal as director.[2] He also denies that his breakup with Grahame influenced the ending to the film.[3] His two films with Gloria Grahame show that he knew how to depict women with both sensitivity and authenticity.

Knock on Any Door (1949)

Ray's first film to be shown at a major New York theater (on February 23, 1949) was actually his third. *Knock on Any Door* ("And You'll Find a Nick Romano"), was based on Willard Motley's long, episodic, John Dos Passos-like novel of the same name. (The movie title should be viewed as a 1950s pop-song title, with the reprised answer in parentheses, following after the main statement: *Knock on Any Door.*) The film, in many ways, was a dry run for *Rebel Without A Cause*, despite the fact, that in Ray's mind, he was telling the story of *one* young individual, Nick Romano, and not of a *group* of teen-agers. Yet, on close viewings, there are striking similarities to *Rebel:* the bitter, hurt, throwaway lines of Nick (John Derek), the pool hall group as an equivalent of Buzz's gang in *Rebel*, the older, sympathetic man (lawyer Andrew Morton in *Knock on Any Door*, juvenile officer Ray Framek in *Rebel*) who tries to help the young man in trouble. There is the Romeo and Juliet-like love story of Nick and his girl friend, which is repeated in a better-told, less sentimental version in *Rebel*. The pacing of *Knock on Any Door* is superb. The camera is youth's camera, looking out, as in *Rebel*. Camera movement and cutting are less 1940-ish and more Ray-like: there is less of an attempt to match cuts, more of an attempt to show parallels between camera movement and anguish, to inform the viewer through cinematic means.

The film was popular. It undoubtedly gave Ray a needed boost to his career, separated him from the pack, so to speak, elevated him above any sobriquet of hack. Here, now, was a director to watch.

A most interesting evaluation of the film is suggested by Andrew Dowdy in *Films of the Fifties*. Comparing *Knock on Any Door* to *City Across the River*, a film on roughly the same theme, post-World-War-II juvenile delinquency, gangs, disadvantaged kids, Dowdy says Ray's film was "the better done of the two" but *City Across the River* was "more realistic." An interesting comparison, especially as *City Across the River* was based on the novel, *The Amboy Dukes*, by Irving Shulman, who would later be the second screenwriter on the *Rebel Without a Cause* project. What Dowdy's comment suggests is that a fundamental difference in approach to the juvenile problem, as depicted in novel or cinema form, existed between Ray and Shulman. In other words, Ray's allegorical style, his *aesthetic* realism (the authentic, rather than the realistic, being what the observer of the movie gets to see) was already there in a sharp contrast to either Hollywood's continuing melodrama or to the documentary realism or sociological realism favored by the young directors of the new avant-garde emerging in the 1950s.

In a Lonely Place (1950)

In 1950 Ray's marriage to Gloria Grahame broke up in the middle of shooting *In a Lonely Place*, starring Gloria and Humphrey Bogart. According to Ray, he wanted Gloria rather than Ginger Rogers for the role. The studio never realized the rift between the husband and wife or he would have been taken off the project. But Gloria never told and the film was completed. It remains one of Ray's finest, besides being popular among modern college couples. Ray still takes pride in the film, of which he has said, "I took the gun out of Bogie's hands"—thus indirectly propelling Bogart toward an ungangster-like part in *The African Queen*.

In a Lonely Place was a terribly personal film to Ray. Outstanding is his direction and use of Bogart as an actor. (Bogart is better here than in the famed *The Big Sleep*.) "Bogart used to say he could only mug for certain looks," said Ray (echoing what Errol Flynn confessed to screenwriter Robert Koch during the shooting of *Elizabeth and Essex*). Ray says that he started Bogart on a new acting line, late in life; then Ray gets misty eyed and stops talking.

Violence in Ray's Early Films

Ray admits to the violence in some of his early films. Later he was to stress that, without confrontation, life was nothing; but that was after 1968—after the word *confrontation* became fashionable. In 1957, asked about his inclusion of violence in his films, he replied "The characters of *In a Lonely Place, On Dangerous Ground, Rebel* resemble each other: they are violent. Absolutely. They have violence in them. It is in each one of us; it is there, in force. The bank teller who leads a peaceful life, counts the piles of banknotes and begins to hate the world; he counts the money up to one day, where, suddenly, he takes the revolver which he had stashed away to protect the cash drawer, runs into the street, and shoots a dozen people."[4]

On Dangerous Ground (1951)

On Dangerous Ground (1951) is Nick Ray's first pre-*Rebel Without a Cause* film that shows the structure he loved to follow. Often a director will "find" his style in one of his early films and then adhere to it, making several powerful treatments of it, then grow tired of it, and make an often unappreciated leap to another structure. Michaelangelo Antonioni, with *L'Avventura*, François Truffaut with *Jules et Jim*, Jean-Luc Godard with *Deux ou trois choses que je sais d'elle*, each found their best style for certain of their themes. Godard and Antonioni had to try to change their styles (only with difficulty) when they came to *Blow-Up* and *La Chinoise*. Truffaut and Ray, once having found their style, never let it go.

Freddy Buscome has defined Ray's style well: "Ray sets up a plot, only to abandon it in favor of a cinematic odyssey . . ." to a special place, a dream world, a mental realm, where actions not ordinarily accepted will seem acceptable and authentic when recorded with the camera. This, of course, is an old Hollywood trick. Ray just does it in a very personal manner, and in a newer style.

In the opening moments of *On Dangerous Ground*, Robert Ryan as Jim Wilson, a bitter, tough, slightly sadistic city cop, is warned twice about roughing up some of the petty criminals he pulled in. He doesn't listen. The masochism of one thug seems to bring out the sadism in him. He has no pity, and, as in the post-World-War-II social film, we are slowly informed why this is the case. So far, the film is not totally distinguishable from the opening of *Kiss of Death* or *Pick Up on South Street:* there is a city and a problem.

Yet, after this talky, twenty-five-minute opening, reminiscent of a TV crime series, the film suddenly moves to the country, the "dangerous ground" of the film, which is the home of a woman (Ida Lupino) and her blond, young, psychopathic brother who has committed a sex murder (because a girl he saw stopped smiling at him). This blond brother, is blind Ida Lupino's "eyes," she says; a seeing-eye human can't be all bad, suggests Ray. In this naive way, he is declared to be redeemable by Ray. But the brother's rescue by Robert Ryan, who—once he understands Lupino's world—becomes

remarkably quickly sympathetic to it (had he found Shangri-La?) is
foiled by the dead girl's father, Ward Bond's clumsy police-like
intervention. (This foreshadows the demise of Plato in *Rebel Without a Cause* almost exactly: Robert Ryan even takes the shells out of
Bond's shotgun in the same fashion and for the same reason that
James Dean takes them out of Sal Mineo's pistol in *Rebel*: to defuse
the situation.) However, this is a very minor part of the plot in *On
Dangerous Ground*; the entire focus is on Robert Ryan.

The contrast between Bond and Ryan occupies the second half of
the film. Bond, appearing as the revenge-seeking, shotgun-toting
father of the murdered girl, is now seen as an extreme case of how
Ryan behaved in the city. Bond even calls Ryan, "the city cop." This
character contrast is so powerful we overlook that we are barely told
why Ryan was sent to the country on this case. But the camera now
tells us that Ryan is in a very new environment. (In the city sequences, Ray shoots *in* through the windshield into the car in which
Ryan cruises through the streets; in the country sequences, he
shoots *out* through the window to reveal the vast snowscapes and
mountains of America.)

When Bond and Ryan track the killer to the cabin the killer shares
with his sister (Ida Lupino), a Nick-Ray-like confrontation occurs.
When Ryan discovers she is blind, he is no longer obsessed with
catching the criminal. Bond still is. Ryan calls down Bond for being
too violent (something he himself had been called on the carpet for
earlier). This is another characteristic of Ray's cinema: the moral
passed on from one character to the next as in *Rebel*, Plato tells Judy
that sincerity is the important thing, Judy then tells Jim that sincerity is important). After Ray has accomplished his character study of
Ryan, he gives us a conventional (but quick) end: the lonely cop and
the blind girl find each other.

Seen today, *On Dangerous Ground* seems like a practice film for
Ray. Yet, if we see Ray as the *author* of the film, it is valuable for
study. Though the dialogue between Ryan and Lupino is not totally
removed from the "come hither" style of Howard Hawks' *To Have
or Have Not*, there is no humor in Ray's film. It is deadly serious and
completely cut off from the romantic comedy. Ray might have been
up-tight while making this film. It is certainly a nervous film. (It
even totally lacks the Shakespearian highs and lows of many of the
films noir, and it tends to culminate in one accelerated push.) The
beauty of the film lies not in the pacing but in its cutting and in its
compositions.

As in many Ray films, the camera often plays with the characters while they play with each other. Secondly, the camera spatially dislocates. As in *Rebel*, we can never successfully reconstruct the living room in which the Ryan-Lupino couple is formed, for the camera is as nervous as they are. Stylistically, Ray's cuts, compositions, and dislocations are as mature and modern as the story is not. Consequently, the film, today, remains fascinating as an eclectic love/crime story, a *film noir* in its first twenty-five minutes, that bursts its bonds and flies out of its static compositions in the city sequence, to become a fluid, cinematically and emotionally moving film in the country sequences, in parallel with Robert Ryan's becoming a more fluid, humanistic person. In the remarkably filmed country sequences, though much happens, time seems compressed and space extended, as if "everywhere" were "now." In its gripping adult style, owing little, outside of dialogue, to the film narrative conventions of 1950 (all Ray's previous films are narratologically more conventional), *On Dangerous Ground* is perhaps Ray's least pretentious, least *tricheur*-like film. This is in part due to the subdued, controlled, understated—almost Expressionistic—performances of Ryan and Lupino, in part due to the camera and its director. The film, while for moments it might look like a Fritz Lang American product, mass paranoia of its characters implied always by their facial *angst*, the dialogue is peppy Hollywood B-film, and, once again, Nick Ray emerges as an eclectic. But the film's finest moments are very much his own style and give away some of his best shots in *Rebel*. These are shots where the actors' looks, some intricate mise-en-scène linked with the terse dialogue that seems to wait until a certain cut for its full force to explode, combine to give a mood through the rhythm of intercut and cut-off looks.

Ryan and Lupino's relationship is told one quarter by dialogue, one quarter by their looks, one quarter by the *juxtaposition* of their looks, and one quarter by the constant reminder, given by Ray's camera, that she is blind. This billowy overlay of effects makes it impossible to see through to what is creating the effect. Ray's nervous style, cutting on the beat, the paroxysm, is not even the reason for the effect, a suspension of disbelief achieved by a constantly shifting emphasis from acting to cutting to pure dialogue to lighting to movement. Too much happens for one to doubt part of the effect. One swallows it, or one has to reject it totally. While it is not a smooth, finely honed and crafted film of terseness and competing wills as is Sandy Mackendrick's *The Sweet Smell of Success* (1957),

America's last *film noir*, Ray's *On Dangerous Ground* is a more savage and primitive film in which the character development is psychologically sound. Whereas you can walk out of *The Sweet Smell of Success* wondering why Susan Hunsecker didn't leave J. J. Hunsecker sooner, you have no doubt, after *On Dangerous Ground*, that the dangerous ground has been covered and the worst is over. Ray's film has the naïveté and the temerity to lecture to the audience, but it does it without any pretension, Ray's moral is presented more in Truffaut's "people are great!" fashion than in Eric Rohmer's moral tale of a clearly discussed premise (as in *Claire's Knee*) that is then illustrated by the action that follows.

For a modern audience, *On Dangerous Ground* is a film too idiosyncratic to plunge into wholeheartedly, but it is an enjoyable film to watch. Film students should see the film, if only to compare it with Sam Fuller's *Pickup on South Street*, and learn from the comparison that Sam Fuller is the Toughie and Ray is the Softie.

If Ray refuses to concede any influence to Fritz Lang, he may have a point, for there is no imitation of Lang's very geometric style (as in *M*) in the mise-en-scène of *On Dangerous Ground*. Ray's playing at creating a *Filmwelt* of his own is more the product of his own romanticism than of any Expressionist horror of city decadence such as Lang displayed in *Metropolis*. Ray's architectural interests in his films seem to have more to do with supporting the drama of the narrative than with an urge to create a new architectural world, a dream world, where things can and do happen differently from the reality. The only exception to this is his later *Party Girl*, which does *seem* to take place in an architecturally invented Chicago of the mind. But, even there, Ray regretted he had not made that film more realistic, by such techniques as better use of jazz on the soundtrack.

Ray's link with Lang, however, is that while Ray is not a stylistic Expressionist, he is an expressionist of the heart, and if Ray were less temperamentally nervous, a greater similarity in his cinematic style to other Expressionist cinema might be evident. As it stands, Ray cannot be well defined here. He (eclectically) draws on impressionistic nervosity for his cutting rhythms, but at the same time, uses very expressionistic techniques in creating a dramatic *Welt*, an interior conspiracy of his actors, all based on what they, the structuring group, decide to do with it. Ray's characters are also always cleanly drawn (sometimes close to being cardboard characters) as in expressionistic theater, even if they live in a dirty *Welt*; they represent Ray and are not concessions to pure impressions of the outer, real world. Ray's film *Welts* can not be seen as existing on uncontrollable metaphoric chessboards of life. The real world, already related to, is expressionistically *replayed* (often, in a conscious and neurotic way, but never in a too self-conscious way; this is the miracle of Ray's cinema: that despite its self-involvement, it is not overly self-conscious). Ray sets up his films to represent expressions of his feelings about our world. And he shows he is a very emotionally opinionated man, with complex, sincere feelings—what we would later call a "James Dean sensibility."

It might here be recalled that Ray never served in the military, simply because he lost most of the sight of his right eye in an accident in the late 1930s. This automatically made him unsuited for military service in 1942, and his contribution to the World War II effort was in a civilian capacity as broadcast assistant to John Houseman's Overseas Information Service. At any rate, Ray's first color film *The Flying Leathernecks* (1951) is a completely incongruous one for Nick Ray to have made, Authorship critics who try to find Ray's signature in this film will find the task difficult if not impossible. As Fritz Lang once remarked, it is often forgotten that directors "have to eat."

The Lusty Men (1952)

The Lusty Men (1952) marks Ray's last film before the McCarthy era (House Un-American Activities Committee Investigations II) and Ray's self-exile to film *Johnny Guitar* in sunny Spain. It is a strong film, dramatically, and though it lacks the cinematic excitement of his later widescreen films, it has great honesty, good characterizations, and strong acting by all the principals, especially Susan Hayward. Ray's film women are difficult to play; they would have become more difficult and more challenging parts as he went on. Hayward here still plays a Gloria Grahame type of part, the strong woman—bitch when threatened—a woman you want to have on your side. Yet, Ray's women are not to cling to; nor do they obtain their ontological experience—their sense of identity—from men: they come forth from lonely places of their own. The Susan Hayward character was superseded by Joan Crawford as Vienna in *Johnny Guitar*, and Vienna is the protagonist of that film. Natalie

Wood next played a complex Judy in *Rebel,* a very tricky and important part, as there was no time to do more than sketch the part of
Judy out, in view of the necessary development of Jim; but Judy is
not a female Jim.

Perhaps Ray's least interesting female character is the blond
Hope Lange in *The Story of Jesse James,* but in Ruth Roman in
Bitter Victory and Cyd Charisse in *Party Girl,* Ray has two female
characters who are personalities, not the superwoman Vienna, nor
the superfemale Judy, to use Molly Haskell's quasi-feminist cat-
egories, but, like Scarlett O'Hara, they are autonomous women.

Ray's depiction of middle-aged love that he began in *On Dangerous Ground,* he returned to with distinction in *Bitter Victory* (1957)
and *Party Girl* (1958). As young, Existential love was then the rage
on the screen, Ray's treatment of mature love was incongruous in
the last era of Hollywood when it was part of the filmmaking process
to show larger-than-life love plots in non-*verité* fashion. Molly Haskell's characterization of Ray as one of "the neurotic and talented
auteurs . . . whose sexual anxieties spilled over into their treatment
of women"[5] does not, to me, describe him well at all. Ray's women
are definitely more "normal" than his men. They are, if anything,
less anxious, less neurotic than Ray. If we are to read anything into
this, we should read that Ray has confidence in women, without, on
the other hand, being a Mom-ist, one of the diseases of the 1950s
that affected other female parts, notably some of the younger girls in
Kazan's films: Eva-Marie Saint in *On the Waterfront,* Lee Remick
and Patricia Neal in *A Face in the Crowd,* and Julie Harris in *East of
Eden.* None of Ray's film females is the "here you can marry your
mother" type. So, from the male point of view, Ray's female characters are all appealing and interesting, with the emphasis on both
character and personality.

Robert Mitchum and Arthur Kennedy are the men of *The Lusty
Men.* Robert Mitchum's acting is naturalistic. Ray used Mitchum's
special off-screen persona well. As Jeff McCloud, Mitchum achieves
the heroism and significance in death that eluded him in life and
traverses the gamut from useless outsider to a briefly remembered
insider, unlike the sacrificial male character in the Western who is
remembered by the stereotyped homesteader couple because "He
gave his life so Nevada could be free." Mitchum dies, not according
to the dictates of a genre, but because he pursued an unsafe profes-

sion. Yet, of course, as in all films of the 1950s about male loners, and in the very heart of the fifties culture itself, for that decade was the time of the male individual in the same way the 1960s was the decade of the male group and the 1970s seems to be the decade of the female individual, in the *American* scene. In the 1950s, the male movie individual often displays a touch of self-pity, one that was intended to be passed on to the audience. The lonely male could identify with such a character, feel sorry for *himself,* and purge himself of the bitterest part of the emotions that made him feel alone.

Arthur Kennedy plays the third major character, the insider, the homesteader, who is married to Susan Hayward, who does not want him to become like the outsider, Mitchum. A love triangle is formed by their conflicting love goals: Haywards' love/respect for the strong outsider, the proud Mitchum, Mitchum's attraction to her, her attraction to what she wants Kennedy to be. Here is a touch of ontological cinema: Kennedy is the future, Mitchum the present. The love triangle ends when Mitchum stupidly but courageously dies in a rodeo comeback attempt he is not prepared for, epitomizing the 1950s' concern for the fate of an individual life, a sensibility lost here in the Chinese 1970s. After this event, Kennedy heroically (for him) acquiesces to his wife's goal, gives up rodeo, and returns to ranching. Hayward's hope is thus cemented by Mitchum's death, the progress of the two characters being informed by the sacrificial death of the third, a kind of chess sacrifice that goes on in all of Ray's films up to *Party Girl,* and one which dozens of critics have commented on and analyzed. Was this not a sign of Ray's pessimism (rather than mere plot device), they asked? Does the hero only make it because his buddy dies?? Or, is Ray showing a brand of neo-realism that didn't exist anywhere else in the contemporary American cinema?

In its way, *The Lusty Men* is the most reality-oriented of Ray's earlier films. In fact, the critic of the French Marxist magazine, *Positif,* said, in a review written in 1956, that he vastly preferred *The Lusty Men* to the then applauded *Rebel Without A Cause,* due to the former's honesty and the latter's mythic phoniness and obviousness. The salient points in this obscure but well-argued review are worth quoting, as they represent the first serious assessment of Nick Ray's cinema that was not entirely favorable. After a long series of comments telling why he finds *Rebel Without a Cause* inauthentic and pretentious, *Positif*'s critic, Roger Tailleur, comes to *The Lusty Men*:

> The one film of Ray's that I admire, the only entire one I like, along with the beginnings of *Violent* [*In a Lonely Place*] and of *Maison dans l'Ombre* [*On Dangerous Ground*] and, with certain revisions made, *Johnny Guitar*, and certain isolated scenes from other ones, and, also, that one in which nothing, or nearly nothing, leads up to those [negative] obsessions of Ray's I've enumerated [in *Rebel Without a Cause*], is *The Lusty Men*. It is here that the style of the director, by its rigor and certainty, is most suited to the remarkable story Ray came up with in collaboration with Horace McCoy. Not having to force his talent, Ray attained—by perpetual disregard for the grand effect—all his goals, resulting in something that moved me: a love quasi-undeclared, preventing sentimentalization; the healthy heros; the pathology as well as the damnation; a rural element; the police; and the modesty of (the director's) self-esteem, of the poetics.[6]

Robert Mitchum's biographer John Belton thinks that the theme of *The Lusty Men* forged "a permanent link of mutual indebtedness for what these three people helped each other achieve." Belton sums up what he thinks Ray's thematic strategy was on *The Lusty Men*: "Director Nicholas Ray uses his characters as archetypes of a distinct class of people: rodeo people like Mitchum, Hayward, and Kennedy have no homes or property, they are drifters. They live in cars and trailers, following the rodeo circuit from town to town." Belton says "the young, eager and ambitious Kennedy [a man a generation younger than Ray, and representing the young, postwar rootless American] contrasts with Mitchum [Ray's age, and cynical] who is easy-going and unaggressive, but whose interest in Kennedy includes his wife. Hayward, the third corner of the triangle, understands Kennedy's dissatisfaction with his present life and shares his ambitious goals, but disapproves of the means he uses to reach them, fearing that he will become, like Mitchum, a rodeo bum." Here we have the "Charlie, I could have been a contender" theme of the 1950s. "The Mitchum-Hayward relationship is built around shared cynicism, toughness, patient determination, and awareness of one another's goals"[7] (as are the Jim-Judy relationship in *Rebel*, the Tommy Farrell-Vickie Gaye relationship in *Party Girl*, and all of Ray's other important male-female relationships.)

The Lusty Men was the last of Ray's black-and-white films. He managed to film it with a sure touch, but the political situation of McCarthyite America had made him uncomfortable, had given him the artist's queasy stomach.

His next opportunity to direct enabled him to escape and coun-terattack, to produce what must be considered the only obvious anti-McCarthy *Western* in existence! It came about principally be-cause Republic Pictures needed a vehicle for its star, Joan Craw-ford, and took on Ray as director and co-producer, to film her in *Johnny Guitar* in Spain. Shooting took place on location near Bar-celona, and the film was completed at the end of 1953. It was shot in Trucolor and widescreen (1:1:85) and released in the United States in May, 1954, when, despite some uncomprehending reviews, it did unusually well at the box office. Within a month, Ray was back in Hollywood, at Warner Brothers, with an office next door to Elia Kazan, and the stage was set for *Rebel Without a Cause*, Ray's highly personal involvement with James Byron Dean, and his one, most personal, bout with trying to write a screenplay. It was the beginning of a pleasant year for him and his life style, thanks to the money he would earn on *Johnny Guitar*. [8]

3

Johnny Guitar

THE ARCHETYPAL NICK RAY FILM is *Johnny Guitar*. It is a film in which Ray indulged himself, using mostly his own ideas. In it he is responsible for more varied lines, architectural nuances, shots, and editing, than in any of his other films. Though *Rebel* is Ray's best film, *Johnny Guitar* is the film one should see just to get acquainted with Ray's work, for here we see Ray the *author* (as opposed to *Rebel*, where we see Ray the *collaborator*), and in this film Ray's strengths and weaknesses are more vivid and evident than in any other work of his.

Johnny Guitar has been considered the strangest Western made. That is true, if one considers *Johnny Guitar* to be a Western, without realizing that it is also something else: an experimental color film, a *political* Western, a film with a female hero (as opposed to a male hero or a female heroine). If truth be told, *Johnny Guitar* is no more bizarre than *High Noon,* which is also now considered to be an anti-McCarthy Western. One could certainly consider two other Westerns equally bizarre: *Storm in the West* (1944) as its screenplay originally intended it to be, and Sinclair Lewis's Western play, *Jayhawkers*, originally a work of Joseph Losey in his first theatrical assignment as director.

There is a fine balance in *Johnny,* between Existential hero all alone on a landscape, a universal landscape, with Peggy Lee's voice singing the lonely title ballad, and the biting satire of a hostile group—the posse which could be McCarthyites but could be any hostile group. While we should see the film as, to some degree, an anti-McCarthy Western, it is also more than that. Like *High Noon,* it is a film made by a man with an offended central nervous system, a film that seems to be in search of a locus, a place to give meaning to its energies. It is the very looseness of *Johnny Guitar,* which—along with its genuine love theme—is its attraction, and its

43

weakness. It is such a loose film that one cannot defend it structurally, and *Johnny Guitar* quite rightly has come to be liked as a "Nick Ray buffs' film."

Johnny also comes as close as Ray ever came to producing an autobiographical film, a film he privately thought of as a kind of motto for his own life, "I'm A Stranger Here Myself." While not going so far as to become a self-referential film in the Truffaut tradition—Ray is too austere for that—*Johnny* has many elements of a politically colored, autobiographical film, and we should take a quick but careful look at that aspect of the director that is revealed in the form of double entendre and allegory, and at its director's politics in the 1950s.

If we are to understand what *Johnny Guitar* is on *one* level—the transparent level of the film's extrastructural "signature," where the director's ego and persona are, in American-Hitchcockian tradition, allowed to be very obvious—a film "about" Nick Ray and Phillip Yordan's opposition to McCarthyism, we need to consider Ray's politics. A whole book should be written on the subject of the Hollywood blacklist and its effect on the American cinema which should, historically, deal with all the conflicting polemics (Martin Ritt in 1976 made a start with his film, *The Front*, about it), for it is too complex a subject to cover within the biography of *one* director. But let us make three points:

First, Nick Ray was never blacklisted himself, but was, he claims, "graylisted." Paradoxically, because of the shadowy nature of the gray list, no one can either doubt him or certainly prove that he or anyone else was ever on such a list. The gray list never existed on paper. (And though the blacklist, containing between three and four hundred names, was written out, each studio had its own version. Ray would have been regarded as "graylisted" after *In a Lonely Place* (1950); and though some critics—notably Douglas Brode— have read anti-McCarthy paranoia into this film, I prefer to think of the film as a reflection of the breakup of Ray's marriage to Gloria Grahame.

After 1951 the graylisted Ray took on himself the role of honorary blacklistee, a political act for which one must respect him. He behaved as if he were blacklisted, even though he wasn't. So while he could continue to make films without acquiring the odium that his friend Elia Kazan did, Ray was as bitter about the blacklist as anyone who had actually lost his job. (Kazan wanted to keep his hand in filmmaking so badly that he named names to the House Un-American Activities Committee.) This is, then, why *Johnny Guitar*, completed before Joseph McCarthy's fall, contains some biting, scathing comments on McCarthyism, bitter comments made by Americans resentful that any American could be told that the freedoms he took for granted no longer applied to everyone. These comments are there to hear, even though they are disguised contextually. They surface especially after one has seen the film more than once. They are obvious comments and not such low-key ones as the anti-Nazi comments in *Les Enfants du paradis* (1945), which had to be really heavily disguised. Yet, if Ray had gone much further, politically, the film never would have been released. Part of its artistic merit is, undoubtedly, as with *Les Enfants du paradis*, due to the subtlety enforced upon it by politics, and the subtle lack of subtlety with which Ray (and Marcel Carné) replied.

Second, it is important to stress that Ray was alone all this time, alone in the decisions he took in regard to anti-McCarthyism. The anti-McCarthy forces of directors and writers, no matter what they now say about it, were never a united group or a front in the 1950s. The human interrelationships here are complex. Ray doesn't like Losey—who was blacklisted! but he likes Kazan, whom some blacklistees despise to this day. Logically, it should be the other way around: Ray should have felt "solidarity" with Losey and not with Kazan. Yet, there is an explanation for this. Apolitical "political" people, like Ray, really always judge these things on personal considerations. Their individuality runs too deep. Ray *likes* Kazan; he *doesn't like* Losey (whom John Houseman says was known as "blue-eyed Joe," a kind of reference to Losey's self-assured purity and his lack of commitment to certain causes). This doesn't make Ray "a bourgeois individualist," and yet it makes us realize that Ray's current interpretation of himself as a radical should not be applied to his 1950s activities either. "Bourgeois individualist" is a meaningless epithet in America anyway. What we should try to keep in mind, while following Ray's film career through this time, is that Ray was an individualist first, a follower of some political or ideological line second. It should then be seen that while *Johnny Guitar* is a *personal* attack on McCarthyism, it is just as much a film about Ray's own loneliness, his personal isolation.

Third, we have to realize that *Johnny* is also a love story. The admirers of *Johnny Guitar*, include among others, François Truffaut, who expressed his pleasant surprise at the "European sensibility" and "romanticism" of Ray, which was in such contrast to the conventional Hollywood product. Bernardo Bertolucci also admired the freedom of one of the shots in the film, paying homage to Ray's 360 degree pan, in his first film, *Before the Revolution.*

While Truffaut and Bertolucci saw *Johnny Guitar* as poetic, the average American critic of 1954 seems to have had tough sledding with the film, and several reviews described it as neurotic. Part of the reason for this was that the political and the love themes don't quite integrate. *Johnny* was no *Casablanca,* and a reviewer in *Variety,* had this to say about the film: "It proves [Miss Crawford] should leave saddles and Levis to someone else and stick to city lights for a background. [The film] is only a fair piece of entertainment. [The scriptwriter] becomes so involved with character nuances and neuroses, all wrapped up in dialogue, that [the picture] never has a chance to rear up in the saddle. . . . The people in the story never achieve much depth, this character shallowness being at odds with the pretentious attempt at analysis to which the script and direction devote so much time."[1]

This review shows a complete misunderstanding of the intent of the film. There seems to have been something the conventional reviewer wanted to find in *Johnny Guitar* that didn't show up. Johnny's return after having abandoned Vienna five years earlier didn't seem to Brog of *Variety* and other critics as enough of a plot. Yet, when the same idea of "return" came up in *High Noon* Phillip French analyzed it to mean that—"the marshall [America] had wanted peace after clearing up the town five years before [i.e., World War II] and [now] reluctantly must buckle on his gunbelt again in the face of new aggression [the Korean War], and eventually his pacifist wife [American isolationists] must see where her true duty lies and support him."[2] Though John Wayne may have misunderstood *High Noon,* the critics and the public didn't, for it fitted neatly into the Western genre convention. Ray's twists on the genre, on the other hand, were just extreme enough to create a camp of those who loved the new "Western" twists and those who disliked them or didn't understand them.

As we have said, *Johnny Guitar* contains much of Nick Ray's spirit. The film has the charm and irony that comes of having been made by someone in command of himself, still young enough not to feel crushed or sorry for himself.

Additionally, we have to consider the degree to which Ray depended on a script. In *Johnny Guitar*, Ray took the active role of filming a finished screenplay, whereas in *Rebel* he insisted on wrestling with the script himself, agonizing over it, and finally having to call in Stewart Stern to complete it, thus elevating Stern to the role of co-author.

In fact, a comparison of *Rebel* with *Johnny* raises the question of whether Ray is better off to film someone else's script (i.e., whether his plots are a bit too shaky, or neurotic, or vague) and just make it into cinema or whether his finest work comes when he starts with his hands in the script.

The answer with respect to Ray seems to be the former, but with one qualification. As with French director Alain Resnais (who fears that he can't write narrative), when Ray finds a screenwriter who shares his views, he gets a double bonus: a screenplay that he doesn't have to struggle with himself and a screenplay similar in certain points of view, thematic development, and types of characters, to what he himself would have written. What Jean Cayrol was for Resnais, Phillip Yordan, in *Johnny Guitar*, was for Nicholas Ray.

Thanks to Phillip Yordan's sharing Ray's cinematic and political views, *Johnny Guitar* then seems to be a simpler more unified start-to-finish Ray concept, fully developed already on the screenplay-thematic level. It therefore didn't require the camera to help the plot come to life. *Rebel* is thus the more cinematic film—the camera had to rescue the film's screenplay—*Johnny Guitar* ends as a less cinematic but more "pure" Ray film.

Let's explain this apparent contradiction. *Johnny Guitar* is anchored by Yordan's screenplay. Ray could then play with filmic devices and decor, to his heart's content, without having to construct his shots painstakingly to inform the film. As we will see later, the screenplay for *Rebel* had none of the hidden cinematic instructions and hints that enable a director just to go ahead and shoot it. Ray had to invent much of the film in the last minute and with the camera. Some other director could have gone ahead and shot *Johnny Guitar*, and while it would not have been a Nick Ray film, it could have become a creditable film, emerging with the signature of another director. In *Rebel*, we have an exceptional case for Ray: one where he produced an inspired film despite lack of a good script. However, given any repetitions of the *Rebel* script crisis situation, Ray probably would have failed to produce any other inspired films.

We've established, then, that *Johnny Guitar* is the ideal Ray film if we want to indicate Ray's strategy in terms of what he tried to accomplish and what he tried to avoid. We have a much easier task in *Johnny Guitar* than in *Rebel*. *Johnny* is simply more revealing of Ray's real abilities—or lack of them—as to his overall narratological effectiveness as a filmmaker. He was free to experiment, and we can take a closer look at those experiments.

The Ray signature in *Johnny* is highly visible in terms of color, lighting, mise-en-scène, decor, pacing, cutting, camera angles, and camera movement, i.e., the filmic elements of the cinema that must fuse with the narrative component to add up to a cohering overall narratology offered to the spectator.

In *Johnny*, the narrative already provides for a good theme: the hero, Johnny (Sterling Hayden), is an outsider who returns, surveying the terrain, looking for some terra firma, and finds himself in a country ravaged by something negative. With his ideas already in the shooting script, Nick Ray could devote himself to building up an architectural locus for the film (he designed Vienna's cafe) and to looking for costumes, shots, and angles to put Republic's Trucolor and 1:1.85 widescreen to good use. Finally, as Ray was an investing co-producer, he had a financial interest in its success.

The Creators Discuss *Johnny Guitar*

"You know how come the film was made? Producer M. Herbert Yates simply said: 'Take Joan Crawford and see that she's happy during the shooting of the film.' We chose Chanslor's novel without using a single word from it, only the title; and we went and wrote a story where the woman was the star, a rare thing in Westerns." This was how *Johnny Guitar*'s screenwriter, Phillip Yordan, described the coming about of the film.

Yordan confirms Nick Ray's intention to make an "anti-McCarthy parable":

Yes. Yes. I was happy that you said that   [that you wanted to produce an anti-McCarthy film] for the anti-McCarthy allusions had given us trouble with the censorship that I told you. Besides, we also played a good trick on Ward Bond, who was, as you know, one of the members of the fascist party in Hollywood. We had him play the role of the head of the posse, an extreme fascist causing a reign of terror. And he thought the character was a hero, a good sympathetic guy. He didn't understand anything. I must say that I've always been obsessed by the theme of *Johnny Guitar*: you live calmly in a quiet place, when, suddenly, an individual comes up to you and says: 'you haven't got the right to live here' for this or that reason, in other words, break camp and. . . . Me I'd like to ask you, why haven't I got the right to live where I want.[3]

Nick Ray described the strategy of *Johnny Guitar* as follows: He made the film because it was pertinent to the mood of Hollywood at the time. The persecution in the film reflects the persecution in America. The film also broke every rule on Westerns; "it was a success after Westerns were out of vogue," he said. "Its success enabled me to do *Rebel Without A Cause.*"

"Republic films was hungry. [They hadn't had a successful film in a long while.] They wanted some old-style female star for *Johnny* and I told them to ditch her. Somehow, Joan Crawford, whom I wanted, got the lead, and Phil Yordan wrote the screenplay with me. The film was made in Barcelona—it split Barcelona down the middle politically. [It's amazing Franco didn't forbid it; but it was at the time of the American air bases for money deal.] Most of the film was improvisation based on the style of the G. M. Cohan—the old time, original Yankee Doodle Dandy—principle of surprise. There is no consummation of the love affair until the very last minute.

"I did much of the design for the film. I designed the back of Vienna's—the Joan Crawford character's—cafe; also, the cabin and the waterfall."

Ray, asked about the cast, commented: "Bart [Ernest Borgnine] was [a] typical [Western character.] Johnny [Sterling Hayden] was the "wanderer." Hayden, at the time, was planning the kidnapping of his own children in real life. At the same time, he was an informer. Vienna [Joan Crawford] also mirrored reality. Under fire from McCarthy, she refused to inform. There was great pressure on the cast, and tension between each of them. The screws were on all of them—it was very tortuous."[4]

When questioned about his opinion of the historical value of *Johnny Guitar*, Ray made these points at a Ray retrospective-film school seminar at the Orson Welles Cinema, Cambridge, Massachusetts, October 1973:

1. It was the first Hollywood Western where women were both the major protagonists and antagonists.

2. It is full of light and color; it was counter to the *film noir* stage of filmmaking of the time.

3. It is a good color film due to its well-handled architectural composition.

4. It is the first color film to use color to its potential.

5. The use of landscaping and design was to maximize the wide-screen [1:1:85] image.

6. It contains quite a few psychological innovations. Men can be seen as cowards and stupid. Women can be seen as leaders.

Most critics would agree with most of these claims Ray made for *Johnny Guitar*. But I would challenge his claim about color being used to its potential. First of all, the Trucolor stock used in the film exaggerated reds and greens. As a result, the film is a symphony of reds and greens in addition to whatever effects Ray intended. Yet I like Ray's Expressionistic use of color; "the palette of fire" that he was to use in *Rebel* is already hinted at in *Johnny*.

Screenwriter Phillip Yordan made these additional comments about the strategy of the film: After confirming that he intended it to describe McCarthyism, Yordan goes on to say that the film attempted to go beyond the effects of McCarthy's blacklisting and get at deeper American dilemmas. "I believe it [*Johnny Guitar*] is an essentially modern subject, a drama owing to the development of the lower-middle-class bourgeois who favor this kind of politics of terror." But Yordan goes on to say that *Johnny Guitar* was not *just* about McCarthyism. "There were other things in *Johnny Guitar*: a violent attack against puritanism, in the character of the old crazy girl, played by Mercedes McCambridge. There was also, for sure, Johnny, the kind of hero of tragedy in the clutch of the Furies, a destiny which comes from below and the arrival of which provokes the drama." To the interviewer's comment that there was a very lyric tone, a great elegy to the history of love, Yordan continued, "Yes. I deliberately constructed a lyric history which permitted Nick the liberty, a free hand, with his baroque ideas. He collaborated with me, less on the theme than on the architectural plan, composing the decor as in the saloon, establishing the geometric relationships of the place. Personally, I found the mise-en-scène prodigious, on top of which we were hardly helped by Republic Studios and their Trucolor."[5]

Thematic Analysis of *Johnny Guitar*

Ray's intentions for *Johnny Guitar* were fairly simplistic. Its theme is that of an aggressive and autonomous woman, Vienna (Joan Crawford), who was abandoned five years earlier by *Johnny Guitar*. Johnny returns to the country/landscape/*Welt* he abandoned—thus we get Nick Ray's "I'm A Stranger Here Myself" theme—and finds Vienna again. She has done well but her self-sufficiency has been bought at a high emotional cost. Vienna reminds the reluctant hero (she is the unreluctant hero) of love. Johnny, the reluctant hero, now learns from the aggressive woman, to love and not so much to fight back but to be strong and authentic. This finally returns him to love. If François Truffaut's formula, a-film-can-be-summarized-in-a-word, is applied to *Johnny Guitar*, that word would be, in film title form, *The Finders* (as opposed to John Ford's *The Searchers*, made three years later).

There are two important sub-themes: the first concerns another aggressive woman, Emma (Mercedes McCambridge), who is Vienna's rival in politics, and who is psychosexually hostile because she is afraid of being frozen out and becoming a loser. (Mercedes McCambridge would repeat this character, next called Luz Benedict II, in *Giant*, also made three years later). The second sub-theme is that of Johnny's not wearing a gun. (He is afraid to shoot someone. He is a precursor of the James Dean character in [*Rebel*] Jim Stark, who once forlornly says: "I don't want trouble.")

So we have enough sub-themes for an epic film; we have enough dramatic conflict for conventional audiences in *Johnny Guitar*, to make it seem like a Western. Actually, the film does not belong to the iconography of the Western so much as to folklore. *Johnny Guitar* is a classical example of a Proppian model for a fairy tale, for it begins, as all such tales do, with a lack, a *manque*, which is then resolved, found out; hence our title *The Finders*. The *manque* of *Johnny Guitar* is Johnny's lack of *emotional* courage. (He is not lacking in *physical* courage; he merely *refuses* to wear a gun.)

In the opening half hour of *Johnny Guitar*, we are given the chance to change our mind several times, as to whether Johnny is a hero, or some kind of a shirker, an emotional coward. There is something about the characters-as-they-are, Crawford's strong face and Hayden's wishy-washy expressions, that thrust upon us an iconography that would contradict anything a scriptwriter had meant to the opposite. Fortunately, the script draws on the reality of the characters; Hayden's Johnny does mirror the star's own personality: his regretting his testimony before the House Un-American Activities Committee is reflected on Johnny's regretting he left Vienna: "Johnny, why did you stay away so long?"

To work himself out of his bind, to satisfy the *manque* of the narrative, Johnny has to act. He takes one thing at a time. We see a therapy lesson on how to stop being a runaway. Johnny returns and is rebuked "for staying away so long" by Vienna, who categorically implies she needed him and had to build her café all by herself. She proudly refuses to tell him exactly how high the price was. Johnny rescouts the landscape (of an allegorical America). Early in the film, he hasn't got the feel of the new lay of the land yet. In response to a question from one of the locals, he replies: "I'm a stranger here myself." But when Vienna becomes threatened, Johnny reacts, love is reaffirmed. Johnny and Vienna then are even able to draw others to their alliance, widening out the alliance, the same implication that Ray leaves us with at the end of *Rebel Without a Cause*. Johnny the outsider has become an insider, and the more permanent outsider, the "doomed character," Emma (like Plato, the "doomed character" in *Rebel*) is wiped out by pistol shots.

Johnny Guitar is a heavily allegorical film. Its chief weakness is that, unlike *Rebel*, its allegory does not exist in enough tension with authenticated events. While *Rebel* has a fine touch of Italian neo-realism, *Johnny* suffers a bit from the fabrication running too obviously through its themes.

Comparing *Johnny* and *Rebel* strictly on one level, we see that the themes of these two films are not very different—they are even quite similar—on the main theme level to Ray's earlier *Knock on Any Door*, and, to a lesser extent, *In a Lonely Place*. Yet, as we shall see, *Johnny* and *Rebel* are visually and cinematically more different from each other than they are thematically, showing that Ray is not a one-style man with the camera and editing. Rather, his talent is for making cinema rather than filming scripts.

Finally, we should indicate that the overall narratological levels of the two films differ greatly from each other. *Rebel* has much more cinematic impact than *Johnny*, suggesting not that its cinema or theme is "better," but indicating that a high amount of cinematic integration between narrative and the cinema's various filmic components must have been achieved. Ray's talent at this time was growing markedly. Within the space of two years, two films with two basically similar themes were made, but with different cinematic strategies, ambitions, intentions, and incorporating within two kinds of soundtracks, with the result, not surprisingly, that the two films differ widely both on their cinematic and overall narratological levels.

But before we leave the theme of *Johnny*, we should make a simple observation. Since the overall narratology is affected by the skeleton of the thematic level (unless the director completely ignores the screenplay and throws it out), it follows that neither film escapes its thematic weaknesses. It seems to me, with the advantage of over twenty years of hindsight, that the problem posed by both *Rebel* and *Johnny* was to authenticate the hurt suffered by each of their central characters, Johnny and Jim Stark, and already a part of them when the films open. (Both films did depend on some belief in a larger-than-life hurt male protagonist, and both films depended a bit on members of the audience feeling sorry for themselves and projecting this onto the characters.)

Neither film perfectly authenticates this hurt, but *Rebel* does a far superior job on the script level and then employs James Dean to complete the authentication. *Johnny* makes a vaguer kind of allusion to the hurt. This is a dangerous way to approach a film audience because they may be too alienated from the central character to respond. But *Johnny*, the far simpler of the two films, does have one advantage.

Although *Rebel* is a far more interesting and ambitious film, *Johnny* has one (and only one) narratological advantage. In it, the love story and the violence problem (which are in a somewhat *over*-eclectic relationship to each other in *Rebel*) are already well integrated on the thematic level. In *Rebel*, the script jumps and dances between the two as it does in Nick Ray's model for this kind of story, Shakespeare's *Romeo and Juliet*.

In *Rebel*, the "Romeo and Juliet"-like aspect of Jim and Judy teaching each other how to love is not perfectly integrated with (or within) the odyssey of the "disturbed" Jim Stark vis-à-vis his family, Buzz's gang, school, police, authority figures, and life's demand for conformity. The love story of *Rebel* (one reason why the film was so popular) on the thematic level, and ultimately on the narratological level, is somewhat gratuitous, tacked on, probably due to Ray's playing it up over and beyond the suggestion explicit in the shooting script. Though interesting and a most mature playing out of a young couple's love story (better done than in Ray's *Knock on Any Door*), the love theme is not well integrated organically into the film. (That is why Eric Rohmer noted in his review that there were two "lyric" episodes in *Rebel* that did not fit into the "five act" horizontal, "symphonic" development of the plot. That is also why *Cahiers* critics like Truffaut raved about *Johnny Guitar*: It was, in all its "European sensibility," a smooth-running film.) Thus, in *Johnny*, the love story is more central to the film than the violence story, helping the final perception of the film as a romantic, unified story.

Cinematic Analysis of *Johnny Guitar*

If we compare and contrast *Johnny* and *Rebel* on the cinematic level, we find the common denominator that shows Ray's particular talent. We know that two different themes, when integrated by similar cinematic strategies, can produce similar overall narratology and thus a similar cinematic impact, despite dissimilarities in theme, screenplay, and screen writer. If, as many have claimed, Ray is an *auteur* (although I will use the word *author* throughout this book to designate the person I think principally responsible for a film in order to divorce completely the concept of authorship from the misleading "translation" of *politique d'auteurs*, which Andrew Sarris and others incorrectly transformed into "the *auteur* theory"), if Ray is indeed the author of his films, then we should look to see how many elements of impact *Johnny* and *Rebel* have in common.

This search is made a bit complicated by the fact (as we will later prove) that Ray is more the author of *Johnny*, on all levels, than of *Rebel*, where he had co-authors, so that the most striking similarities between the films are to be found only on the cinematic level—the similar use of cuts, tilts, and pans to inform, signify, and suggest; the generally similar use of color to create icons and indexes with a subtler life than if these were verbalized; the use of the camera to duplicate or run ahead of what is said, thus giving the narrative a push into the poetic/aesthetic realm that goes beyond the mere conveyance of information. The two films do not duplicate

each other cinematically; in each Ray uses different shooting strategies and tricks. The greatest dissimilarity is in the acting. *Johnny*
still features Hollywood acting; *Rebel* appropriates Method acting,
using it throughout.

In *Johnny*, the ontology is more obvious, less integrated than in
Rebel. This is why *Johnny* so strongly bears Ray's neurotically flashy
signature, for a director's signature is what stands out beyond and
apart from the intended text. The successful integration of the narrative with the filmic components never seems total in a Ray film.
What, for example, does the 360 degree pan late in *Johnny Guitar*
mean? It is a dramatic shot, but it stands out too much. It is not
nearly so well integrated into the film as Godard's similar famous
360 degree pan at the opening of *Deux on trois choses que je sais
d'elle* (Two or Three Things That I Know About Her), where the shot
informs the narrative and vice versa; nor is it half so well integrated
with the narrative as Ray's famous upside-down shot of Jim's mother
coming down the stairs in *Rebel*, a 180 degree vertical pan. In 1953
Ray was still excited by the camera and wanted to be daring with it,
so that this gratuitous shot in *Johnny*, taken from the top of the hill
where a gang is hiding out, is part of Ray's signature. Such a shot is
referred to as a "show-off" shot by the character in Bernardo Bertolucci's *Before the Revolution* who speaks of it with breathless
admiration.

If a comparison is made of camera movement, cutting, tempo of
cutting within the sequence, mise-en-scène, use of color, etc., between *Johnny*, *Rebel*, and *Party Girl*, three Ray widescreen color
films made within a period of five years, certain authorship
similarities emerge. First, there is a repetitious use of color strategy: characters are always dynamically color-coded; they graduate
from one color to another, with meaning. Yet, these colors in themselves mean nothing; they are not icons. Red does not always symbolize passion and black, death in Ray films. But note that Johnny
rides in wearing an off-red shirt, Jim Stark puts on the Red Cross
red jacket when he refuses to wait for his father's advice, Vickie
Gaye in *Party Girl* wears red when she really wants Tommy Farrell.
Mercedes McCambridge wears black and white in *Johnny Guitar*,
Plato dresses in a dark jacket throughout *Rebel*, as if he were El
Greco going to a funeral, Tommy Farrell wears dark, conservative
suits in *Party Girl*. Jim Stark begins *Rebel* with a dull brown dap-

pled sport jacket. One could say these dark colors are an index of people in trouble, rather than that dark is the icon of death. For the latter two characters survive and the former don't. But beyond these repetitions, an evolution toward a certain maturity can be progressively found in the three films.

Ray in *Johnny* introduces his idea of the horizontal grouping to fill the longitudinal axis of the wide screen; and he tries out a clever widescreen idea of quick, crude crosscutting between a large hostile group and an endangered small group—between the posse and Vienna in *Johnny*, between the gang and Jim in *Rebel*. Both films are very much horizontally composed. *Johnny*'s horizontal structure is novel, but amateurish; in *Rebel*, eighteen months later, the same horizontal style is used again to brilliant effect.

As *Johnny Guitar* was made away from Hollywood scrutiny (no studio executives on the Catalonian set) and was such a personal exploratory film, venting most of Ray's loathing for Senator Joseph McCarthy, it is a dangerous film to force into a mold or to use to read Ray's other films. As we have suggested, much of Ray's widescreen style is already here in embryonic form; but the film student or buff, unfamiliar with Ray, the serious student of filmmaking, or the aspiring film director would all be well advised to see *Rebel Without a Cause* and then *Johnny*. The style of *Johnny* would then be obvious. (Without an author theory, it is almost impossible to understand Ray's earlier films, even after several viewings.) *Rebel*—Ray's most accessible film—should then be compared with *Johnny* and then the rest of Ray's films seen chronologically. Embryonic, full-grown, and menopausal Ray films can then be compared, authorship studied, and developments in cinematic narratology evaluated.

The major differences between the twenty films Ray did could then be understood. As in *Rebel* vs. *Johnny*, it is not so much major stylistic differences that distinguish one Ray film from another; nor do we always experience a complete, total recognition of a dominating style, as with Hitchcock. Ray films differ from one another *depending on what Ray's preoccupations were at the times*. One sentence could define Ray's preoccupation in one film, but *not* in all his films. For *Johnny Guitar*, the sentence would be "You're living calmly . . . and, all of a sudden, for this or that reason, somebody tells you you can't live here anymore [Phillip Yordan]. And you return to the land you left and someone asks if you know your way around and you answer, 'I'm a stranger here myself' " [Nick Ray].

This suggests that *Johnny* would have to have an open structure, to use Leo Braudy's term—something like a horse opera onto which these "insights" of an America in pain could be hung as content. *Rebel*, on the other hand, was to be about "a group," not "one teen-ager (I'd already done that in *Knock On Any Door*," Nick Ray told Dr. Robert Lindner); and teen-agers going on a "blind run," Ray's term for they know not what they do. The preoccupation of that film was to give the public a more closed structured moral lesson, without being "trite," on how a rebel without a cause becomes a rebel with a cause. If *Johnny* is about blind lashing out, *Rebel* is about lashing out with more control, purposiveness, and chance of success. This is, at least, how one feels the films were intended.

Comparative Cinematic Impacts: *Johnny* and *Rebel* Tested by Time

It is only natural that the impact of a "symphonic" film like *Rebel* is greater than that of a "lyric" film like *Johnny* (using Kandinsky's distinction between the two).[6] *Rebel* has four characters whose intertwined fates we become concerned about; *Johnny* has really only one such character, Vienna, and she's not enough. The lack, I believe, has much to do with the unfortunate personality of Sterling Hayden, who plays Johnny. One does not really sympathize much with him, even though he is supposed to be the co-protagonist and a positive character. Hayden plays Johnny a bit like a dazed Marine Corps officer who has lost his unit. He also belongs to the Jane Fonda–Henry Fonda wooden Indian school of acting. As the *beloved* of the film, he falls short; Joan Crawford as the *lover*, by contrast, is loving and—though grotesque—very sexy. As Vienna, she does what the script demands, doing justice to a difficult role. As a result of Hayden, *Johnny* delivers only half of its message. It is flawed as an Expressionist film, for the *Welt* in which the Expressionist hero and heroine are supposed to function is too thin (see Fritz Lang's films, for comparison). Ray recognized this, and he hoped that he could use the film's thinness to advantage by making it into a fairy-tale-like lyric. As a result, we have an eclectic film: some of the seriousness of purpose is there, but some has been sacrificed to the necessity for balancing off the flimsy props with lightweight narrative and getting it done. *Johnny Guitar* thus ends up as a lyric film with mostly good intentions, a hybrid between a serious film and the Czech spoof-Western *Lemonade Joe*. Yet it is still a beautifully photographed film, marked by creativity in its cutting and in its ontological use of color that somewhat makes up for its yé-yé acting.

Already evident in *Johnny Guitar* is Ray's dislike of shot-countershot as the means of visually showing a conversation. Contrast the shots depicting the first major conversation between Abra and Cal as they become friends in Kazan's *East of Eden* with Johnny and Vienna's conversations in *Johnny* (and Judy and Jim's almost "confessing-to-the-audience-frontstage" love episodes in *Rebel*), and you will see Ray's self-divorce from Hollywood's late 1930s-early 1940s smooth, mobile, matched mise-en-scène. Ray definitely developed his own uniquely different cutting rhythm as one apart from Hollywood's epic cinema in order to suit the action/hesitation/action/hesitation life style of the middle-class American 1950s people he always showed so authentically in his cinema.

The main weakness of *Johnny* is really that it is a long "lyric" film, and its ending suffers due to lack of impact. *Rebel*, a more "symphonic" film, has many thematic sub-texts, musical and ontological threads, culminating by accumulating the main characters and problems together at the Planetarium, and resolving all their problems; this at least partly, compensates for the lack of any integration (unity of meaning of the sub-texts) of the themes earlier in the film. (Why Judy helped Jim mature and how, is never developed in *Rebel*; why and how Vienna helped Johnny grow *is* developed in *Johnny*. She basically suggests to Johnny that his problem is not speaking out!)

Rebel is a much more complex film than *Johnny* and uses one clever device that *Johnny* could have used to advantage. In *Rebel*, Plato likes Jim because he is "sincere." He tells Judy that Jim's outstanding quality is that he is "sincere." Judy later tells Jim that "sincerity" is the most important thing. We already know this, because Plato told us. *Rebel* gives privileged information to the audience to involve us. *Johnny* doesn't. We have to watch.

Overmuch has been made of the "kid" Turkey, in *Johnny*, as a forerunner of a James Dean character. Turkey is there to identify with, but he is not part of a sub-theme, as even a minor character like Crunch is vis-à-vis Moose and Goon, in *Rebel*. Turkey is more of a symbol of value—youth—than a real character.

So we can say that *Johnny* occasionally lags and uses much screen time to impart its sparser theme (than *Rebel's*). *Rebel* also gives us more than a thematic ending; it delivers its crescendo more on its overall narratological level—Jim's red jacket is placed over the fallen Plato, an empty gun lies on a lawn, the sun rises, everybody goes home, a solitary figure walks to work, and despite the fact that you have been briefly shown that man alone doesn't have to stay man alone, you see the solitary figure at the end, and wonder if he isn't alone after all. Nothing at the end of *Johnny Guitar* produces this effect; its ending is that of a Western that is weary of its plot.

The weaknesses and strengths of *Johnny Guitar* are attributable to its two personal authors, Yordan and Ray, who indulged their whims in a very personal way. This helped make *Johnny* a good *Zeitgeist* film, but it by no means made it a classic. (It is not substantial enough to stand the test of time.) It still deserves inclusion in any study of the political American Western film, and it deserves more scrutiny than this book can give it, as a specific reaction film to the Hollywood blacklist. It, correctly, will take second place to *Rebel Without a Cause*. But, considering *Johnny* was the earlier film, it must be studied by authorship critics of Ray, and Ray must be given much credit for his pioneering efforts in *Johnny,* particularly for his use of the wide screen and color for ontology rather than effect, the benefits of which we can readily see to greater advantage in *Rebel Without a Cause*.

4

"Movies Without a Cause"

HOLLYWOOD'S FILMS of the early 1950s failed the emerging generation, but so too did the youth films of the middle 1950s. The before-dawn, latent generation, described by one writer as "more idealistic, less cynical than the present one," was the one that would provide the box office for most of the youth films that would be thrown out at them. It would also be somewhat synonymous with the generation that Dr. Robert Lindner in his books *Rebel Without a Cause* and more specifically *Must We Conform?*, described as being like no previous generation of adolescents. They were waiting for some information or some emotion with informational content, in film. But Hollywood, never able to lead, could not give them anything, that had not become a trend. Instead, Hollywood did what it always does in such situations: it created the "youth film." It quickly made up a "department" to spin off youth films, in effect, a slightly more liberal branch of itself, and gave some men the green light and money to go ahead and make some films that might attract the audience that wasn't going to see *Singing in the Rain* or *The Moon Is Blue*, or gaze at the wondrous new CinemaScope in *The Robe*, or empathize with Judy Garland in *A Star Is Born*.

The significance of the creation of a new genre of movies like *Rebel Without a Cause* (1955) was that the first films of this genre were rushed, muddled, and yet mythic, and had precious little to do with what the studios, like Warner Brothers, thought they were putting out. While it was one of the first of the youth movies on "the rebel without a cause" theme, Ray's film lacked the clear message of Albert Camus' book, *The Rebel*, (1951), which said rebellion is good and revolution is bad. The film, for example, was most certainly regarded by its studio as a James Dean youth movie, a showcase for a new star, and perhaps, a box-office answer to the emerging cult for

A production still showing James Dean (Jim Stark) and Corey Allen (Buzz Gunderson) taunting each other. The composition and facial expressions in this still do not occur in the film. credit: Warner Bros.

61

another studio's star, Marlon Brando, as well as just another in a
series of Warner Brothers action pictures.

In fact, it is downright amusing to read what the studio *thought* it
was filming. Highly-neo-Freudian in tone, screenwriter's Stewart
Stern's synopsis of the film was a self-deceptive homily to the need
to have a special genre of film dealing with the emerging generation. Stern thus described the characters in *Rebel*:

Jim: [James Dean] The angry victim and the result. At 17 he is filled with
confusion about his role in life. Because of his "nowhere" father, he does
not know how to be a man. Because of his wounding mother, he anticipates
destruction in all women. And yet he wants to find a girl who will be willing
to accept his tenderness.
Judy: [Natalie Wood] The victim and the result. At 16 she is in a panic of
frustration regarding her father—needing his love and suffering when it is
denied. This forces her to invite the attention of other men in order to
punish him.
Plato: [Sal Mineo] Son of a divided family . . . he feels himself the target of
desertion. At 15 he wants to find a substitute family for himself so that he
need no longer feel cold, and especially a friend who will supply the fatherly
protection and warmth he needs.
Buzz: [Corey Allen] A sado-masochistic boy of 17 who acts out aggressively
his idea of what a man should be in order to hide his real sensitivities and
needs. He was probably rejected by both parents and must constantly court
danger in order to achieve any sense of prestige or personal worth.[1]

To understand properly how the mythic youth film genre,
"Movies Without a Cause," crept up on Hollywood unawares, we
have to set *Rebel Without a Cause* against the background of Hollywood in 1955.

Two facts characterizing Hollywood of the early 1950s have already been well documented and do not specifically enter our study
of "Movies Without a Cause." Nevertheless we need to keep them
in mind while reading this chapter, for they are the essential background. They show the McCarthyite influence and effect on a conservative Hollywood. The film industry, reactive as ever, kow-
towed more to McCarthy than many other American institutions,
and was severely shaken up. Many of its talents were driven away,
but, after 1954, almost as a result, a temporary opening in its infra-
structure appeared into which new talent could pour. In addition,
TV competition had to be continuously fought by scheme after

scheme; one way of doing it was to put James Dean in the movies and draw him away from TV. A temporary respite to this problem was effected by 20th-Century Fox head Spyros Skouras' successful one-man[2] pioneering of the CinemaScope process, an act that quickly helped boost the flagging box office for Hollywood films. By 1955, eighteen short months after the introduction of the process, *thirty* Scope films had grossed over five million dollars apiece. By winter 1954–55, the success of CinemaScope was obvious, McCarthy had been checked, and one could definitively say then that the movie industry's biggest problems were no longer McCarthy-HUAC interference, or money, or TV, but "Where is Hollywood to go?" and "What to do to replace aging stars and win the new 15-to-25-year-olds over to the movies?"

If we want to know how much progressivism and change we could have realistically expected from Hollywood in 1955, we must recall what the United States motion picture industry was like at this time. According to the man who composed the musical score for *Rebel*, Leonard Rosenman, Hollywood was not the land of *auteurs* and new ideas. "You have to realize, the era when I started in Hollywood [with *East of Eden*, 1954] was a time of dizzy broads and Cinema-Scope as a marketing gimmick. Somehow, accidents happened in both the best and worst of films to make parts of them better."[3]

Despite Rosenman's uninspiring snapshot of Hollywood in 1954, two new groups were coming into their own in cinema arts. First, there was a delightful new crop of actors: Montgomery Clift was already there, Brando arrived next, and James Dean entered in the summer of 1954. These would appeal to the new generation and were—especially Dean—*part of* this generation. As François Truffaut wrote in March 1955:

East of Eden is the first film to present us with a Baudelarian hero, moulded by vice and honor, that family of I love you and I hate you at the same time. This is James Dean, freshly cut flower of evil, whom it is necessary to speak about in any survey of cinema. James Dean, who *is* the cinema in the same style as Lillian Gish, Chaplin, Ingrid Bergman.[4]

Second, there was, a half-generation older than the teenagers, an American avant-garde, neither mainstream nor Beat generation, who were frustrated by having lost some of their youth to World War II, men who all had probably read Albert Camus' novel *The*

Rebel, men who would have liked Jean Cocteau's film *Les Enfants terribles*. They ranged from disenchanted romantics to latent mythomaniacs. They were ready to join forces with the younger generation, and they were especially important because of their potential for giving Hollywood new themes and ideas. These were men such as Steward Stern, born in 1923, a staff sergeant in World War II and thirty-one when he started work as the final screenwriter on *Rebel*. The assistance of these "fellow travelers" (the oldest of whom was forty-four-year-old director Nicholas Ray) in reaching out to the needs of the younger generation (James Dean was born in 1931) was highly significant, once they joined forces. Many of the myths embodied in youth films and the very films themselves would have been impossible if this half-generation of older and talented artists had not united with the talented new actors in the youth projects. To the older group belonged Stanley Kramer, who produced *The Wild Ones*, and the youth-film, horror-film director, Roger Corman (born in 1926). These men characterized Hollywood at the time that Elia Kazan began *East of Eden* (Dean's first picture) and that Nick Ray returned to Los Angeles from his self-imposed, anti-McCarthyite exile in Spain.

We should point out critiques contemporary with the youth films that would make up the first wave of the "Movies Without a Cause," (and launch a second wave of rock-and-roll movies and a third wave of European reaction to youth movies). It is fascinating to note that *Rebel* got a sociological whitewash in England, despite skepticism about its authenticity in the United States. It also was totally accepted in France and Germany, not for being accurate sociology, but for being good, convincing myth. None of the contemporaneous U.S. and British critiques that I have seen have emphasized or mentioned at all the importance of the mythic input into these "Movies Without a Cause," including *Rebel*, which has one foot in the genre and one foot outside it. These critics failed to see the basis for the creation of a new film genre, as important a genre *sociologically* as the New Wave.

French reviewers, such as Truffaut and Rohmer, were quite aware of the mythic sensibility of *Rebel*. Curiously, in America no one was aware of this, possibly due to the schism in America at that time, between movie criticism and "highbrow" literary criticism. Phillip Rahv, for example, in 1953, warned of the increasing popularity of myth in American literature, but no one connected this to *Rebel Without a Cause*.

After *Rebel* was released, some theorists discussed it, *Blackboard Jungle*, and *The Wild Ones* as a series of related films. But until *Rebel* suggested the trilogy, reviewers fished in the dark. No one at the time related specific youth films like *Rebel* to non-youth-oriented films with similar themes. The father-son problem, for example, was equally dynamically illustrated in *The Rack* (1956), in which Paul Newman's adult performance can be contrasted with Dean's teen performance in *Rebel*, though Newman (born 1926) was actually only five years older. No one was then aware that a genre of film was forming, though several critics in obscure publications came close.

A recent study of Don Siegel (born 1912), who was the same age as Ray, suggests that Ray was the exception to his generation and Siegel was the rule, in the way they developed in the 1950s, the theme of the anti-hero facing his environment. It has even been suggested that Siegel did not much bother to distinguish between hero and anti-hero, as he went merrily on his way with increasingly violent films. Siegel thought that the anti-hero as well as the hero must punch his way through, and greet violence with violence; Nick Ray felt that the anti-hero must strengthen himself in a new, positive, and somewhat mythic way and only then stage a resurgence to remove the obstacles in his way. Since Ray's movies' endings fitted Hollywood as well as Siegel's filmist endings, critics such as Bosley Crowther can be (almost) excused for neglecting to see the essential difference in the structure and intent of the two directors' films. Now it is easy to see that Nick Ray abandoned the *film noir* tradition with *Johnny Guitar* (1954) and *Rebel* (1955) but that Siegel carried on the bitter *film noir* tradition *ad nauseam*, and that in his film world there is very little difference between heroes and anti-heroes, indicating no or little concern for the way the environment relates to the protagonist, but concentrating, much as John Ford did, on how the protagonist deals with the environment. It is easy, then, for Siegel to bring in violence as from a world not of the hero's making, and continue the 1940s crime-film tradition of violence meeting violence, aggression meeting aggression, and an "eye for an eye" leading to revenge, hostility, and *Dirty Harry* (1971). An interesting generalization is that those directors like Siegel and

Frankenheimer, both of whom made important youth films in 1956 that were *not* mythic, were the directors who adhered to the *film noir* tradition or world and who developed the violence in their films straight from the premise of dog-eat-dog *film noir*. (A good synchronic typology would soon discover that *The French Connection* is *a film noir* even though it was made in 1971, and *Force of Evil* [1947] is not a *film noir*.)

Another exception to his generation was director Richard Brooks. Again, the same age as Ray, he belongs with Ray (and not with Siegel, nor with Frankenheimer, a younger man who fits with the older generation) as one of the mythmakers. Brooks, as a convert to the mythic youth film, is even more interesting than Ray, for he had a much longer Hollywood past. It seems that Brooks gave up on the *film noir* tradition just about the same time as Ray, and that his studio was more responsible for the inception of *Blackboard Jungle* than he was. Yet his development of the film was a highly personal one.

Blackboard Jungle was made under similar circumstances to Ray's *Rebel* as a studio quickie (twelve weeks from conception to finish), but it neither influenced *Rebel* nor was influenced by it. (Its two directors never met to chat about the two films.) It was the simultaneous appearance of these two films (within six months of each other) and their peculiar similarities (the gang versus the individual, the knives, etc.) in contrast with their different mythic aspects[5] that launched the "Movies Without a Cause," but also threw the critics off the scent. These two films, even though they both, obviously, deal with the parameters of mindless violence and teen-agers, had no obvious *mythic* elements that linked them to the same genre. As a consequence, critics linked their *themes*, but failed to find and note the synchronous topology that really connected the two films, just as they later failed to find the link between Kubrick's *Clockwork Orange* and *Barry Lyndon*. Faced with films with difficult topologies, most allusive critics end up saying both films had guns in them. So it was the most critics linked *Rebel* and *Jungle* to *The Wild Ones*, and nine out of ten of them thought *Rebel* was the finer of the two, as they thought it was *de rigeur* to praise James Dean. As Bosley Crowther said in his *New York Times* review of *Rebel* (October 27, 1955) "Like *Blackboard Jungle* before it, it is a picture to make the hair stand on end." Thus, critics started to link these types of films in genres that had little to do with why the films drew a wide audience and perpetuated themselves.

Why did "The Movies Without a Cause" last for twenty years, from roughly 1954 to 1974? The answer is complex and will be developed gradually through this book, but generally we can compare the continuance of the genre to the continual thrust of a multistage rocket. Just before each stage would have died, a new thrust pushed the next on. First came the films such as *Rebel* and *Blackboard Jungle*. Then came the combination of film and rock 'n' roll. Then came the mutation of these films in Europe. Then came the return of the products of the mutation, from Europe. At last came a serious weakening of the genre, followed by a final nostalgic wave, the British rock documentaries, the death of the rockumentary split-off, and finally, the desire, even on the part of much of the genres' prime audience, for a return to historicism. In short, the genre seems to have lasted about a generation, suggesting that it is adherence to a certain generational idea (such as rock music) that perpetuated the "Movies Without a Cause" for so long.

In addition to underestimating the mythically inclined, neurotic director's personal inputs into the text of these films, (Eric Rohmer had already written in 1956, that psychiatrists would have a field day with Nick Ray's symbolism in the mansion sequence in *Rebel*.) Many writers and critics have *over*estimated the commercial bind Hollywood was in at the end of 1954 as a cause of the youth film genre's appearance. This "quick buck" theory again underplays the cravings of certain directors and screenwriters to get their personal myths into film, and gives much too materialistic an explanation of the "Movies Without a Cause." The "quick buck" theory, as expressed by David Manning White, goes like this:

Other factors were at work during the Fifties which hindered additional serious youth films even if there had been producers who wanted to make them. It was a period of severe economic upheaval in the film industry. In the wake of television's usurpation of America's leisure hours, theater attendance fell off from a peak of 80 million weekly in 1945 to about half that number. . . . Attempting to win back the lost audiences who defected to the 21-inch screen, Hollywood held up the carrot of the superscreens of Cinerama and CinemaScope. Productions from the major studios hit a 40-year low point in 1954. Compared to 1935, for example, there was a 60% decrease in the number of films released by the major companies. The need to fill the screens of neighborhood and drive-in theaters that were still keeping afloat was met to a large extent by (my italics) *quick-buck productions* that capitalized on youthful violence and the more "frank" films permitted by the relaxation of Production Code strictures against certain sexual themes, drugs, and other titillating keyhole subjects.[6]

The problem with this description—besides not going deeply enough into the matter—is that it only fits the shaky years between 1949 and 1953. In 1954, the decision, pioneered single-handedly by Twentieth Century-Fox's Spyros Skouras, to gamble on Cinema-Scope paid off commercially. At this point the recovery of the film industry was obvious even to Warner Brothers, the studio which had been particularly heavily hit by financial troubles. Furthermore, the fact that few films were produced in 1954—as White says—is misleading. There were fewer films than previously, but because some of them were CinemaScope "big screen" the revenues of 1954 in relation to production costs showed a decided upswing. Far from being desperate to make a whole host of cheap films to save their skins, producers more likely felt an urge to make films with mythic input by directors and screenwriters from the in-between generation because of the time-honored Hollywood practice of starting a genre whenever a film like *Rebel* seemed to hit a public nerve center of response. As White himself admits, "If there were no Gresham's Law [bad art drives out good art], Hollywood would have invented it. In the message film, as in other types of Hollywood's movies, one box-office success breeds imitation which in turn breeds imitation *ad nauseam*.[7]

Ultimately, to be fair, we must emphasize that by late 1956 not everyone had failed to see "Movies Without a Cause" for what they were. A careful study of the criticism of *The Wild Ones, Blackboard Jungle*, and *Rebel* discloses that by October, 1956, about a year after the third of these films appeared, it was becoming clear to critics that a genre had been born, reflecting a new American preoccupation—mythic violence. About one out of ten critics found and pinpointed the inconsistencies in these films quite well, but their influence was minimal. Their articles were often located in the more esoteric publications, so that their comments did not feed back into the mainstream. How many teen-agers read *Film Comment*? But the point must be made that not *everyone* in 1956 failed to see the "Movies Without a Cause" for what they were. Eugene Archer really hit the nail on the head when he observed in *Film Comment*[8] that "It is known . . . that there has been an increasingly large number of cases of adolescent violence, in contradiction to the generally acknowledged trend toward conservatism in the adult population." And he saw Dr. Lindner's argument clearly when he explained that the post-World-War-II atomic era imposed a bit too much conformity on the youth of the day, so that "the trend toward violence represents a revolt from a too rigidly circumscribed environment."

Archer offered by far the wisest assessment of *Rebel Without A Cause* at the time when he wrote in 1956 that it was

. . . less pretentious than its predecessors *(The Wild Ones* and *Blackboard Jungle)* and more valid than either. Without probing deeply into the causes of delinquency, or offering any solution, it nevertheless makes a clear and interesting comment about the situation and raises the issue of moral responsibility in a manner that deserves attention. Unfortunately, the issue which is raised is not answered [earlier, Archer had said quite honestly, "The actual extent of the increase of juvenile delinquency since World War II is unknown, and the possible causes are subject to controversy."] and the result is a superficial comment on a serious theme.[9]

Archer then saw *Rebel* as not going far enough to suggest a solution to the premises it presented; the film, in effect, got a generation to identify with it, yet had nowhere to lead it. One begins to suspect that the motive of the film might have been that a group of overage teen-agers were trying to make contact with a new group of "themselves" in the new generation and win their sympathy. For only the enemies of the teen-ager are ever clearly brought to light. As Archer says,

[*Rebel Without a Cause*] places the blame for delinquency on the parents, and this, as far as it goes, is sound enough. . . . In themselves [the three cases of Jim, Judy and Plato] are all interesting enough; but when presented as causes for the urge to violence on the part of the adolescents involved, they are inadequate. At the film's conclusion, particularly, when the henpecked father announces for the hundredth time that he will try to act like a man, and a happy ending is implied, the script seems pat and contrived.[10]

But one must remember that all the dry, sane, historically accurate comments about *Rebel* and most of the similarly skeptical ones about *Blackboard Jungle* fell on deaf, young ears. The mythic lure of James Dean's iconic face in the former was too strong for young people to resist (even Hemingway blessed the film: "James Dean comes down off the screen and into the audience"); the adult opposition to the latter (it was banned in Atlanta and pulled out as the U.S. entry to the 1956 Cannes Film Festival) helped create a sympathy for it (akin to that for rock 'n' roll) among those who felt adults banned what kids like. (Even Ronald Reagan didn't mind *Blackboard Jungle* and naively said its violence would just turn people off.)

Finally, both films kept their complexity level down, especially through their pat endings. This one-dimensionality helped them commercially. It also helped them pass into mass culture as successful "Movies Without a Cause," for, as Hitler cunningly observed, a good myth should only deal with one thing at a time; otherwise, people lose track. But, by fixing mass audience on one track, these films achieved a kind of triumph of the violent revenge motive, as in *The Count of Monte Cristo.* However, both *Rebel* and *Blackboard Jungle* failed to transcend their own interesting premises. Even more fateful for the American movie-going experience, they successfully inaugurated a genre of "Movies Without a Cause."

5

Rebel Without a Cause — From Idea to Shooting Script

"A boy wants to be a man, quick,"

"Make sure the unities are comprehended."

"Try to follow the classic form of tragedy."

"Through a tragic irony, the escape that James Dean found was total and absolute. But he is mourned through the image of Jim Stark, whose escape was the one he really hoped for, constantly searched for—a full, complete realization of self."

"After seeing *Rebel Without a Cause,* many people drew parallels between the character of Jimmy Dean and of Jim Stark. In the letters written to James Dean, and after his death, to me, the two are identified to an extraordinary degree. In these letters, Jim Stark and Jimmy Dean became one and the same person. In life they were and were not. . . ."

"The last time I saw James Dean (alive) was when he arrived without warning at my Hollywood home about three in the morning. That evening we had met for dinner. We had talked for several hours of many things, of future plans, including a story called 'Heroic Love' that we were going to do."[1]

Nick Ray

"My heroes are no more neurotic than the audience," replied Nick Ray to a challenge about his always having neurotic characters in his films. "I always do my own casting," said Ray in response to whether he's ever been contractually stuck with a "studio property," that he was forced to use. From these two statements, we can deduce that Ray's plots are his own creations, but concocted to become vehicles the audience can experience. Despite his love for teamwork—"film is a collective art"—Ray's statements on that sub-

73

James Dean and Nicholas Ray. Speaking of Dean in a *Cahiers du Cinema* interview, Ray said, ". . . working with him was a joy."

credit: *Cahiers du Cinema*

ject are almost tearful evocations of John Donne's "No man is an islande." The fantasy for one of his projects seems to originate *in Ray's head* rather than in group discussion, or from modification of an idea tossed out by a friend.

Ray gave the best answer to the eternal question of how he (or anyone else) goes about creating a film in a 1961 interview:

"I simply think whether the story ought to set in motion harmony or dissonance. . . . It is very difficult to define. Every story which I attacked was always, for me, the occasion of throwing out a probe which would affirm or reaffirm an idea, or it might expose a contradiction, which seemed worth the trouble to follow through. But to define the reasons that motivate this feeling is to come back to trying to define oneself, and that is, for me, impossible. It is not that I am any more complicated than another person, but I think that very few people have the necessary qualifications for introspection and objectivity towards themselves." Ray, thinking the question led up to his being expected to make a statement as to what, of himself, was in his films, concluded: "Every film reveals only but a fragment of ourselves."[2]

Ray seems, then, to have thought out his film in scenario form, sketching out a dramatic treatment of his characters, as in a play synopsis. How did he get a screenplay out of this? The answer is: others did it for him. How did he proceed to deal with and modify a completed screenplay, either one he co-scripted or one done by hired screenwriters?

It seems that, not even in *Rebel*, the screenplay which owes the most to himself, did Ray ever incubate the film in *shot form*, or, like Jean-Luc Godard, draw it out in storyboard form. Mostly, he let the script form be done by his screenwriter for the studio. He would then film the script, changing dialogue or continuity that did not fit his cinematic concept. Ray, in other words, does not think in script form, in decoupage form.

Ray, lucidly as ever, seems to have again provided an answer to the paradox: how does a director who is so visual, avoid thinking in terms of shots ahead of the time of the drafting of a script, when he provided an answer to the question: how does his screenplay then take visual shape? When asked, "what purpose do you assign to the breaking down [of a film] into shots?" Ray said: "In my opinion, a script is broken down into shots, essentially to help production people and management to estimate the duration of the film: they thus have an idea of the number of days of shooting required and can better estimate the approximate cost of the film. When I collaborate on a script, or write a script myself, I put it into shot form for reasons of economics, but also, a little bit, to note down my feelings toward the evolution of the film at that moment, the visual ideas which, at that stage, seem to me the best: but everything changes when I am on the verge of doing it—because the circumstances, the different actors chosen, modify my point of view. That which every writer imagines to be at the heart of a black room must be submitted to the trial by fire of the reflectors, to the whir of the projectors, and still more, to the imagination of all those participating in the enterprise."[3]

What does Ray think is the significance of editing to the final finished film?

Montage must be seen as a new form of poetic creation. Very often, it is nothing. In effect, in America, except on rare occasions, and only where the director is also the producer, the final montage is at the mercy of the distributor. In our generation, as there are very few great writers, great poets, great playwrights, there are also very few great editors: and thus, whether the director is wrong or not, he must be the one to decide, in the last instance, whether the montage expresses, puts into play, the intentions of a sequence or not. Modifying the sense of a sequence through the montage seems to me on reflection, imprudent, maybe contradictory to the efforts deployed during the shooting, and is not justified except as a measure where, in the making and execution of the very same sequence, the director made a mistake. The montage must not do more than reinforce the primary intentions of the director, not modify them. To modify them seems, to me, to be the role of those who do not understand the film.[4]

The above revelation definitely puts Ray out of the category of a director of the montage school, but does it put him into the opposite category of the two, that of the mise-en-scène director? The *Cahiers* critics all seemed to think so, but, in my opinion, Ray comes in between these two opposites: he is not exclusively concerned with the mise-en-scène of the shot. He certainly did not think of using the mise-en-scène of a long take instead of a series of cuts, to create a more realistic effect. He is equally if not more concerned with the dramatic role of the shot in the overall film and with the pacing or tempo of certain sequences, something that shows he *is* interested in the montage structure of a film. In the above interview, he probably meant he thinks the montage or editing problems should be taken care of by the script and not be "invented" in the editing stage. He is obviously bitter at the damage editing did to his films and about the privilege of final cut being usurped from the director. Obviously, the only way a director could protect against such a system (ideally) is to shoot a film that was perfect or one that could not be edited. Yet, Ray's comments are revealing in that *his system* of making a film (to the probable disappointment of film buffs who love Ray) is very much the same as that of many other Hollywood film directors.

This all, superficially, puts Ray somewhere between being an *auteur* and an enlightened Hollywood director. Yet, I would hesitate to put him in such a nebulous category, or in any other category, because of his eclecticism. His formal elegance as a person enabled him to impress Hollywood and work with stars such as Bogart. But, inside, he was a serious rebel of the Camus type, and realized better than most rebels who never had any power how far he could go and how far he could not go. Considering the 1955 Hollywood mentality, *Rebel Without a Cause*—the way Ray did it—was as far as "they" (the studio) would let him go. Ray, to his credit, did, in the case of this film, push his ideas through at least one level of resistance successfully. But then and there he hit the limit; pushing further would have caused Warners to drop the film. So credit must be given to him both for pushing and for knowing how far to push.

Ray has said: "Good films somehow get made . . . to object to the movies because they are 'commercial' is idiotic; to accept that honesty and originality are necessarily 'uncommercial' is impossible."[5]

Yet let us not make Ray into an Establishmentarian director, either. As John Houseman says in *I'm a Stranger Here Myself*, a documentary film tribute to Ray, "Ray was at his best when he filmed stories of people oppressed by society." Houseman also ventured the guess that Ray was such a person himself and that he—as opposed to his colleague, director Elia Kazan whom Houseman felt was "tough as nails"—was relatively ill-equipped to deal with the insensitivity of the Hollywood system.[6] One could hardly then call Ray a "Hollywood director." Ray's quips on Hollywood's men who smoked bad cigars or said, "It's a color picture . . . why aren't there any pretty flowers on the table?" leaves you no doubt how he felt about them.[7]

Then there is Natalie Wood's story about the studio executives at

Warner's watching with horror the scene being filmed in *Rebel*, in which her father doesn't want to have her kiss him on the mouth anymore because she's turned sixteen.[8] All these things make us realize that it is a miracle that *Rebel* was filmed at all in the way Ray wished it filmed.

Ray, himself, has told admirably the next part of the story, how he incubated the idea of doing a film on juvenile delinquency and Warner's gave him the green light to go ahead. Even though the evidence shows that the film came entirely out of Ray's "Blind Run" script idea and had nothing to do with the book *Rebel Without a Cause*, Warner's still used the latter title. (Even after the success of the film under that title—and perhaps, *because* of that title—Ray, perversely, took no credit for the title: "They called it that; I called it 'The Blind Run.' ")

Ray, some time in the late summer of 1954, by his own account, told Lew Wasserman, a Warner's executive, that he wanted to do a film on juvenile delinquency. Wasserman told Ray that Warner's already owned such a property, the rights to Dr. Robert Lindner's book, *Rebel Without a Cause*. Ray called Wasserman back and said he didn't want to do a film based on the book. As Ray told the story, "Wasserman said: 'They know that you want to do a film on juvenile delinquency and they didn't understand your reply. Do you wish to go and see them about it?' " Ray did.

The work began when Ray went to a meeting with Steve Trilling, Warner's production chief, and told him how he had interviewed judges, talked to kids, delinquents, etc., whose problems he felt he sensed. Then Ray said: "There is the film . . . A few afternoons later," Ray continued, "Trilling called me and asked me to put my idea on paper. . . . Without a synopsis, a film didn't exist in Hollywood. The rites for the birth of a Hollywood film had to be observed . . . both the audience and the studio would be impatient for something to be put on paper; for the studio, a subject didn't exist without a synopsis, and for the director, the 'marvelous idea' didn't become a reality up to the moment where he could work on something—a process, then, where 'a canvas was born in a few hours of dictation to a public stenographer or in a session with a dictaphone.' Several people (Jim, Eve—later called Judy, and Demo—later called Plato) and several situations took form, and if the details were lacking, the general line took shape. At four in the morning I was finished with 20 pages of a story called 'The Blind

Run'; at seven-thirty, it was typed, and at the end of the day, Warners offered to buy it for $5,000."[9]

We must now also consider Ray's subconscious motives in crafting *Rebel*. Here, we have to consider his political convictions—the strength and vehemence of which would surprise the uninitiated but which do not *overtly* emerge in Ray's cinema in the form of political films. They run as undercurrents. For example, he said in an impromptu Cambridge, Massachusetts appearance at the Orson Welles Cinema in front of forty people, on January 2 1975, that the studio wanted Ginger Rogers to play in *In A Lonely Place*, but not only did he feel his wife of the time, Gloria Grahame, "could play the part better," but he knew that Ginger Rogers and her mother, Mrs. McMath, helped finance one of the "red" books that listed supposed Communist affiliations and contributed to the HUAC-McCarthy purge of directors and screenwriters. Ray concluded, with finality, that, today, he wouldn't let Ginger Rogers "on his stage" or "in the door." Thus, not only the appropriateness of an actor's skill, but also the degree of his or her honesty, and political commitment, surely ranked as simultaneous factors in Ray's sense of whom he wanted to have work with him, or wanted to cast in a particular film. After 1951, and McCarthyism, Ray increasingly preferred to film themes about outsiders, based on his feelings of revulsion about that period. Yet, as much as Ray's mood was affected by America's political climate, one must not look for an *overt* political message in *Rebel*. There was none.

Critical Misunderstanding of Ray and *Rebel* in the 1950s

In the postmortems on *Rebel*, to which Ray contributed by his 1956 writings and interviews, he never makes the slightest political claim for the film; but in his post-1970 comments he, unfortunately, does make some dubious political claims for it. He told a reporter from *The Real Paper* that James Dean would have gone to Chicago in 1968 and that the Chicago Seven "had all seen *Rebel* at least fifteen or twenty times."[10] Leonard Rosenman totally discounts this claim that *Rebel* was political, saying that "James Dean was apolitical and so was Nick Ray."[11] Ray is not, after all, a polemicist. His talent is elsewhere, as a depictor of an individual, personal mission and not of motives for activism.

Ray was, I feel, a 1950s rebel right out of Camus, not a 1960s revolutionary. This is nothing to be ashamed of; Ray was a damn good rebel for his time. As an Eisenhower era rebel, Ray did his share to focus young people's attention on the coming of America, which would be artificially held back by the McCarthy era. As a "within the system" rebel, knowing how far he could get, and pushing for it, he was terrific. But when he began imagining himself as a 1960's scenaricist of revolution, his scenarios inevitably mixed up 1930s comradeship with 1960s *Weltschmerz* and failed to weed out the hypocritical young from the committed ones. Some of the things Ray said about *Rebel Without a Cause* after 1971 detract from what the film was and was really meant to be about.

In 1954, "The Blind Run"/*Rebel Without a Cause* was to Ray, "an original idea for a film, without dramatic structure but with a point of view." The point of view was "The main action should be compressed into one day, beginning for Jim Stark in trouble and confusion, but ending, for the first time, in something different." The form of the narrative would be "classical"; the content would be the odyssey of Jim Stark: "A boy wants to be a man, quick"; the feeling to be evoked: "I wanted a *Romeo and Juliet* feeling abut Jim and Judy—and their families. *Romeo and Juliet* has always struck me as the best play written about 'juvenile delinquents.' "[12]

As it was, Ray's main thrust in *Rebel* was to deal with young *upper-middle-class malaise,* and we must never lose sight of this in "reading" the film. To this end, he valiantly campaigned to find just the right screenwriter. As it turned out, Robert Lindner—for a few, brief minutes, Leon Uris, Irving Shulman, Stewart Stern, and James Dean, in that order, all had their hands in the pie. The final credits (Story: Ray; Adaptation: Shulman; Screenplay: Stern) were an oversimplification of fact, which we will clear up in the next chapter.

When we come to Ray's concept and development of Jim, the central character of *Rebel Without a Cause,* who would show the upper-middle-class malaise to the public, we must realize the fine-spun workings of Ray's mind: even though it was a story, he would put it in a social, moral context. It would be an object lesson. That character would have to be right to convey that lesson: he would have to be honest, appealing, but also convey something of Ray, of Ray's internal "gut" feeling. James Dean must have been a Godsend to Ray here, for he fitted all of Ray's fantasies about such a character.

Happily, the requirements that all three criteria must be met in a Ray film, were more satisfactorily met in *Rebel* than in any of his works.

One must then obviously appreciate that, because of all of these obsessions to fulfill his vision, a Ray film must be devilishly hard to make, since his standards for himself are so amazingly high. His liking bright young actors—like the crop he discovered for *Rebel*—is obviously a vital ingredient in Ray's style of filmmaking, because in his open-ended way of planning, he needed such fresh input badly. Actors' experiences, like Dean's, were desperately needed to authenticate Ray's most personal films. Thus the invariably excellent results achieved in *Rebel* are a deceptive triumph for his filmmaking style, for it was a triumph he never could repeat.

What he went through to get his results, how well and thoroughly he rehearsed and prepared sequences, how surefootedness and improvisation were blended (all Ray's cinematographers, including Erny Haller, whose shooting of *Rebel* Ray later praised, were professionals, veterans), how he cast characters and worked with them, how he had an advanced sense of Method acting, and how all this jelled is very obscure, despite mid-1950s critics' growing interest in Ray's films.

Other than V. F. Perkins, who had written most perceptive comments on Ray in the early 1960s, contemporaneous critics writing in English said little that helped make his cinematic output understandable. Although over one hundred reviews of *Rebel* were published, virtually none of them showed any interest in Ray's cinema.

John Houseman, for example, thought that Ray's skill was a balance of arrogance and humility that made him a good director of actors. Ray lent "omnipresence to a cast," said one chronicler of the Hollywood scene, which offset his "neurotic" themes and erratic track record. This reputation was fostered by the fact that Ray was a grand thespian himself. I have rarely encountered anyone who can top him as an actor; and, unlike Fritz Lang, he was not above acting out a part for some of his fledglings. Hence it was easy to mistake him for a poseur.

It was, of course, Ray's modern, theatrical preparation of actors in *Rebel* that helped lift some of the better parts of the film above the typical mid-1950s Hollywood product. But that he backed this distinction up with innovative cinema remained unnoticed even by the more astute observers in 1956. *Rebel* became notorious for James Dean's performance, and its theme was excessively scrutinized: Were there really upper-middle-class delinquents? How violent was the film? Contemporary critics never sought to "read" the film through its cinematic techniques. The Romeo and Juliet theme was totally missed. Dean's acting was not seen as experimental, but Brandoesque. Totally missed was Ray's progress in working out new methods to develop and train film actors.

Obviously, in making *Rebel*, there was, for Ray, the challenge of developing some of the new crop of actors that were appearing in Hollywood at this time. Few knew that Ray might have been a secret mentor of a very young Tuesday Weld, a mid-1950s newcomer to Hollywood and a novice in a TV series. His fatherly attitude toward Sal Mineo, Jimmy Dean, and herself on the *Rebel* set has already been well-documented by Natalie Wood and we need not elaborate on it here.

Perhaps Ray's most "radical" act in *Rebel*, after his casting of James Dean, was giving Dean *carte blanche* to improvise acting and dialogue. With James Dean's auteurist improvisations, the script was much less of a problem than it would have been without Jimmy's amazing work and dedication. A constant process of rescripting took place on *Rebel*, which went on until that last day of shooting, something unusual for Hollywood in 1955, and Dean was the key to this. Jim Backus and James Dean rescripted all of *their* sequences, vastly improving on the screenplay. Only the puns and irony of *Rebel* seem to come from elsewhere than the rehearsals; they are in the Stern script.

Of Jimmy Dean, Ray says: "Working with him was a *joy*." Ray reports in the documentary film *I'm a Stranger Here Myself* that Elia Kazan even complimented him later: "The nicest thing Gadge ever said to me was, 'How did you get such a spontaneous performance out of Jimmy?' "

When, in December, 1954, Dean became Jim Stark—provided *Rebel* could be completed by June, 1955—the final link between Ray and Dean was complete, a link forged through the series of mutual friendships that surrounded them both. (The ones between Ray and Liz Taylor, and between Liz Taylor and Dean, somewhat predicated that there would be a good relationship between Ray and Dean.) The signing of Dean for *Rebel* was thus based on a lot of little things, mostly, the idiosyncracies of Ray, and the people in Ray's social circle, Elizabeth Taylor's liking of cats and her not caring how often Dean changed his shirt may have had more to do with James Dean's volunteering for a Ray & Dean combination than anyone realized. Ray's famous quote that when he met Dean, they "sniffed each other out like a bunch of cats," may have been a pretty good description. The high respect Ray held for Dean as an actor is hard to document in specifics, but one pertinent quote on the subject exists, and shows how well Ray quickly grew to understand Dean's sense of his life being led under compressed time, cinematic time:

> . . . but what allowed the actor to bring such a fine, intense perception to his role was that Jim Stark, like himself, was jealously seeking an answer, an escape from the surrounding world.
>
> [James Dean] rode a motorcycle. There were days when he did not shave. He dressed casually, untidily, which was invariably interpreted as a gesture of revolt. Not entirely true . . . it saved time, and Jim detested waste.[13]

Thus it came to pass that Ray's organic style of finding a theme, letting the cast assemble around it, and using his actors' "essence of the moment" (Dean's and Natalie Wood's personal rebellions, Sal Mineo, Jr.'s hero-worship of Dean, Dennis Hopper's sullenness, Corey Allen's stylized Method acting, etc.) led to the ideal casting of *Rebel Without a Cause*, as "the group of authors in search of a play" finally found their film.

6

Rebel Without a Cause: From Script to Film

SINCE *REBEL* BECAME A MILESTONE *Zeitgeist* film, it is interesting to speculate—as with films like *Gone with the Wind*—who gave what to it during its incubation period and during its filming between July, 1954 and May, 1955. Answers to this question are important, because if there is ever a claim for Nick Ray's authorship of a film, it is here that it must be settled.

We have given evidence that Ray is not the sole *auteur* of *Rebel*. Nor did he intend to be. His "communal" policy was never more successful than with this film. *On the Waterfront* and *East of Eden* are one hundred percent Elia-Kazan-authored films; and it is ironic that the *auteur* theory has been applied so loudly to Ray and yet not to Kazan. But Ray suited the framers of the *politique d'auteurs* in that he was concerned with investing a film with his signature, rather than filming a screenplay. But Ray's approach was so strongly oriented toward implicating other people in the creation of his films that it is amazing that his "co-*auteur*" approach has been neglected. At any rate, the authorship of *Rebel* is widely distributed; and through semiotic analysis a surprisingly great contribution can be seen to have come from James Dean. (I support Jim Backus's observation that Dean functioned, *in places*, as a directorial influence.)[1]

In the Kazan films it is hard to make any case for the authorship of the authors. I do not mean to disparage the trust that existed be-

Production still from *Rebel Without a Cause*. Ray describes *Romeo and Juliet* as the best story ever written about adolescents and paid homage to it in *Rebel*. Here Natalie Wood (Judy) tells James Dean (Jim) that she loves him. Judy/Juliet assumes the active role while Jim/Romeo passively accepts her declaration. Castellani's *Romeo and Juliet* (1954), made the year before *Rebel*, includes a shot exactly like this one except that the positions are reversed with Romeo above and Juliet below. *credit: Warner Bros.*

tween Brando and Kazan and that led to a special bonus, shown in
Brando's performance in *On the Waterfront*, but rather to suggest
that people be more careful about throwing the word *auteur*
around. One only has to document James Dean's contribution to the
final film (versus the final script) in *East of Eden*—which was nil—
with Dean's contribution to *Rebel*, which was of major importance,
to see that Kazan *is* the *auteur* of *East of Eden*. Words, shots,
editing effects are all Kazan's. *Rebel* has such a disparate smattering
of different vocabularies from different sources that it is an integrated film only in those specific sequences where Shulman's original idea, Stern's rewriting, Ray's reworking of the dialogue, Dean's
acceptance of such dialogue or improvisation of new, Ray's shooting,
and Leonard Rosenman's musical score coalesced. The great surprise was that *Rebel* is not more disjunct than it is.

As Wolf Rilla said in his book *The Screenwright*, "the screenplay
should give the director something to film, not make him invent
what he should film."[2] But the relation of screenplay to film should
be open-ended, the screenwright should give the director the sand
with which to build his castles, but he should know what kind of
castles the director likes to build and not give him unreasonable
sand.

Rebel Without a Cause seems to have grown through a stage of
successive scenarios, the first being an idea latent in Ray's head. *All*
of the versions of *Rebel* are interesting; particularly Ray's twenty-
page treatment. (There are several misreported versions of what
this treatment said; the only acceptable, accurate version is published in *Arts et spectacles* 619); Leon Uris's notes; the Shulman
script; and the various stages of Steward Stern's final screenplay, the
one used in the film. (There seem to have been at least *three* versions of Stern's shooting script.) All of these versions of *Rebel* are
interesting because all of them were somehow inferior to the way
Rebel was finally filmed (not always the case) and because the collective version made by the group around Nick Ray was superior to the
treatment Ray put on paper, in lonely isolation, illustrating how
much he needed the collective and how little he was a screenplay
auteur. Even the final shooting script and much of its dialogue are
not carried into the film, showing not only Ray's skill at last-minute
cinematic improvisation but also his deference to James Dean's special way of speaking, his *insistence* that Dean be allowed to revise
his own dialogue. That the "on the screen" version is uniquely

superior to the final screenplay is not only an indication of Ray's talent *once a screenplay existed*, but a justification of his collective way of working or wanting to work.

Here are the six screenplay stages of *Rebel Without a Cause*.

Robert Lindner's Contribution

There is the true case-history book published in 1944 by Dr. Robert M. Lindner about a juvenile delinquent named Harold whom he was treating at Lewisburg Federal Penitentiary, Pennsylvania. Warner Brothers bought the screen rights to the book in 1947. No more than two percent of *Rebel* is based on this book. Mainly, it is its title, *Rebel Without a Cause*, that was passed on to the film. The basic idea could also have been passed on; as it is, it is not. The two percent of Lindner's book found in the film is represented at the few moments in *Rebel* where you get the idea that a character did not know what he was doing, as was the case with Harold, the subject of the original study. The social context of the book has little if nothing to do with *Rebel*, the film, mainly because it did not interest Ray.

Even the sense or gist of the all-important title that Lindner's book contributed is *not* the same. Lindner's was a literally true (not a metaphorical) title. Lindner's patient, Harold, talked only under hypnotherapy and did not know why he committed those crimes. The only touch of this (the two percent) that shows up in the *Rebel* script is not in the case of the main character, Jim, but when a police officer asks Plato, "Why did you shoot those puppies?" Plato doesn't know.

Ultimately, the conclusion of Lindner's book which—very significantly—*was not* carried over into the script, was that only if an individual had a sufficiently strong ego, could he avoid becoming a teen-age psychopath or a "rebel without a cause." Later on, Lindner was to affirm this thesis again and again. This is why he volunteered to act as an advisor to the film. But Ray refused to let Lindner work with him, for reasons Ray himself gave.

Lindner has never received the credit he deserves because as Leonard Rosenman pointed out, "He was too journalistic for The American Psychiatric Association and too psychiatric for the journalists"—and readers of popular articles. Lindner understood the historic situation in 1954, when he gave a lecture called "Mutiny of the Young" (later published in a book called *Must We Conform?*). Remarkably, even while Nick Ray was floundering around with his *Rebel* script, Lindner was giving his lecture at an American Psychiatric Association meeting in another part of the very same city of Los Angeles—a remarkable case of myth and reality being co-present.

To no one's surprise, Ray and Lindner did meet at a cocktail party sponsored by the Hacker Foundation at the Beverly Hills Hotel. But the two men totally disagreed as to how Lindner's core idea should be filmed and presented to the public at large. Both men seemed to sense they were sitting on a potentially important project, a milestone film. As Ray tells it, "There was, naturally, some tension to overcome at our first meeting. He knew I had rejected his book, though he soon made it clear he was not piqued—only genuinely bewildered." And Lindner should have been bewildered. He was sincere. And it has taken literally half of the 1970s decade to clear away, for America to clear itself of, the fallacies and confused premises of the youth-to-power myth that started in 1955.

Ray continues:

His own book, he told me, contained the most searching basis possible for any film on delinquency. "You must do it this way. You must make a developmental film." In his lectures he was going to discuss *the conflict between protest and conformity*, that faced young people today [i.e. 1956]. The problem of the individual's desire to preserve himself in the face of overwhelming demands for social conformism was, he felt convinced, at the heart of the subject.

Lindner pleaded in vain with Ray, and too soon. It was thirteen years before the debunking documentary approach even had a chance against the youth myth, and eighteen years before debunking it became popular and established.

Ray completes his story of his encounter with Lindner:

As this nervous handsome man in his early forties [his remarkable career as a criminal psychologist was to be abruptly ended by death a year later] talked excitedly of protest and rebellion, I could not restrain the impression that he was grappling with a delayed rebellion of his own. The idea of filming his study of the young delinquent who related fantasies of violence under hypnosis seemed almost to obsess him. He almost begged me to do it; he offered his services as a consultant.[3]

Ray never accepted these services. Lindner as a consultant would only have gotten in Ray's way. Furthermore, Ray had a pragmatic reason to do *Rebel* his own way, about a group of boys and Jim, caught between them and his father's lack of leadership: "I explained that one strong reason for my not wanting to film his book was that I [had] already made *Knock On Any Door* about an adolescent boy who drifts into crime as a result of poverty and wretched upbringing, and I didn't want to repeat myself." Besides Ray was obsessed with delinquency in the middle class, partly because it was truly the newest California rage and partly because it fitted his own middle-class "delinquent" conflict with established society and the recent impositions McCarthyism had made upon him. Ray winds up his account of his meeting with Lindner: "His security, however, was unshakeable. So, in its way was mine—though behind it, lay some pressing doubts."[4]

Was it a mistake for Ray to have rejected Lindner? The answer is *yes*, if Ray had intended to make a serious film about *juvenile delinquency*. In his lecture and essay, called "Mutiny of the Young," Dr. Lindner indicted total conformity, said it would make everybody revolt, and stressed that the new adolescent generation differed from all the past ones by its tendency "to act out" demonstratively "their feelings of isolation" rather than suffer them silently and by doing this "running in packs," where no identity or ego-strength, the goal toward which an adolescent should strive, could ever be achieved. The New Adolescent's behavior was an honest reaction; but it was counterproductive. It was hopeless to behave in such a way without getting lost, for the two tendencies contradicted; the gang instinct, Lindner argued, was dangerous to the adolescent, because he or she would not develop any ego-esteem in a herd or a gang. The problems of conformity, however, is in the film, and how the new generation was revolting against it is at the film's core, especially after Stern revamped it. To sum up, Lindner said the rebel without a cause *acted* out his or her feelings, instead of hiding them and suffering or else he or she ran around in a mindless herd of other adolescents, rather than suffer isolation. Thus the two new manifestations could in cases, lead to violent, senseless crimes. More importantly, the rebel could not cure his or her own behavior problems. At this point Ray's film leaps away from Lindner's model. Jim in *Rebel* does act out his feelings and survives; but Buzz tries to both act out his feelings and run around as a member of a herd and does not survive. Lindner had a good point here. But it is not evident in the film that Buzz's contradictory ideas are the reasons why he is violent and finally dies. In short, Steward Stern's final screenplay touches on all these matters, but really does not clear them up, leading to what Leonard Rosenman calls the "cardboardness" of the characters. As an authentic treatise on adolescent psychology, *Rebel* doesn't make it.

As for the bizarre kind of incidents that adolescents were newly causing, the film tries to include many stereotyped examples of them, like those that can occur when adolescents relieve their tension by "acting out" their sense of isolation: the opening shot, of Jim lying on the ground playing with a toy monkey is an especially bizarre shot that works well and is rendered all the more bizarre because the shot before it, that was supposed to open the film and "explain" this shot, was cut by Warners; Plato having murdered some puppies with a pistol; Jim's mimicking the police siren in the police station. The running in the pack comes across symbolically in Judy's witless running around with Buzz's gang (for thrills? as protest? she doesn't know) until she is verbally and psychologically challenged by Jim: "You always hang around such rank company?" during the switchblade fight sequence.

However, there are only these tiny elements of Lindner in the film *Rebel Without a Cause*. Jim Stark, the rebel character, is a bit more complex than that, as he is an extension of Nicholas Ray's inner persona. But Ray Framek, the juvenile officer—representing Ray's sense of liking to give advice—and a character who functions as a pragmatic alter-ego for Jim—is not *unlike* Lindner, in his open, verbal, yet dignified sympathy *(vide* Lindner's *Must We Conform?)* for the adolescent who feels he or she is the victim of adult society. On that score, Dr. Lindner felt the problem was that adults insisted on too much conformity; everywhere the adolescent turned, (in 1955) there was a "No."

Warner Brothers' Option

In 1947, Warner Brothers bought the screen rights to Dr. Lindner's book. A Warner's executive went to New York and signed Marlon Brando to play in the film on the strength of the rave notices that Brando was receiving for his acting in Tennessee Williams' *A Streetcar Named Desire*. Warner's never exercised the Brando option. After it expired, however, the studio held on to the rights to the book.

Ray's Synopsis

The Wild Ones, starring Brando, was produced by the adventurous Stanley Kramer and released by Columbia in January, 1954. Meanwhile, Nick Ray, who had been affected by the McCarthy lists, was still in sunny Spain, finishing up his color "Western," *Johnny Guitar.* After the film was completed, Ray returned to Hollywood. *Johnny Guitar* was released in the United States on May 28, 1954. Ray joined Warner Brothers as a director, where he was given an office next to Elia Kazan's (who was then filming *East of Eden* with James Dean on an "A" budget). Ray snooped around and decided that he was interested in juvenile delinquency. He thought of doing a film to be called "The Blind Run." Warners thought in terms of a money-making success on juvenile delinquency to be called *Rebel Without a Cause.* By August, 1954, the two trains of thought collided.

A twenty-page synopsis that Ray developed for "The Blind Run" was as far as he got in developing the story line himself. Despite being assigned a sympathetic producer, Dave Weisbart, he couldn't move it further by himself—the details just didn't come—and the rest of the story of completing the script is of a collective effort. The agonizing Ray found a screenwriter with whom he worked out a script and quarreled over it.

Leon Uris's Conception

Early in the autumn of 1954, Leon Uris (author of *Battle Cry* and *Exodus*) was assigned by Warners to work with Ray on the *Rebel Without a Cause* project. He and Ray were apparently on different wavelengths. Uris proposed a communal network in action, a macropicture, something like what later was filmed in *Exodus*. With this in mind, he constructed an imaginary town in which Jim Stark was to live. He did research to make this town typical and started to blueprint it brick by brick. This did not fit Ray's conception which was to film a boy's state of mind. Nor did it fit Ray's trust in romantic allegory rendered authentic through cinematic means rather than a cast of thousands. Ray's style of allegory was designed and meant by him to be rendered powerful through cinema, not through sociology. *Rebel*'s "radical message" to youth and its Romeo and Juliet theme were to be gotten across simply, carefully, systematically, by improvisation and good acting emanating from an organic community of young actors that he would set up on the spot.

Compare *Rebel Without a Cause* (1955) with *Exodus* (1958) and you will instantly see the difference in approach. (The Uris approach in depth is also evident in *American Grafitti* and other pseudodocumentary "youth" films, whereas the sparse Ray approach was a bit stiffly continued by Peter Bogdanovich in *The Last Picture Show*.) The difference in approach was fatal. It was not just one of scale, but of a personal, Carlylean concept of history (Ray) versus the Tolstoyan (Uris). Do heroes or events make history? Ray opted for the former. He asked for another writer, and Uris left the project.

Irving Shulman's Contribution

To do the second screenplay version of *Rebel*, in October, 1954, Ray brought in Irving Shulman, author of a novel about teen-age violence, *The Amboy Dukes* (basis for the film *City Across the River*). He and Ray were in immediate agreement to transfer Lindner's lower-middle-class rebel of Polish descent to an upper-middle-class California context. This was a stroke of genius on the part of whoever thought it up. (Probably Ray and Shulman both had the notion independently.) This set *Rebel* apart from *The Wild Ones* and *Blackboard Jungle* and would give it its distinctive identity. Shulman is further credited (by every one of the various accounts of the shaping of the film) with introducing the planetarium sequence (which Leonard Rosenman feels is the key to the film and should have been developed more) and the "Chickie Run" sequence, the latter based on a newspaper account of an incident Ray and Shulman read.

According to Nick Ray, "Later on, I had the idea of another sequence in the planetarium. At the climax of the story, when Plato believes that Jim, his only friend, has abandoned him, I thought he should return, at night to seek refuge under the great dome with the artificial sky. It was the kind of dramatic end that to me was essential to the story; classic tragedy suggested it to me. Shulman, on the contrary, had a completely opposing opinion. He insisted that Plato would seek refuge in the mansion. To my eyes, this was a major point, because it showed evidence of a development more violent than I wanted, something Shulman seemed incapable of admitting to. This led me to understand that our points of view were essentially different. Despite the precious elements Schulman brought to the scenario, once again, we were at an impasse. We were now at the end of November, 1954.[5]

Stewart Stern's Synthesis

What really counted, according to Leonard Rosenman, was that in December, 1954, Warner's rejected Shulman's script. Although this contradicts David Dalton's statement in *James Dean: The Mutant King* that Ray fired Shulman, Rosenman is probably correct. Rosenman, who had been assigned by Warner's to do the musical score for *Rebel* (and who personally knew James Dean) now suggested his friend, Stewart Stern, to help Ray perfect the script.

According to Ray, who immediately and gratefully accepted Stern: "I noted: Dave (producer Weisbart) and I must plan to get a young, beginning screenwriter, one who stays on our side and works with us until the final curtain.[6]

Stu Stern was to be a major factor in *Rebel*. Some consider the intellectual, young—then only 31—Jewish, Freudian, the co-*auteur* of *Rebel*. (We will consider this supposition in detail later.) At any rate, by March, 1955, Stern laid down the final skeleton—one that ran over 250 shots—a skeleton which was then continuously improvised upon. The final script has so much meat on it, some could (and was) pared away to make it the right length, easier to follow, and mythically powerful. Other shots in the script were omitted or juggled because Ray had no or other cinematic plans for them.

Where neither Ray nor James Dean had a last-second brainstorm or change of mind, the original Stern script shows through. After about twenty viewings of *Rebel*, this becomes apparent. Jim and Judy's first conversation is an interesting example. It sounds different from the style of the Stern-like opening sequence; it "reads" as if Ray had written Judy's part and Dean had written his own. The same goes for the father-son confrontation sequences. They sound as if Ray wrote Jim Backus's lines and Dean again wrote his own.

Barring a complete semiotic investigation, these observations are very general ones. But the point can be made that the overall narratological level of the film often shows a lack of integration between the screenplay (narrative component of the film) and the cinema (visual realization). In many of those cases, the film is saved because the cinema is so overwhelming (or beautiful) that its inconsistency or incongruity with the script remains unnoticed or unobserved.

Elizabeth Taylor was pregnant with Michael Wilding's son from August, 1954, to May, 1955, so that Nick Ray was provided with James Dean who had been scheduled to star with Taylor and Rock Hudson in *Giant*. Meanwhile, Ray's *Johnny Guitar*, of which Ray for once in his life was a co-producer, had been released by Republic Pictures in May, 1954, and was running to mixed reviews, but good box office. This stroke of fortune enabled Ray—during the brief week in early March, 1955, when Warner's ditched the black-and-white CinemaScope version of *Rebel* and revived it as a Warnercolor project—to threaten Warner's that he'd film it himself!

Though finding James Dean for *Rebel* was extraordinarily lucky for Ray, I feel he would have made such a film anyway, and regardless of whom he cast, the film would have worked. Yet all evidence suggests that it would not have succeeded had not Dean helped it at the box office, where it grossed approximately five million dollars. (Two million people have seen *Rebel* in CinemaScope. In addition it is often seen in adulterated form on television, where one sees only about sixty percent of the image area.)

Once the studio came to a decision to start work on *Rebel* in autumn, 1954, about the time Warner's was beginning to see glimmers of a juvenile box office topping by far that of Stanley Kramer's *The Wild Ones*, Ray needed a final screenplay fast; and he could not write it out himself. When Leonard Rosenman, *Rebel's* studio-assigned musical director (a natural who had already worked with Dean—scoring *East of Eden*—with Warnercolor, and with CinemaScope) suggested his New York cohort, Steward Stern, to put the Shulman treatment of "The Blind Run"/*Rebel* into final form, Ray said yes; and his project was saved.

Ray's final piece of luck was that Dean was available to work, thanks to Liz Taylor's pregnancy. Though Dean had been contracted for *Giant* on the studio's faith in the rushes of *East of Eden*, and shooting was scheduled to begin the moment Liz Taylor recovered, Dean had no feature film commitments from

October, 1954, to June, 1955. It is this temporal accident, and not
the *auteur* theory, that would make *Rebel Without a Cause* one of
the most written about and talked about films in American cinema
history.

7

Rebel Without a Cause: Analysis of the Narrative

THE TOTAL RUNNING TIME of the final version of *Rebel Without a Cause* is given by various sources as 110 or 111 minutes. The film can be broken into eight sections of roughly fifteen minutes—give or take a few—each. (Segmentating a film into its obvious filmic, non-filmic, or "filmic like" components, according to a method devised by Vladimir Petric and modified by the author, is useful not only in order to see how the film under analysis was constructed narratologically, but to begin the precise assessment of how the narrative is supported by the filmic components the director used to build his film. Does the director use any cinematic integration to build his film toward a cinematic form of expression? Or, did he merely film the narrative? We must obviously begin this process by stating what we think the narrative is. Step one in this process is segmentation.)

In this chapter, then, we shall attempt to give the background for a thorough reading. Particular attention is paid, for example, to the first quarter of the film (segments 1 and 2) because it is here that a film's shot vocabulary is disclosed. This may become very complicated, for a unit of shot vocabulary can be merely a narrative one, or it can be a very complex narrative component-film component combined, a truly cinematic unit, which is made up of many, many combined sub-units, and which, while it functions in the film to give expression and information, can seem like a moment of culmination, high impact, without any further "work" to do. In written analysis, we also are faced with the problem of reducing a dynamic interaction to separately stated "bits," which puts an intolerable burden on a reader's mind, if he or she wants to reconstruct this film in the light of what we have said. Therefore, the purpose of this, and the next, chapter is not to read *Rebel* so much as to demonstrate why

oduction still from *Rebel Without a Cause*. Dennis Hopper
oon), Natalie Wood (Judy) and James Dean (Jim) look over
e cliff where Buzz has just gone to his death. Sequences like
is, which exclude an adult point of view, made the film popu-
· with teenagers. *credit: Warner Bros.*

97

and how it is cinematic and not mere filmed narrative, why the film was a classic case of aesthetic realism taken seriously, with a special case study of how James Dean helped authenticate the part of Jim Stark so that people thought the two of them were synonymous on the screen. It is most interestingly, to demonstrate how a film which is not authored by one person can go through an organic (rather than merely mechanical) process that actually creates a product superior to what the director would probably have done on his own. This is, then, a case study of *Rebel*, as a creation, and only an analysis insofar as I feel it necessary to defend the film against those skeptics who have never given it its due.

With this in mind, let us follow through the narrative of the film, segment by segment, with particular attention to segments 1 and 2, where several sub-themes are introduced, compressed, and started off, in such a time-compressed fashion, that we know we could not be observing such concurrence in any coherent fashion on a stage. *Rebel*, I invite both students of cinema and of theater to note, breaks with both the Hollywood narrative tradition of 1938–1955 and uses autonomous subplots to give the feeling of *Zeitgeist* rather than of theatrical unity of time and place. It is thus an attempt to escape the chains of genre cinema; it could never have been a play.

The eight segments of *Rebel Without a Cause* useful to a discussion of the film:

1. Police Station Sequence; Jim, Judy, and Plato, and Jim's parents all brought together in one place.
   Jim meets Plato (but forgets him and doesn't recognize him the next time he sees him).
   Plato meets Jim and remembers him.
   The camera introduces Jim and Judy.
   Jim will recall Judy; Judy won't recall Jim.
2. Jim and Judy's second encounter;
   (A) Judy rejects Jim in favor of a group; first day at school;
   (B) Planetarium lecture, leading Jim and Plato to the balcony, which sets up the Switchblade Fight Sequence.
3. Switchblade Fight Sequence.
4. First confrontation between Jim and his dad. Jim puts on red jacket, and goes to chickie run. Parallel sub-sequence between Judy and her dad.

5. Chickie Run Sequence. Death of Buzz.
6. Jim's fight with father and mother. Second confrontation with dad.
7. Judy and Jim and Plato in mansion. The Artificial Family Sequence, disrupted by the appearance of Crunch, Goon, and Moose.
8. Return to the planetarium, where Plato is killed. Judy and Jim are united as a couple, Jim's dad promises to try harder, and Jim is the welder of a new temporary alliance of Jim, Judy, and Dad.

(Detailed analysis of Sections 3 and 5 will be reserved for the next chapter.)

Taking key speeches from these eight segments, we find that each sets up a dilemma that is seemingly resolved and then, suddenly, creates a new dilemma that will be resolved in the next segment. This enables the film to cover a lot of teen-age dilemmas and also keeps the narrative going. However, *Rebel* is not *Tom Brown's School Days* and does not take place "late at night in a teen-age underworld of violence, romance and death," as has been written by David Dalton in *James Dean: The Mutant King*. It takes place in a split-level upper-middle-class Los Angeles milieu. From the very first shot, of a sport-coated James Dean lying in a gutter playing with a toy monkey, an elegant teen-toy, material world is flashed at our consciousness. Despite the first shot of the version we see being the second shot of the planned film (the first shot showing a bit of ritual Friday night violence, was cut by Warners) we see the first "word" of the shot vocabulary of the film. The shot is only image and music; its composition "says" the hero is *inarticulate*. When shots like this repeat, they mean our hero is mute.

After the credits, a progression of themes begins. One theme: In the police station sequence, it looks as if Jim Stark's problems with his father will come to a head soon. Will he solve them? Another theme: His sudden desire for Judy creates a new problem on top of his old one. In his first attempt to get to know her, in Segment 2, he is rebuffed, which triggers off a new feeling of isolation, and adds to the problem of his not wanting to be like his dad that he outlined in his rap with the sympathetic juvenile officer, *Ray* Framek (Ed Platt), to whom he confessed he'd love just to "get through *one* day without being confused." The key spoken sentences here serve as second articulations of already dramatically developed themes, and bridge these themes. *All* these themes are about "being confused."

Now we know what *Rebel* will be/should be about: Will Jim Stark get through one day? Segment 1 informs the film, so, during the next seven segments, we can *join* with Ray in meaningfully following his film. *Rebel* lets us participate in it, but observe carefully how, at the same time, we are being manipulated into an Expressionistic *Welt*, one where we do not *see* so much as have a vision.

Segment 1: Police Station Sequence

Segment 1 begins with problems Judy and Jim have in common. They are excerpted from a composite of all teen-agers, and singled out as special cases (Jungian as well as Freudian) of those whose problem is their fathers. (Resnais will develop this fully with Bernard and Marie-Do in *Muriel.*) As they appear in Ray's film, they are sociological types and no longer screen writer Stern's melodramatic types.

Jim is brought in and booked for common drunkenness (something that, in 1977, we have to recall could and did happen in 1955, and still happens in New Hampshire.) While Jim sits drunkenly on a police bench, waiting for his father to come to the station, Plato appears. He, too, has the look of someone who has been picked up for a crime, but, with Plato, it seems as if his offence could only have been thought-crime. Then we see Judy, wearing a red coat with red lipstick, sitting opposite Officer Framek. What has she done? Right now, we are just outlining the dramatic tension to be produced by the narrative. The camera here is doing its work; it is panning away from two people talking in medium shot and searching for one of the others, often seen through a glass partition in another room. As the words define the first articulation, the camera suggests but by no means defines a possible second articulation. Our imagination is engaged, we are involved, by the camera. Later on, in Segment 6, the watchword will be: "We are all involved." At least three shots in this long sequence build this metaphor, whose precise meaning here we can later retroactively assign. We are lured into a *Welt* by the seeming open structure of the film. As it progresses, the door of multiperception closes, and we are aware of ever more and more specific meaning.

Framek is sympathetic to Judy, but he is also doing his job as police officer very thoroughly and is trying to hit her with specific (Freudian) questions. She has been arrested for wandering around the streets at 1 AM in a California suburb, a community where everybody drives. The implication (plus her red coat and equally red lipstick) is that she might have been soliciting. (Actually, her red coat is indexical *color coding, a foreshadowing* that she belongs to the same class of people who rebel, a parallel to Dean's wearing his red jacket later in the film.) She, however, tells quite a different story as to why she was wandering around at 1 AM.

Officer Ray: What makes you think [your father] hates you, Judy?
Judy: He looked at me like I was the ugliest thing in the world. He doesn't like my friends. He doesn't like one thing about me. You know what he called me? He called me a *dirty tramp!* My *OWN FATHER* (cries.)
Officer Ray: Do you think your father really means that?
Judy: Yes . . . No . . . I don't know.

The above four lines show both sides of the "rebel" situation—the adolescent who is certain why he or she is being picked on and the adolescent who becomes less certain when asked whether he or she might have misunderstood, misinterpreted, or missed seeing the sympathy that might be available to her or him, even from one who seems an enemy, or conformity figure (father, high school principal, authority figure, police officer).

When Ray Framek deals with Jim, it is entirely another situation. Judy has been "cleared," and her mother called to take her home. She, however, is very annoyed that Framek didn't call her *father* to take her home, as he promised her he would.[1]

Natalie had a minor car accident while out cruising around with Dennis Hopper and some others—Ray encouraged the young cast to go around as a group. She was taken to a hospital, was called a "juvenile delinquent" by the doctor there, refused to ask for her parents, telling the hospital to send for Nick Ray instead. The hospital doctor's calling her "a juvenile delinquent" becomes "he called me a dirty tramp" in the film.

The police next find Plato much more remote than harmful (even though he committed the kind of senseless act of violence that Ray while researching the film found so many teens were committing. Plato has shot some puppies with a pistol. This episode tells us that Plato has access to a pistol. The police officer now recommends a "shrink" for Plato, only to find out he already has one, and it hasn't done much good (something Dr. Lindner would not have allowed to remain in the script).

Jim now enters the chamber of "The Grand Inquisitor." Jim is
sullen. Ray challenges him aggressively:

Officer Ray: Why aren't you wearing your boots?
Jim tries to punch him. (Dean's acting keeps it believable, but this scene
only plays well due to heavy protection from the music, Dean's Method
acting, and the fact that it takes place in an inner room, reminiscent of the
Hollywood night club or place where the dream world begins.) Dean fails to
connect, as Ray blocks the punch.
Officer Ray: Too bad you didn't connect. You would have landed right in
juvenile hall. That's what you wanted, didn't you?
Jim: What for?
Ray challenges Jim. He suggests he *wants* to get sent to juvenile hall. Jim's
reply is defensive, defensive of his own perverse desire to get sent to
juvenile hall.)
Jim: Leave me alone.
Ray: No.

Ray now tries to convert him into an ally, and succeeds (because
the film must show how a rebel without a cause becomes a rebel
with a cause). By the end of the confrontation, they are friendly.
(This will occur once more in the film, *after* the fight between Jim
and Buzz, where the two boys start to become confederates.)
Officer Ray, in fact, plays the Dr. Lindner type to perfection,
especially with Judy. Yet, with Jim, Officer Ray Framek plays rather
the political ally, "Let's form an alliance, shall we?" and in that way
more approximates the anti-McCarthy side and consciousness of
director Nick Ray. Two things happen at once here. Jim Stark, then,
is not a documented case study at all. (Perhaps he is James Dean's
Expressionist vision of himself, but it is impossible to prove this.)
Rather, Jim Stark seeks not only to examine the cause and the
backbone of loyalty, but also how it is formed, to whom it is given. It
seems that Nick Ray, through this character, is asking: Can an extension of trust be achieved between a member of one group (the
police, for example) and another group (adolescents)? He answers
this question (realistically? Expressionistically? both ways at once?)
by saying that aware members of both camps can become friends
and symbolize trust. The character Jim carries both the questions
and the beginning of the answers, but within the limits of the narrative, he could not have solved the problem of loyalty. The director
intervenes at the end of the film to endow Jim with unearned wis-

dom. As Jim Stark's extraordinary lucidity is not anchored on his character development in the film, his "magical insights" in *Rebel* are often falsely attributed by youth-mythologizing biographers (such as David Dalton in *James Dean: The Mutant King*) to James Dean alone; the Nick Ray insights given Jim Stark to mouth are seriously overlooked. Leonard Rosenman commented, Nick Ray was "a derelict" himself.[2]

As Ted Perry has observed, the best neorealist films (and *Rebel* in its way is a neorealist film) express a tension between a contrived aesthetic realism and documentary-like shooting style. The fantastic realism in *Rebel* which, in the 1970s, fathered a pictorial art movement all its own, should be familiar enough to anyone who reads novels, goes to movies, daydreams, etc. The enormous liberty Ray took with the main character of *Rebel* fits with the way anyone who has a strong vision would like to create a character. While granting synchronicity between James Dean and Jim Stark, let's not, on the other hand, forget that Jim Stark is also no more James Dean than Scarlett O'Hara is Margaret Mitchell.

Who Jim was in *Rebel* is never so clear as what he thinks of others. The narrative reveals this nicely. Ray Framek "convinces" Jim (and the audience) that *he*, Framek, understands that Jim's *father* is the problem. Ray has converted Jim into an ally by the token application of classical Greek politics: offer to join someone against an enemy, and you find an ally and a friend. This fits with Nick Ray's feelings or convictions that no man can operate alone. (Here Ray connects with François Truffaut's sensibilities, and the content of most of Truffaut's films.) If he does stay alone and he is talented, he is wasted.

For Jim Stark to become a productive member of society, his isolation should be resolved, yet he challenges all the terms by which alliances can be made. He tells Officer Ray he "never wants to be like *him*" (his father). This is the watchword of Segment 1 and this theme will be continued in Segment 4. The police station sequence ends Segment 1, suggesting a new odyssey for Jim on new terms.

The realistic, talky, fairly immobile and documentary-like beginning to *Rebel* is significant in its order of appearance in the film because, as a *Cahiers* interviewer once said to François Truffaut, "People don't mind a realistic story becoming melodramatic, but they do mind a film that starts as melodrama and ends up going beyond it."[3] It is very important that *Rebel* start realistically if it is to be a successful film. Stewart Stern's screenplay must be given credit for imposing this beginning onto the film. And unlike the semidocumentary beginning of a film like Nicholas Roeg's *Performance*, which does not integrate with its more allegorical second half, *Rebel*'s first fifteen minutes have enough camera mobility to suggest that the pace of the film will now quicken.

Segment 2: Part A—Jim Meets Judy

Moving into Segment 2, which starts when Jim wakes up to a "new day," we see him in a friendly scene at the family breakfast table. We feel the promise of a new day. Everyone is standing around Jim, giving him a kind of physical support, emphasized by the mise-en-scène of the actors. Even Jim's father is trying to give him support for his first day at a new school, "Dawson High." (Segment 1 suggested that in his last school Jim had "messed up" a kid who had called him "chicken" to provoke a fight. His mother, we learn in Segment 6, insisted on the move to a new location.)

During the breakfast conversation, Jim looks out the window and fleetingly sees Judy go by, walking her dog. Judy seems like a breath of fresh air and the music helps us realize it; so does the change in color composition—we suddenly see greens. Jim now leaves for school, after being warned by his father: "Be careful how you choose your friends; don't let them choose you." Much of *Rebel* has key lines like this spoken either before or after their prime applicability to the action; in *Rebel*, much of the verbal signification predicts or retroactively informs; as a result, there is a sense of a maze.

Now comes a short, moving, and important bit of dialogue between Jim and Judy, as their paths cross on the street. This is one of the two sequences Eric Rohmer considered a lyric interlude, i.e., a portion of the film apart from the film proper, as, say, a dance number would function in a non-musical film. We accept it mostly just because it is there.

The conversation between Jim and Judy is indicative of the way that Nick Ray might have imagined the first conversation between Romeo and Juliet. Also, it is the first time in the film where the persona of Nick Ray quite obviously appears. James Dean probably wrote his own lines here; Ray probably wrote Judy's, and an improvisational session at rehearsal worked out how to make it sound authentic. The result is semantically superb, a true teen face-off.

Jim proposes, exposes, expounds; Judy denies, evades, rejects. We see the 1950s male-female dilemma at its worst. The boy is eager, and then, when rejected, saddened that his sincerity of enthusiasm fell on deaf ears; the girl arrogantly knows hers is the power of rejection. Yet she wants to coax the boy to expose himself so that she can find out what he thinks about her before she rejects him even if she suspects she will reject him at the end. The conversation here is not so much to give us teen dialogue but to show how Jim is hurt by the general style of behavior that Judy at this moment, represents. (It is here, of no concern to us, that the real-life James Dean was guilty of some of the very behavior that Judy exhibits in this sequence.)

Later on, in Segment 7, there is a sequence which retroactively informs us what was going on in Judy's head while she was relating to Jim here. Jim first confesses how he felt about Judy the first time he saw her; Judy then shares with him, and confesses how and why she behaved as she did during their first little conversation.

Jim: You know somethin'. I woke up this morning, you know. And the sun was shining. And it was nice. (whispers to himself . . . ah . . . happy thing! . . . .) The first thing, I saw *you*. (whispers to himself . . . . she's nice . . . . she loves you. . . .) Boy. This is goin' to be one perfect day—so you better live it up—'cause, tomorrow, you'll be nothin'. (whispers. . . . see, I almost lost you. . . .).
Judy: I'm sorry. I'm very mad I treated you mean today. You shouldn't believe that thing I was saying. Nobody, nobody acts sincere.

The confession Judy makes is remarkable, for two reasons. First, because it uses the key word *sincerity*, which she learned from Plato who got it from observing Jim. This shows a tutorial side of the film, even though it is disguised in action dialogue. Second, it is a kind of class indictment against a whole group of people. She is implying she is just an indexical symbol of a whole group of Judys. It also suggests that, removed from the conformist influence of Buzz, she can start to "believe" what she is saying. Now let's return to Segment 2, and how she and Jim spoke in their first encounter. (At this moment in the film we do not yet realize that Judy's negative way of dealing with Jim here is a result of her brainwashing by the non-think of Buzz's gang):

Music (romantic, opening up of possibilities, light theme, never used again)

Jim: Hi . . . Hi . . . Wait a minute. (catches up to her.) Hi . . . I saw you before.

Judy: Well . . . stop the world.

Jim: (inaudible)

Judy: Now that's true. But life is crushing in on us.

Jim: (mocking, theatrically) Life . . . can be . . . beautiful. Uh. I know where it was. (Quickly) Where I first . . .

Judy: Where what was?

Jim: Where I first saw you. (music: Jim & Judy love theme. It suddenly erupts softly) Everything goin' O.K. now? (music over this) You live *here*, don't you? (music again)

Judy: WHO *LIVES!*

Jim: Hey. Where's Dawson High?

Judy: At University and 10th.

Jim: (very softly) Thanks.

Judy: You want to (hesitates) *carry* my books?

Jim: (quickly as if to hide nervosity) I got muh car (Dean's Indiana accent is suddenly given free rein here). You wanna go with me?

Judy: (solemnly) I go with the kids. (Screaming of kids in the background. It's Buzz and the gang down the street in two cars.)

Jim: Yeh. (disappointed) Yeh. I bet. (resentfully) All right. (said more friendly) (Car screeches to a halt down the street.)

Judy: (turns to him and squeezes off the line) I bet you're a real yo-yo.

Jim: I love you too.

Gang: Hey . . . (shouting)

Cookie: What's that? (meaning Jim)

Judy: Oh, that's a new disease. (She exaggeratedly stresses her solidarity with the kids.)

Buzz: A friend of yours?

This shot sequence, at first glance, seems to be more Brando than Brando. Everything is broken up into short, five-word Brando-like speeches. But note the way the music and dialogue counterpoint each other and form an organic whole, as in a well-scripted radio play, where music is used as cues, and something new is started every three seconds, to compensate for the audience's lack of visual cues. The above sequence remains one of the most unusual Hollywood film sequences, and it is at points such as these, that one begins to sense that a leap from second-generation cinema to third-generation "ontological" cinema is under way.

Also, this is one of the highly improvised parts of the film, worked out in rehearsal, and not just laid down by the screenwriter. A careful reading of *Rebel* would soon expose which sections were improvised and which were not. Note that there are two different orders of signification in the film. The more improvised order of signification conspires to draw the spectator into the action, and, at moments, has little to do with advancing the narrative. Fortunately, narrative continuity is always maintained, but as we have hinted, Ray does this often in *Rebel*, by retroactively supplying the missing narrative links. Segment 7 "explains" and gives the narrative signification of Jim and Judy's first encounter. Judy's "I'm sorry. I'm very mad I treated you mean today," confessed in Segment 7, changes the retroactive signification of segment 2 to "I am now being mean. I am not acting sincere." This is the signification of her dialogue in Segment 2. Crucial to whether *Rebel* is a successful film is the question: does this signification work? The answer is difficult. I sense Ray's camera tries hard to protect the fragility of communication at moments like this. During the first half of this exchange between Jim and Judy, the camera travels with them as they walk along together. When Judy asks him whether he's making a romantic approach ("You want to *carry* my books?"), Ray switches to a rapid series of countershots, showing them from lots of angles, showing them constantly in new positions, until their spatial dislocation jars us, and we feel Jim has "lost his footing." (Note that here Ray does not ever use shot-countershot more than one time in one location.

Jim next drives to Dawson High. The gang, whom we have briefly met (the shot vocabulary of the film has fused a sight-sound "sentence" of two significations: Judy's "I go with the kids" and the image of Buzz, Cookie and several kids in a car, along with Judy, who entered it. This gives us a pre-interpretation of the gang we are now again to encounter on the steps of Dawson High, as they give Jim a highly ominous new-kid treatment. They go out of their way to show he is an outsider. At the same time, we learn nothing about them, they are a repeating sentence, a Greek chorus. As Leonard Rosenman has observed, "they are cardboard characters." This would bode ill for the narratology of the film, which could completely lose its thrust here and degenerate into *High School Confidential* if the filmmakers had not fallen back on professional know-how to develop its continuity. Fortunately, not improvisational brilliance, but the steady hand of the scriptwriter's skill takes over, and Plato is reintroduced as a character at this point in the film.

He is introduced visually, as the script had a very awkward *way* of having him come up to Jim and say, "You remember me?" We see, instead, Plato combing his hair while looking in a school locker door mirror, above which is taped a cut-out of a magazine picture of movie star Alan Ladd. Jim's face suddenly appears in the mirror (next to the icon of Ladd) and Plato smiles. We now know Jim is Plato's hero. Moments later Ray's camera cuts to a detail of a school bulletin board announcing (to both the characters and us): "Juniors and Seniors. Planetarium Field Trip. 2 PM Sharp." Fritz Lang's famous dictum, "The script creates a film, but the director creates a new film," is applicable here. The "script film" said: "You must reintroduce Plato now"; the "director's film" modifies this anew, saying "Yes, but in this new, meaningful way, where we not only introduce Plato but foreshadow his importance to the planetarium sequence by creating a shot metaphor: you see Plato; cut; you see the word "Planetarium." This linkage is no longer the primal shot vocabulary unit we were talking about, but an attempt to create cinema, by setting up a filmic equivalent to a simile or metaphor. Whether we "get this," depends on whether what we see and hear in the film is intrinsothemic to what the director or author had in mind. Nick Ray has indicated he wanted Plato's home to be the Griffith planetarium. Ray's reputation, then, rests on whether his metaphoric intentions were successfuly conveyed, intrinsothemically, by the film, through devices of linking filmic manipulation to narrative. The above example shows a typical way Ray used to achieve this linking.

To continue. By bringing back Plato, Ray not only has rescued the narrative but has pre-signified Plato's symbolic association with the coyly named Griffith Planetarium, to which the film now dissolves. (Note here that Plato does not fit into the Hollywood iconography of being the sidekick, a sidekick of Jim; his character is a genuine if incomplete attempt at cosmic symbolism.) All of the people involved in making *Rebel* disagree on how successful a character he was, Nick Ray saying, "Plato had his own story to tell," meaning he could have been the subject of another youth film;

Frame enlargement from *Rebel Without a Cause:* the planetarium sequence, James Dean, Sal Mineo, and in the back, Nick Adams, luminous in the darkened planetarium, react to the lecturer's speculation on the end of the world.

Leonard Rosenman praising Sal Mineo's acting, but feeling the potential of the planetarium idea was not realized; scriptwriter Shulman wanting Plato to be more psychotic and less cosmic. Let us just say that his was the most difficult character to realize, as his function always tended to be somewhat outside the narrative one. Whenever he appears, he suggests a cosmic implication to ordinary events. He is thus symbolic and what he says should always be taken more metaphorically than literally (i.e., if he said "I'm a star," we are invited, always, to interpret it differently than if Jim had said it). We see this particularly in the planetarium sequence: on Jim's left we have the creepy icons of Buzz's gang; on Jim's right, the symbolically cosmic Plato. Jim, in the middle, is very alone; in the planetarium he is cut off, (whereas Plato is self-isolated) and he will stay alone, until he finds Judy, which he ironically does—in a reversal of the Romeo and Juliet situation—as he goes out on the balcony and catches the first smile Judy ever gives him, from down below.

Segment 2: Part B—The Planetarium Sequence

The planetarium sequence—despite music director Leonard Rosenman's feeling that more could have been done with it—is a high point of the 1950s Hollywood cinema.

The planetarium turns out to be a mighty symbolic place, where the lecturer, a Dr. Minden, informs the class from Dawson High about entropy and the fate of our planet, inviting them all and us to examine the metaphoric meaning of the word *star*. Unfortunately, as Jim Stark/James Dean walks into the hushed auditorium just a split second after Minden says: "For many days before the end of our earth, people will look into the night sky and notice a star, increasingly bright, increasingly near. As this star . . .," Stern has Dean say "*Star*k, Jim Stark," reducing the symbol to Hollywood icon. (This seems overexplicit, even for Hollywood, and more like a pun directed to the audience as it would mean nothing to the characters in the film.) Minden continues: ". . . as this star approaches us, the weather will change. . . ." This is beautifully implicit, but the word *star* has unfortunately already been de-symbolized by Stern's pun. James Dean's ascendency to Hollywood stardom is being signalled rather than Jim Stark's odyssey; there is a bit of tension between the script and image.

The image itself, however, is beautifully rendered, an artificial ceiling of stars, and Buzz, Judy, Jim, Plato, all levelled by the cosmos, forced to acknowledge it. Buzz, Judy, and Goon get restless and start to make jokes; Jim tries to join in and is rejected. Plato suffers: "What do they know about man alone?" A crescendo of sound announces "the end of the world," and also the end of the dreamlike quality of the sequence. Only Plato has taken it all seriously.

Yet the narrative requirements have forced the script to overlap the cosmic mood with the sexual competition for Judy, and it shows us that Jim's attempt to "horn in" on the gang will provoke them to attack him. For Jim and Plato must later be trapped in the planetarium in such a way that they will first appear on the balcony—looking for a way to escape—so that Plato can first point out to Jim the mansion—to which they will later go—and they can then descend to the parking lot, where the switchblade fight will later take place.

We have concentrated on the narrative of the first quarter of *Rebel Without a Cause*, simply because I feel that within the first half-hour of a two-hour film, the film must establish its shot vocabulary.

Instead of attempting a detailed reading, I have attempted to imply how Ray set up the shot vocabulary of the film, to show at what points the script allowed him to make cinema, and to suggest how he related the camera to the script.

I have suggested that Ray's filmic "sentences" are built by a series of cuts, linking a specific and a more general meaning to a group of shots. The specific meaning will serve the needs of the narrative; the general meaning will be his attempt to create metaphor. As Ray's metaphors are very space-time oriented, they easily fit into cinema. This is why we feel the personality of Ray in the ontology of his films.

But the most curious thing about *Rebel*, a veritable maverick among Ray's films, is not the way its shots deal with space, but the way the film deals with time. The duration of the story told by the film is about thirty hours. The first quarter of the film—approximately the thirty minutes we have already described—covers fifteen hours of the narrative's duration. This leaves eighty minutes of real time to tell the last fifteen hours, so that we actually have *more* screen time in which to finish the story. Yet, the film accelerates its pace, and we experience the psychological time of the rest of the film as very fast. In fact, the amount of activity and information still to be conveyed is enormous! My point is that *Rebel* has more than enough material for one film; all of Ray's other films are thinner in content. *Rebel*'s richness, which we notice, right after the planetarium sequence, is the sign of a symphonic composition with many rich sub-texts, each already quite satisfying. My firm contention is that the best films are often overgenerous, like this, in their content, and their brilliance lies not just in their form.
Segments 4 and 6: Jim's Two Confrontations with His Father.

At least half the concentration of *Rebel* is on the hate-love relationship between Jim Stark and his father, Frank Stark. As played by Jim Backus (who was the voice of the cartoon character Mr. Magoo and a good comedian), Frank Stark is slightly more sympathetic than pathetic. Even when he is raked over the coals by Stern's script (Stern later confessed to Mike Steen that the biting, scathing criticism of the father in *Rebel* was not so much the taking to task of Frank Stark, but a critique of his own father, whom Stern desperately wanted to reform), there is hope for him. Implied at the very beginning is a positive note. The relationship between father and son has some of Howard Hawks' world of male camaraderie, a world which men can share with each other. Even though Jim in the opening segment says of his father "I never want to be like him," one senses his real mission is not to kill the father but to convert him. The treatment of the father-son relationship was enough, though, to antagonize many an adult in 1955. I gasped when I first saw Jim Backus hit the floor under James Dean's choking hands. (Slow-motion analysis on the Steenbeck editing table and analyzer discloses that James Dean really is choking Jim Backus.) There is this much violence in *Rebel*.

But to call *Rebel* unconciliatory to adults (as many teen-agers "read" the film at the time) is to overblow the nihilism merely suggested by *part* of the title, "Without a Cause." As we have already explained, a double negative is involved, for Jim Stark negates his negation, as the film progresses.

The two father-son conversations, Segments 4A and 6 of the film, are set up by Segment 3, the switchblade fight sequence, to be analyzed in detail in the next chapter. After Jim defeats Buzz in a ballet-like knife fight, Buzz, to save face, must challenge him to a repeat match, the chickie run. Jim goes home and wants to consult his father and ask his advice on whether he should go to the chickie run: "Dad, what do you have to do to be a man?" In Segment 4A, his father fails to answer this question, except to provoke Jim to mock his father's way of dealing with problems. When his father wants him to make a list of *pros* and *cons*, when he advises Jim that ten years later, he wouldn't have wanted to have ruined his life, Jim flies into a rage at the very thought of playing it safe, screaming *"ten years"* as if that were a useless eternity, and puts on the red jacket that would, with Dean's blue jeans, become a national youth costume.

Sandwiched in this segment is a brief parallel sequence of Judy having a run-in with her father over whether she can still kiss him on the lips now that she is sixteen. Natalie Wood recalls that the studio executives who watched this scene being shot were shocked. Yet this is necessary to the narrative, as it must be shown that Jim's story parallels many other teen-agers' stories. The handling of the film here is a bit clumsy. The difficulty of parallel plots is that they demand equal time for every important character. Alain Resnais solved this problem seven years later, in *Muriel* by having no one character the main one. But Jim is the main character of *Rebel*, and Judy's role is a bit too compressed to give us the feeling it is her story too. (Feminists would be wrong if they said that Judy does not have equal weight in the way its makers intended; her role is only limited because of the time limits of the film.)

Segment 6, the father-son confrontation, is, in the opinion of many, the finest sequence in the film. Narrative and picture are superbly integrated. All of Ray's filmic tricks are needed to sustain the power of the narrative so they do not stand out. Nor does the narrative skeleton stand out, cinematically unsupported. Do we here have second-generation Hollywood cinema at its best? Or do we already have a touch of the 1960s third-generation ontological cinema, a cinema investigating the language of film?

After having made a careful study of the difference between the screenplay version of this sequence and the film as shot, I have come to the conclusion that *every* change made in dialogue in this sequence was an improvement and that every line seems to function within the rhythm of the mise-en-scène. When the characters speak, the camera lets them speak. When the demands of the mise-en-scène require motion, the dialogue is as terse as the movement. This gives the sequence a tightness where every punctuation mark becomes an exclamation point and one feels at the end as if something is going to explode. Yet, despite the fact that the mise-en-scène is reproduceable on a stage, this is a narrative that could never ever have been staged. Why? Because the emphasis constantly alternates between what Dean says or what someone says to him and where the camera takes him. The cutting constantly sets up emphasis on who will speak and who will listen, normally the function of the mise-en-scène. Lasting only a little over six minutes, this sequence is a three-way verbal brawl, in which the wishy-washy liberal position and the openly cowardly position (father and mother respectively) are touchingly assailed by Jim, who ends by pushing his father down and running out.

The advantage of having this moment of highest impact so late in the film (approximately ninety minutes from the start of the 110-minute film) is that the narrative does not have to carry the film through so many moments of routine cinema, such as was terribly evident in most Hollywood 1950s films. *Rebel*, remarkably, has the pace of *The Big Sleep* (1946), the aura of CinemaScope, the feel of a coming to an end of the Freudian film dialogue epoch.

Segment 7. The Mansion

Jim, Judy, and Plato play artificial family in the mansion on the hill, that Plato had pointed out was "a place they can go," when he and Jim were trapped on the planetarium balcony. It is the same mansion that was used in *Sunset Boulevard* (1950), but used quite differently. Jim and Judy go there after Jim's fight with his father. The "You Can't Go Home Again" dialogue between Jim and Judy in the driveway outside their homes is touching; now that they feel sincere, how *can* they go home again? The mansion sequence is not a Huckleberry Finn romp so much as an experiment with a nuclear family: Jim, the father, Judy, the mother, Plato, the son. Natalie Wood recalls that Nick Ray gave them all Thomas Wolfe's novel, *You Can't Go Home Again* and asked them to read a particular chapter of it together in rehearsal.

Before arriving at the mansion, Jim and Judy fleetingly are reminded of Buzz's death. It is announced to them again, ironically through a car radio blaring out a dedication from Buzz to Jim of a song "Milkman's Serenade," which becomes a sad icon of the dead Buzz. Judy, practically, however, reminds Jim that the gang will be looking for him, and they go to the mansion. Plato, tracked down by the gang, also heads there, to warn them the gang will soon come.

The tone of the film now becomes flowing, moody, and almost chaotic. It foreshadows the last segment, the death of Plato, Jim and Judy, the new couple, the reconciliation with Jim's dad. Ray achieved this by using low-key lighting during moonlit Californian spring nights.

Plato arrives just as Jim and Judy get cozy and relaxed, and sexual tension results, only momentarily dispelled by *Judy* incorporating Plato into the artificial family. Judy then dramatically declares her love for Jim after the two of them have gone *upstairs,* leaving Plato by himself, *downstairs* (alone, just like Jim *was,* in the Stark family living room). Plato is vulnerable as (the gang) Crunch, Goon, and Moose make their entrance. They chase Plato, who finally shoots Crunch. Then, as he is about to fire at Jim for deserting him, Jim calms him down. The scene only works because one has become convinced that Plato is a bit insane (now definitely a rebel without a cause) and Jim (now definitely with a cause and definitely no longer a rebel) is justified in abandoning Plato for Judy.

While they are acting out the new family *upstairs,* Judy and Jim tell the audience a moral tale. (This is the second of the two lyric episodes which French critic-director Eric Rohmer has pointed out, are extra to the film proper, and are added for the sake of their lyricism. It is also the sequence Rohmer said would "give psychiatrists a field day with Nick Ray's psyche.")[4]

Throughout the sequence Judy has given the girl's point of view on how she felt about Jim and her previous behavior toward him. Not even a women's liberation advocate can accuse her of passivity at this point. (Marjorie Rosen gives Judy grudging credit in *Popcorn Venus*, but Molly Haskell in *From Reverence to Rape* does not even bother to mention her as a female character ahead of her time.) Yet, to those who conceive of male-female relationships as fifty/fifty propositions, Jim and Judy achieve that.

Judy: (sitting up, while Jim is lying down, so that she is looking down at him) . . . and all the time I was looking for someone to love me.
(She has discovered the active voice in love.) I love you Jim, I really do.

She says this in a most Romeo-like way; Jim mumbles his agreement. It is not so much a love scene as a point made. Through the script, Judy gets the point across; it is she who lectures Jim in soliloquy fashion, on the falseness of her earlier quest. She now has got it straight. Love is active, activity, confrontation.

Segment 7 shows that both Jim and Judy have learned their "moral lesson." This lesson is easy for us to accept, as it is told with innocence. (Rohmer's *Claire's Knee* would later be a perverse form of this quest; in *Claire's Knee*, touching Claire's *knee* proves that one can touch a demystified love object without any sincere purpose and thus exposes the cynicism of the hero and suggests the insincerity of setting up a goal that is no goal at all.)

Plato and Jim's father remain to be dealt with. Segment 8 will kill off Plato and satisfy the film's *manque*, reconcile the wayward father with his son.

Segment 8: The End

The police enter, as they discover there are prowlers in the mansion. Plato exchanges shots with them and flees to the planetarium. Jim's parents are cruising around in a police car with Ray Framek, looking for Jim. The police find Plato has fled to the planetarium, and inform Framek "a boy" has been seen to go in there (i.e., it could be Jim) and in this fashion, Framek is directed to the planetarium, serving the narrativity by bringing Jim's father to the place where Jim and Plato are.

Ray's 1955 police are kind people. They carefully announce they don't want to harm Plato: "Come out, you haven't killed anyone yet." Plato hides in his symbolic home, the planetarium. Jim enters, with Judy, to coax him out. Dawn threatens to break. The last segment is in real time; it all elapses in minutes of both screen time and psychological time. The story and reality are now one. At least, this identity is successfully conveyed, as Eric Rohmer acknowledged in a glowing description of Segment 8, in his review of *Rebel*: "Jim's odyssey becomes our odyssey, and we march along with it."[5]

Some have complained that Plato's death is contrived. Peter Biskind, in *Film Quarterly*,[6] has gone so far as to suggest that Jim betrayed Plato. We do have to deal with this accusation, though Plato's death works perfectly on the narrative level. Jim took the bullets out of Plato's gun. The nervous police shoot him, not knowing this. Jim screams a moment later, a moment too late: "*I've* got the bullets." He covers Plato with the red jacket, now no longer his symbol: "He was always cold." (Sal Mineo has stated in interviews that James Dean was extraordinarily protective toward him the day this scene was shot.) Plato *was* always cold, symbolically. Like the star-child he was intended to be, he never had a chance on this earth, given his faulty psychological equipment. One should accept that he was a doomed character and not seek political implications for Jim Stark's abandonment of him.

At this point, on the narrative level, the film could end. But, like certain rock music songs of the late 1960s, it has two "false" endings followed by a third, final, ending, the last one bringing us a silent, Hitchcockian appearance by Ray himself. The first ending is the death of Plato. The second ending shows Judy and Jim standing at the front of the planetarium, and being joined by Mr. and Mrs. Stark. Jim, still ignoring his mother, achieves reconciliation with his father; and, symbolizing his new loyalty to Judy, he introduces his father to her: "Dad, this is Judy." This is not a satisfactory place to end the film, especially on such a Hollywoodian cliché. And, fortunately, Ray doesn't end it there. But, I argue, the first ending would have been satisfactory. That there are three endings gives me the feeling that the filmmakers sensed they were doing something important and did not want to leave out anything that might deny them making an "instant classic," a popular film.

The final ending is purely visual: the sun rises higher. We have seen all the people (who suddenly seem as if they were but actors on the stage of life, recalling the cosmology lecture in the planetarium and looking ahead to Antonioni's *Blow-Up*) (Jim, parents, police) literally disappear. The planetarium sits like an icon. Then a solitary figure, seen from above, in a crane shot, makes his way, with rain-coat and briefcase, to the planetarium. At first we think it is Dr. Minden, the lecturer, or some other planetarium employee, but then we cease to try to identify *who* it is and merely and humbly become aware that life goes on. The figure is actually Nick Ray, signing his name by personally appearing on the screen. After one finds out that it is indeed Nick Ray (who is only seen from behind and remains incognito) this appearance gives off vibrations of humil-ity rather than arrogance.

The third ending is ontological in its implications. It suggests that Nick Ray takes his solo walk to the place where in the film the cos-mic and practical worlds collide and produce the ultimate question for our lives: Is the world chaos or disorder?

But Ray's walk is also realistic, not melodramatic, and returns us to "the man alone" theme of the first ending, Plato's death. The first and third endings say "man is alone"; the second ending says "man can have ever-shifting temporary alliances." My feeling is that end-ing two is the screenplay's ending, endings one and three are Ray's. Endings two and three, at any rate, remain in conflict with each other and produce a conclusion that tends to undercut itself. Many who saw the film feel this. Even David Dalton, who does not seem to understand that even punks saw that the film *was* a moral alle-gory, is not convinced by the second ending, nor were Eric Rohmer and other foreign critics, who showed a brilliant understanding for the film. Apparently, one needn't have been a hip American to see through the American dream-making power of CinemaScope. "The conclusion of *Rebel*," writes Dalton, "is only an apparent happy ending, one of those cinematic sleights of hand Ray practiced throughout his career. We cannot really believe that Jim and Judy's problems are finally over. What we see is only a lull in the battle, setting the stage for a new one."[7] Or, put much more succinctly by Eric Rohmer, "The eroticism of Nick Ray is nonetheless suspicious of that which it wishes."[8]

8

The Filming of *Rebel Without a Cause*

IN THIS CHAPTER we try to give you the feeling of being behind the camera, of seeing how filming a script *is* making *another* movie, a new movie out of it, and of how Nick Ray did this, made the camera do even more than necessary to get across the basic rudiments of plot. In *Rebel,* Ray uses his two filmic shooting trademarks to do this: dislocating cutting, and mise-en-scène that continues after the interruption by the cut, to great advantage. This he also did in others of his films. But that is not all that he did in *Rebel.* He created for this, which he considers his best film, a unique spatially abstract shot vocabulary for the one sequence in which Buzz accuses Jim Stark of being too abstract. A visual message is given out by the camera, a reinterpretation of the script that adds a symbolic dimension to the iconical-indexically defined events in the narrative.

In so doing, Ray often recreated, in cinema, particularly in the switchblade sequence on which this chapter will focus, a communication equivalent to philosopher Charles Peirce's arbitrary sign, one which signifies equally in the iconic, indexical, and symbolic dimensions. Thus, what we see and hear is neither too specific to be banal nor too abstract to be unclear. (We will also describe, at the end of this chapter, a sign in the planetarium sequence, where there is some debate as to how it works, whether it helps the cinema of the sequence, or undermines it.)

Our focus on the switchblade sequence will not only show it to be crisp and symbolic, but demonstrate that it has a hidden structure, a structure that cannot be seen but only experienced while viewing it at projection speed, as the several elements of composition are so

James Dean on the set of *Rebel Without a Cause.* Screenwriter Stewart Stern is the man in the left background wearing a jacket and tie. Dean, 24 and Stern 30, were the combo that put the myth into *Rebel*—Stern deliberately, and Dean, inadvertently—that led to the James Dean cult.

119

symphonically overlaid that at any one moment of viewing you cannot watch them all evolving at the same time.

How Ray made cinema is clear in slow motion, however. The
development and evolution of the sequence can be seen structurally. Ray's strategy is one of emphasizing five filmic devices: (a) architectural blocking: against what building backdrops do which
characters appear, when, and in what order: (b) spatial blocking:
how do we split up the characters into different groupings; (c) setting up cuts that do not match but dislocate; (d) having the cut fall on
movement; and (e) composing the frame for CinemaScope, which,
in this film, meant using groups in single lines across the screen or
putting an outsider character like Plato in the middle background to
show him off against a couple, Jim and Judy, in the right and left
foreground—which also meant taking advantage of the heightened
kinesthesia that cutting in CinemaScope produced even if the lens
was only changed from 40 mm to 75 mm.

This shooting strategy underpinned the film. After all this was
provided for, Ray could then rehearse his cast, knowing how their
bits would fit into his cinema. (And he could show a shooting script
to the studio, for economic purposes, one he never would closely
follow.) As much as script rehearsals, then, produced *dramatic* revi-
sions of the narrative, and a kind of organic acting where everyone
played off a center, James Dean, *Rebel's* real power lies not in just
the acting. Ray's shooting strategy was the real power that created
Rebel's tremendous cinematic impact.

**The Switchblade Sequence: Illustration of how Ray expands his
shot vocabulary for the balcony-parking lot confrontation segment
of this sequence.**

The central idea of Ray's composition in the switchblade sequence, besides his using the three-shot (a shot tightly framing
three people, invariably a medium shot) for Buzz, Crunch, and a
third male gang member, and the two-shot (a shot tightly framing
two people, and invariably a medium-close shot) for Jim and Plato,
is his widening out what we see through Jim's eyes. Helen and Judy
are also in two-shot, ostensibly so that we can see their faces in more
detail but, compositionally, to fill up the huge CinemaScope frame
(Jim and Judy are thus already united by virtue of being in the same
shot scale, even while they are spatially separated).

Ray does not order his shots like this.   Instead, he orders them like this.

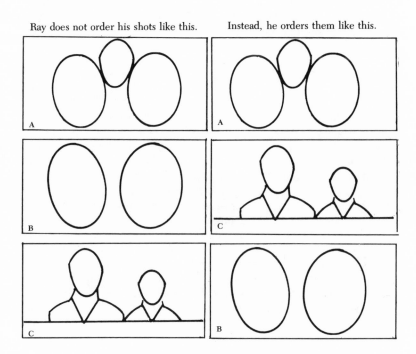

A model of Ray's style of cross-cutting.

Next, if we were to crosscut between the differently scaled two-shot of the girls and the three-shot of the boys of the gang, we would sense something phony and unnatural. This Ray never does. Alternating the cutting between the three-shot of Buzz and the boys, and Jim and Plato, and cutting between the two-shot of the girls and Jim, Ray makes his manipulated images seem really natural. Even the difference in scale between the Buzz three-shot and the Judy two-shot is accepted, because of the order in which they appear and their separation from each other. The two-shot of Judy and Helen is, in fact, the most highly manipulated image of all. All this manipulation has a very cinematic purpose.

Though we only see the Buzz and the Judy compositions in alternation and never as a medium long shot showing them all in a line (as we do after Jim descends from the balcony), we are shown that they are together by a long shot later in the action, which confirms our sense of their standing in a line. But, even before this delayed "establishing" shot, we feel that they are always there standing next to each other in a wider panorama than we ever see. This gives us "the feeling" the screen is two CinemaScope lengths long. Ray suggests that we are seeing the double-length CinemaScope frame and gets away with it, as we never doubt when we watch Buzz in one shot that the not-visible Judy is in fact next to him, and vice versa. So, while we sense real space, we accept the narrative manipulation of Jim and Judy being joined (though not through spatial connection; they remain fifty feet apart in space) in what has been known as an invention of neo-realist cinema, but which has long been practiced by many directors, including Nick Ray—the device of aesthetic realism. The shooting strategy in this segment, then, is to create a contrived relationship in real space, by spatial blocking.

In the next segment, this strategy is no longer needed. Ray wisely shifts to another strategy and features dislocating cutting. From the moment when Jim comes down the stairs from the balcony, with Plato a step behind him, the shooting strategy shifts from (b)— spatial blocking to (c)—dislocating cuts. This is because a good director never wishes to overdo or overexpose his methodological skeleton. This is his business and not the audience's.

In the parking lot segment, Ray cuts and cuts and cuts. Space is also used differently. As Eric Rohmer observed in a brilliant review, at this point in the film we see "a fight with knives, where the scenic beauty of the countryside stands out against all the roughness, the game of street urchins."[1] Space is concrete but it is not static. The moment Jim and Plato reach the parking lot and walk into a composition where the gang is seen in a line at the right of the frame, there is a cut on motion, while Jim and Plato are walking. We soon lose track of where they are, on what ground they stand. Jim is next seen walking towards his car—Buzz has slashed one of his tires (in the original script four gang members did it)—and we will soon see Jim take a tirejack out of his trunk to defend himself. When we see Jim, after the cut, he is still walking toward the car, but the angle is different, by approximately 30 degrees, and, if we look for the gang, they are not where they should be, in relation to the 30 degree shift

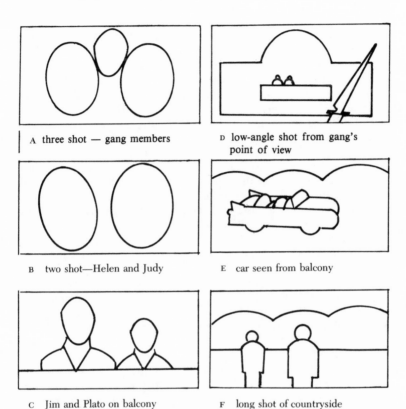

A three shot — gang members

D low-angle shot from gang's
point of view

B two shot—Helen and Judy

E car seen from balcony

C Jim and Plato on balcony

F long shot of countryside
from behind Jim on balcony

Ray created a vocabulary of six shots (A–F) for the balcony-parking lot-switchblade confrontation sequence. He used these shots to spatially direct the viewer's attention between two narratives going on at the same time: the love interest (B–C) and the group-individual conflict (A–C), both involving Jim Stark, (C). (A–C) is later resolved by the fight, and (B–C) triumphs.

of position of the rest of the composition, Jim, Plato, and the parking lot and car. This dislocation has the impact of an extra burst of speed, tension, spatial confusion, which tends to give the viewers an insight into Jim, by giving the dynamic perspective of the tension of the character. If not done too often and if the dislocation is not so great as to be perceived as a director's mistake or is not there gratuitously (as are some of Ray's similar cuts, notably in the action sequence on the attack on "Rommel's Headquarters" in *Bitter Victory*), dislocation shots create not merely psychological but ontological tension. At any rate, it is on shot successions like these, that cinema operates so very differently from theater, to create point of view, empathy, and suggestion of what is to follow, in a cinematic way. No director who passes up *every* chance to use these devices can be considered "cinematic."

This is not to say that Ray is anti-talk. *Rebel*, in a semantically important way, shows a great concern for the use of the camera to "protect" the signification of the dialogue. If the words of a shot become very essential to the narrative power, Ray backs up the narrative with loving care, and, at points where the dialogue is crucial, he lets the pace of the film slacken, so as to let the dialogue make itself heard. Here is an example, according to the script.

87. FULL SHOT CAR
  SHOOTING between group and Buzz toward backs of Jim and Plato, who are looking down at car which rests on its rims. Jim turns and moves toward group. He *stops* (my italics) looks from one to the other and smiles nervously. Then he looks straight at Buzz.

Jim: (wearily) You know something?
Buzz: What?
Jim: (reproachfully) You watch too much television (Changed in the actual film to:) You read too many comic books.
Buzz: Ahhh . . . he's real abstract. He's . . . um . . . he's different . . .[2]

This is the real heart of the film. Here, Ray has shifted (eclectic that he is) to the labels the American conformist and non-conformist of 1955 would have thrown at each other. The non-conformist angrily calls the conformist a victim of comics and TV. The conformist smugly calls the non-conformist "abstract" and "different"—in other words, un-American, as Americans are pragmatic and similar to each other.

The next segment of the sequence has to justify why Jim gets violent toward Buzz. In becoming violent, he must still have our respect. Ray has to proceed carefully, to justify his extreme provocation. He does it, dramatically, by the trigger word, "chicken." It seems Jim can take all the other insults but that. But this is just a plot device, for, as we shall see later, Ray himself believes *everyone* contains violence within himself/herself and at this point in the film admirers of James Dean have to decide whether the real Dean would have condoned the very violence the script asks him to condone and play. (We now follow the dialogue of the film, through a few shots, without reference to change of shot.)

Jim: That's right. That's *right*. And I'm cute, too. (GOON starts clucking softly like a chicken. One by one the others pick it up. Buzz, the last, crows. Silence.)
Jim: Is that meaning me? IS THAT MEANING ME? CHICKEN! (This is more violent than in the original script line, which read: Meaning me?)
Buzz: Yes.
Jim: You shouldn't call me that. (Walks over to Judy.) What about you? Are you always at ringside? No, I mean what are y'hanging around such rank company for?
Buzz: (incredulously) What!?! (shocked at Jim's "impertinence." Grabs him and pushes him. Jim has—in actuality—gone on the offensive and put Buzz on the defensive.)

suspense music

Jim: I don't want any trouble. [In the original script, this line came *before* Jim challenged Judy to break away from the gang, a placement that perhaps makes more sense. Here, the line is ironic.]
Crunch: The blade game, huh, Buzz?!?
Jim: I thought only punks fought with knives. [The script next contained the line, to be spoken by HELEN in French: "les jeux de courage!"—"the games of courage," which would have acted as a narrative comment on the action. Ray wisely left it out, for few would have understood it.]
Buzz: Who's fighting? I'm not fighting. It's examination time, man. . . . It's a crazy game.
Yeh. Go and get'm a knife. . . . Give it to him. Uh. Give 'm a knife. (A member of the gang throws a switchblade at Jim's feet.) PICK IT UP!
Jim: (calmly, making Buzz seem hysterical by contrast.) I don't want any trouble.

Buzz: *PICK IT UP!*

[suspense music, to crescendo]

Pick it up!

[other theme of suspense music eerily comes in]

[Buzz calls Crunch to come over. He stands next to Buzz and grins sadomasochistically while Buzz has his arm around his shoulder, and jabs him with the switchblade to illustrate what he's going to say to Jim. It is one of the most bizarre, memorable visual scenes of the film.]
Buzz: Just a little *jabbing*. That's all. (CRUNCH laughs spasmodically.) What's the *matter?* What are you waitin' on, Toreador? I thought you wanted a little action . . . Or are you crum chicken? . . .
Jim: [savagely, aggressively] Don't call me that. (And he flips open the switchblade he is holding.)

The above shows Ray at his best as a thespian and cinéaste combined. Note that the speeches of the characters are very rhythmic, as if they were a few notes of jazz, bursting out here and there. Cut from the dialogue are some strange lines, such as:

Crunch: (wetting his lips) Machismo, Machismo.
Jim: Machismo?
(Just before Ray returns to:)
Buzz: Somebody find him a knife.

Lines such as these are interpretative and slow down the real action. As this segment of the sequence stands, it is the finest action segment, next to the father-son confrontation sequence, in Ray's entire cinema.

In this segment we come close to getting an ontological discussion of violence. Ray never denied including violence in *Rebel*. Once, in a discussion when someone pointed out that the characters of *In a Lonely Place, On Dangerous Ground, Rebel* resemble each other: they are violent, Ray replied, "Absolutely, they have violence in them. It is in each one of us; it is there, in force. The bank teller who leads a peaceful life, counts the piles of banknotes and begins to hate the world; he counts the money just up to one day where, suddenly, he takes the revolver which he had stashed away to protect the cash drawer, runs into the street and shoots a dozen people."

When in *Rebel*, Jim is holding the unopened switchblade and Buzz calls him "chicken" for the second time, Jim Stark also reaches the breaking point. He is also, at this moment, completely alone. The result is that Jim Stark momentarily behaves like Ray's hypothetical bank teller.

Ray's interrogator continued, "In your films, the theme of violence is always linked to the theme of loneliness." Ray replied: "Of all that I have read, that which touched me, moved me the most was my . . . personal label made for always: 'I am a stranger here myself.' [Or, as it literally was recorded in the *Cahiers* interview: 'I am a stranger here below.'] The first poetry I wrote in my youth was on this subject. The search for a full life is, I believe—paradoxically—a solitary one. I also think that solitude is very important for a person, for as long as it doesn't harm him, that he knows how to primitively partake of it as . . . It is a very personal feeling: it is too difficult to talk about it." And yet, this is where we are, at this very moment, in the odyssey of Jim Stark. Aside from having been alone enough to think, what will rescue Jim Stark is his non-conformism, which is the healthiest side of him. Ray concludes, "I love non-conformists; the non-conformist is healthier than that . . ."[3] (than the man who suddenly takes his revolver and shoots a dozen people, healthier than Buzz, the gang).

In the rest of this segment not only does Jim defeat Buzz in the switchblade fight, but he throws some of his health at Judy: "You always at ringside? You always associate with such rank company?" To Buzz in response to Buzz's "You know what a chickie run is?" Jim replies teasingly "That's all I ever do."

Ray's Use of Spatial Composition to Create Additional Shots

Shotwise, we have four obvious options in filming the confrontation leading to the switchblade sequence: (A-B) the gang seen head-on, on the lower level of the parking lot; (C) Jim shot head-on on the balcony; (D) a low angle shot, from the gang's point of view, up at Jim; and (E) a high angle shot from Jim's point of view, looking down at the gang. To this, Ray adds a fifth shot (F) from behind Jim, looking straight out over the landscape. (The balcony is deep enough so that a camera could be put behind Jim, while he stands at the railing.)

By adding F (and only using D once with great shock effect) and by breaking up composition A-B into a left half (A): boys (sexual grouping and gang menace) and a right half (B): girls (sexual grouping and love interest), Ray spontaneously created two more shots to expand his vocabulary from four to six shots for this particular segment, and to serve the narrative/plot demand by setting up the two shots he needs to use alternatively throughout the whole sequence to advance the love interest (B-C) and the group-individual conflict (A-C). Ray has now given himself six shots for his working vocabulary: A, B, C, D, E, F. (He has also avoided the predicament of being forced to use shot-countershot, (A-B)-(C)-(A-B).

The balcony-switchblade fight sequence entails over seventy shots and is so complex as to need a detailed shot analysis (a "book in itself") to explain it.

Next notice another reason for dividing the gang into two groups: Composition A: a boy on the left, Crunch, and Buzz, with Goon (Dennis Hopper) leaning forward on the hood of the car; and Composition B: the girls: Judy and Helen.

While shot A-B never appears in actuality, when we see shot A, we always understand that the girls are there to the right of what we see, and when we see shot B we always understand that the boys are to the left of what we see. Exploiting the great length of the CinemaScope screen, Ray turned a disadvantage into an advantage. He first showed us the gang spreading themselves out along the car.

Composition A

Then, he could chop up the composition and show detail, trusting we would always bear in mind the rest of them were there.

As Elia Kazan told Michael Ciment about his tricks in overcoming the problems of the C-scope frame while filming *East of Eden*:

> . . . I made up my mind that films are essentially an art of cutting. In other words, no shot has a significance by itself; it gets significance by what it's next to and what it follows. That was the theory I had then. Now, without my thinking too much about it, C-scope made it impossible to cut as often. The face didn't fill the screen so I did a staging that was much more relaxed, more like a stage—more 'across', more at ease. It was not intentional; I was forced into it by the aesthetics of that shape. I also did something else; I combated the shape. I tried to get inner frames. In other words, I would put something big in the foreground on one side, something black, that you couldn't see through and put the action on the other side. The next time I'd have the action in a corner over there and something blocking it here. . . . I tried to make an asset of my problem; but I never liked the C-scope frame. I think one-six-six is a pretty good ratio.[4]

Nick Ray also made "an asset of [the] problem," but needless to say, Ray did it differently.

To remind you that there are nine or ten people in the gang, Ray belatedly refers us to high angle shot E, the entire grouping around the car. Later, during the switchblade fight, this car is our reference

Composition B

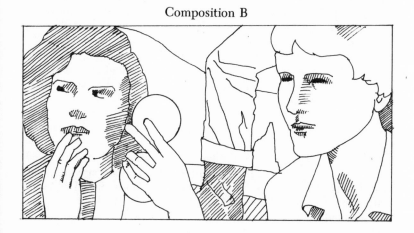

point, as in an arena. For the moment, Ray shows us the gang relationships and develops them. He features Crunch and Buzz, like partners in a ballet, and he likewise features Helen and Judy as a pair. I particularly like his keeping Helen's frozen face and Judy's changing face together in the same shots. Only twice does he resort to a close-up of Judy looking up at Jim to give you their relationship. After repeated watching, one notices a strange synchronization of Jim's nervosity and Judy's. When the air is let out of Jim's tire, Judy lets her breath escape in awe; Jim up on the balcony is also wheezing nervously. Occasionally, we are reminded that Plato is with Jim, but mostly he is cut out, and Ray favors a medium close-up of Jim in profile on the balcony. (Romeo and Juliet in reverse?) At any rate, both the romantic interest and the fight interest are kept going simultaneously, and the cutting is so fast it seems they are both happening at once, which is the way it does happen in real time.

Ray here wants to violate the long frame he is otherwise restricted to. And by breaking up the gang, he can get them both into medium shot, even medium close-up with the two girls, and does not have to repeat the long shot, which would become boring. This gives the impression, along with the medium shots of Jim, of facial detail, of the equal importance of both groups (the boys and the girls), and of confrontation, while at the same time not neglecting to use the wide screen as wide screen.

By excerpting two medium shots out of the horizontal Cinema-Scope frame—in effect a gentle zoom, Ray has broken up that overly horizontal look to give us cameos of the actors. When Jim comes down from the balcony, Ray will return to the mass ballet and choreography that the long screen allows for, and we will see all of the gang (on occasion) most of the time during the fight, except for the two key shots of Buzz versus Jim alone. Particularly noteworthy is how Judy relates to *both* Buzz and Jim, showing she was, for those days, not an entirely unliberated girl.

The Fight

The actual fight footage is that of a beautiful ballet, with a 360 degree swing in action. Jim and Buzz go in a circle, at which point Jim knocks Buzz's knife (sword) out of his hands, in a Hollywood cliché made nonetheless effective and fitting, for the fight is in every sense an allegory. Buzz even plays overconfident villain, tossing his knife from one hand to the other. Jim knocks it away from him while it is in mid-air, and Buzz suddenly finds himself knifeless. It is made clear that Jim has contempt for knives: "I thought only punks fought with knives."

Ray, here, uses at least two very Wellesian low-angle shots to backdrop the fighters against the sky. We get the feeling the fight is off in space, i.e., that it is a ritual of abstract proportions. As we said before, a masterful film comments on itself. Buzz's comment that starts off the second half of the sequence ("He's real ab-stract . . .") turns into a prophecy as the sequence ends in that very abstraction.

Unresolved Resolution at the End of the Switchblade Sequence

And yet, as the switchblade sequence ends, Jim has started be-friending Buzz, or, shall we say, Buzz has started befriending him. (As someone has observed, to a 19-year-old in 1976, Dean would seem a lot tougher than Buzz in the knife fight segment. It is obvi-ous that Dean is the new leader, the new heavy.) But why is Buzz befriending Jim, when they both are interested in Judy? Another triangle, even before we have the Jim-Plato-Judy one resolved? It is in such segments of his films that we become aware of Ray's ten-dency to see the world's need as one of forming ever-evolving al-liances.

The end of this sequence, a killer sequence in itself, leaves more *un*resolved than resolved, leading to the need for another sequence to burst the balloon. This is the famous chickie run sequence, that everyone remembers. Who could forget Buzz's leather jacket sleeve caught on the door handle, as the car races over the cliff to doom? And just when we started to like Buzz. On the popular level, the chickie run is the most famous sequence in the movie. But the switchblade sequence is the finest cinema in the film.

Why? Because of its massive use of all of Ray's shot vocabulary, his arsenal of cinematic "tricks." In the switchblade sequence, the cinema carries the narrative. The chickie run sequence, by contrast, depends on the cinema to make some unbelievable narrative palat-able. For example, Buzz taunts Plato about Jim, calling Plato "chicken little"; yet, three screen minutes later, Buzz is saying to Jim: "You know, I like you," and, like Cybelle in *Sundays and Cybelle*, Buzz has given Jim the supreme gift of his name, he tells Jim "I'm Buzz *Gunderson*." We accept this, but only because of

Ray's camera. When Jim and Buzz share a cigarette and question why they have to do the ritual of the chickie run (Jim: "Then why do we do this?" Buzz: "Well, you have to do *something.*") it only works because Ray has shot them both backdropped against the Pacific Ocean, isolated from the land, recognizable space, and has given the shot the quality of the Hollywood night club dream sequence. The aesthetic reality of the switchblade sequence gives way to stylization in the chickie run sequence; it is the switchblade sequence that tells us the most in the film. It, and the father-son confrontation sequence, tell us who Jim is, by a narrative so supported by tornado effects and active silences, that we learn the odyssey of Jim Stark as a cinematic experience.

What Ray knew how to do, and did, then, throughout the switchblade sequence was to keep the double rhythm of the fight interest and romantic interest going simultaneously. He does this both with cutting and mise-en-scène. While Jim is up on the balcony, the fight/romance simultaneity romantic interest is kept up mainly through cross-cutting. When Jim comes down, the focus switches to mise-en-scène. Judy never speaks to Jim the entire time: he says three sentences to her; she answers by lowering her head; again, through mise-en-scène, not dialogue. Ray effectively has produced a visual, non-verbal Romeo and Juliet.

Because of his (1) intricate A, B, C, D, E, F alternatives, *and* because of (2) the *speed* of crosscutting—sometimes only two seconds or forty-eight frames which make an important statement within the montage—it is virtually impossible to see how it is done while you are watching it. In fact, as Lincoln F. Johnson says in *Film: Space Time Light And Sound:*

> The film maker's art comes most fully into play and his authority or lack of it is most clearly revealed in the way he shapes structures in space–time. Basically, he exploits two variables, harmony (or likeness) and contrast, both of which can appear in any dimension of the film—in spatial organization, movement, time intervals, emotional and intellectual content, and, of course, in sound and color. The film maker may not, of course, wish to maintain smooth continuity in either the movement from shot to shot or the nominally continuous action. He may, for a number of reasons—*to provide information, to intensify the visual excitement, to inject a visual shock, to modify the rhythm, or simply to introduce variety*—he might reduce or eliminate the harmonious elements.[5]

Ray does all the above five things to reduce the harmony in the switchblade sequence.

After a relatively conventional opening to the film, mystery and reality suddenly become (both simultaneously) great, in the switchblade sequence. You really don't have any idea of how it will come out. The answer is NOT obvious. The dialogue is very explicit, direct, primitive, and final. The visuals are complex (as opposed to simplistic, in their internal composition and in their montage relationship to one another), and are designed both to elucidate and foreshadow, simultaneously.

To understand the beauty of the switchblade sequence, we have to go into a bit of film theory.

To the rhythm of a film, which we can define as (1) speed of cutting integrated with (2) whether the film is harmonious or contrapuntal, we next have to add the degree to which a film creates (or *re*creates) apparent motion. There can be (1) fast pacing and (2) very highly contrasting, disharmonious shots, but very little (3) apparent motion. For example: suppose we had rapid cutting to different groupings of people in different cities all seated around an identical table with a bottle of wine on it, not moving and not drinking it. Or, we could have the opposite: the same group constantly either rearranged between shots, and also moving in the shot, drinking the wine, pouring again, poking each other, etc. The latter example would be far closer to the rhythm/apparent motion of the switchblade sequence, the apparent motion coming from both mise-en-scène movement and cutting.

Ray's style uses much apparent motion. This creates an overload, i.e., so much is happening at once that the viewer cannot keep track of what has just happened. This is an extreme use of apparent motion, one used to show turmoil effectively, and it is here that cinema is furthest away from still photography.

As Andreas Feininger says in *Color Photography*, "The eye can not stop very rapid motion, can not retain the image of a subject that is no longer there, and can not combine a number of images in one impression. The camera can do all three. As a result, a photographer can either stop a subject in motion, symbolize motion graphically thru blur, or indicate it *through multiple images*—thereby expressing movement in heretofore unknown beauty and fluidity of form."[6] Ray uses the last technique, to force the eye to see discontinuity.

To sum up: What did Ray then accomplish by setting up this double rhythm of shots? Why did he keep the fight interest and the romantic interest going simultaneously? Because of his (1) intricate and unexpected A,B,C,D,E,F, alternations *and* because of the speed of crosscutting (sometimes he allows 2 seconds, 48 frames, and no more, for a shot) *and*, because he often returns to what apparently is the same composition—but it has been slightly changed—characters have slightly moved their positions in ways that would have taken them longer than if real time had elapsed. This out-of-phasing creates a spendid nervosity of movement that perfectly serves the nervosity of the plot requirement. And cinema has been created! It is virtually impossible to see how this sequence is done while you are watching it. It totally defeats self-consciousness. Mystery and reality fuse in this great sequence. The dialogue adds the final touch. It is very explicit, direct, primitive, and final. The visuals are complex (as opposed to simplistic) and are designed both to elucidate and to further and foreshadow the next action. David Dalton is not too far off when he calls the plot of *Rebel* a "series of concentric rings"[7] Jim must break through. *Rebel* shows us Jim Stark's life as a link of interconnected linear events, like a chain reaction, which doesn't stop till human life stops. The only pauses (pauses without trouble—troubles without a pause) are right after Buzz dies and right after Plato dies.

To conclude, we have to praise James Dean and Corey Allen for their acting. Both handsome in different ways, it was a stroke of genius to cast them together. The lighting used by Ray made them even more effervescent. Apparently, though the sequence was shot in bright spring daylight, Ray had the entire planetarium area ringed with bright lights to eliminate shadows. We see Buzz and Jim with shadowless faces of adolescence, and the memorability of these faces has, at least in my case, lasted for twenty years.

Sound in the Switchblade Sequence

It must be emphasized that the dialogue is so great during the switchblade sequence, it confirms the visuals. We become sure of what we see. (In the usual Hollywood fare, we ordinarily look for the visuals to confirm the dialogue, as is chiefly the case in musicals, and typical in genre films.) Then, in reciprocation, the visuals, integrated compositionally with watchwords, become stronger than

mere words, they become icons. Dialogue is short, befitting the
shortness of the shots. (In *Rebel,* characters almost always finish
their speeches in one shot.) Leonard Rosenman's music is like
libretto-backup (or even like dialogue itself) and also serves to overlap two shots and connect them, even while driving their
momentum by the quick, jazziness of the theme. This sequence
could have served as a model for *West Side Story* (1962).

The word "chicken" is used as the sequence's detonator. The
knife fight is triggered by Buzz's speaking the word "chicken," and
it is a bullfight that emerges, that corresponds to Buzz's other taunt
word to Jim "toreador." (Jim is bombarded with nasty words:
"chicken," "Moo," "abstract," "different," "toreador"; the song dedicated to him by Buzz is "The Milkman's Serenade"; more importantly, each word is connected with a visual image. Within many of
the shots of this sequence, we hear a taunt word thrown at Jim, and
see his *physical* reaction, within the confines of short shots.) In the
battle that follows, Ray likens the game of teen combat to the an-
cient ritual of the bullfight. The camera pans after Buzz and Jim *as if
they were in an arena.* Buzz's remark, "hey, toreador," informs us
what *we should see:* the moment of truth in a *corrida.*

After Jim gets so angry that he seems suddenly more powerful
than Buzz, the climax occurs. He succeeds in knocking the knife out
of Buzz's hands, in an Errol Flynn-like move, and now comes out
from under and threatens Buzz with a knife to his throat. "Have you
had enough, or do you want more?" Buzz now has to save face and
challenge Jim to a chickie run. The pace totally slows down. Nor-
mality is returning. Jim seems to consent, and Buzz asks him: "Have
you ever *been* on a chickie run?"

Jim: (with Nick Ray irony) "Yeah, That's *all I ever do.*" As in
Shakespearian comic relief, we see the seriousness mirrored in ex-
post-facto comic comment.

These two lines further show that what *Rebel Without a Cause*
does here is (and dozens of films would do this in the late 1960s and
in the 1970s) comment on itself. Like Nick Ray's personal appearance at the end of the film, this gave people the feeling that Ray had
not just made a "B" movie for fun. His film commented on *how* film
language should be used, or, as Bob Setlik put it: "all films are really
about film."[8] In 1955, hardly anyone knew what an *auteur* film was:
such comments as were found in *Rebel* were to most people self-
conscious, civilized, and sociological remarks, rising to an almost

ontological level. This time when Hollywood and the general public had barely accepted Freud, left one with the feeling one had seen a milestone film. *Rebel Without a Cause* exists thus on at least two levels: a higher, ontological level, where individualism is discussed, and a plot-narrative level, where plot runs the course of a "B" story film, and strives to entertain. Ray's compositions, however, deal more with ontology than plot, and that is why they are sometimes more mysterious and complex than needed merely to advance the story.

To demonstrate to the reader that this idea of levels is not a mere fabrication, listen to what Fritz Lang had to say about his murder/suspense film, *M*. "On the lowest level, my picture *M* is a cops-and-robber story. On a higher level, it's a police procedure. On a still higher level, it is a documentary of the times. And on a very high level, it is an indictment of capital punishment."[9]

In conclusion, the coordination between the framing of shots and the movement, acting, and dialogue within them in the plane-tarium-switchblade sequence is nothing short of remarkable. The shots are so fluid in composition, that the location, mostly a parking lot, is hardly noticed. So much happens all the time in one place that one always thinks one is time travelling. *Rebel Without a Cause* is perhaps the most time/space compressed of any film made before Fellini's 8½. For this reason this sequence belongs with the most modern of second-generation films.

And as an odyssey of youth, the amazing amount of information compressed into this 110-minute film seems to say everything that needs to be said about adolescence.

The combination of all the valid information about youth, and the technique Ray used to compress space and time, makes *Rebel Without a Cause* a timeless achievement; in short, a classic.

In this chapter we have attempted to call attention to Nick Ray's film as a "novel of adolescence," to alert film students and viewers to the fact that, as early as 1955, Ray introduced some of the elements that would create *third*-generation cinema some five years later. The most notable of these elements are: how to compress time and space at will and to make the compression comprehensible cinematically (not just in the old story-narrative way). This method, as we have tried to hint, presents and uses apparent motion exquisitely. It foreshadows the "anthologies of experience" that were to become rock songs. And it flawlessly avoids the "gonzo" or ego-based editorializing that later on would wreck the very nature of the truth presented.

Semantic Analysis of the Father-Son Confrontation Sequence

Nick Ray has written lucidly on the writer-director relationship in film: "The writer needs the director for his story to be realized; the director needs the writer to give him a story in a form he can realize." At the same time, Ray jealously guarded the director's right to override the writer's film (and make, in effect, a *second* film, the director's film) and expressed skepticism about the writer-director. "The writer-director is much too indulgent to the writer, reluctant to cut a word of that brilliant dialogue, a sentence of that verbose scene."[10]

The following illustrations are 16mm frame enlargements from the father-son confrontation sequence in *Rebel Without a Cause*.

1. After the chickie run in which Buzz has plunged to his death, Jim returns home. In this shot Jim eyes his sleeping father with whom he desperately wants to talk. He feels guilty and seeks his father's— emphatically not his mother's—help.

2. Frank Stark, played by Jim Backus, dozes in a living room chair. In this bleak moment, he has failed his son who badly wants his advice and convinces the boy of his moral cowardice. This sequence which encapsulates the mid-fifties iconized idealism of sons who are so sincere they want to reform their fathers, caught the imagination of a "pre-hip" American generation who felt morally superior to their parents. After 1969 this conviction of the moral superiority of the younger over the older generation vanished.

3. Jim sees his mother, played by Ann Doran, come down the stairs, upside down, cartwheeling counter-clockwise into his vision. Her intrusion into the conversation Jim wants to have with his father is shown this way by Nick Ray. This director's point of view shot was the first time in Hollywood history that someone was shown upside down and then righted by a 180° pan.

4. Jim, weak from seeing his new friend Buzz killed in the chickie run, hangs his head in a moment of stasis soon to be interupted by the entrance of his mother. Nick Ray's mise-en-scène was never more brilliantly constructed than in this father-son-mother confrontation.

1

2

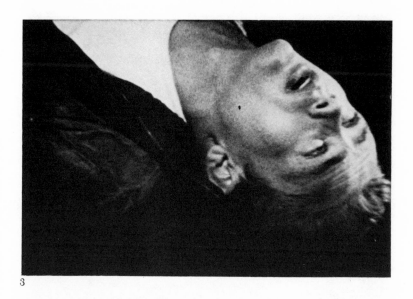

3

4

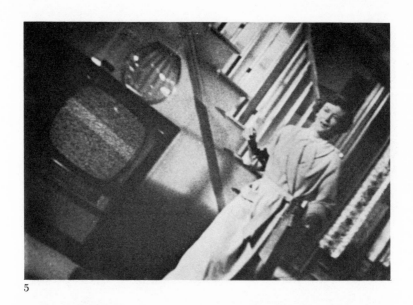

5

6

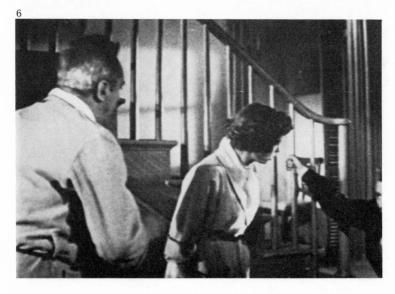

7

8

This brings us to the point of our semantic analysis of a sequence in *Rebel*. Did Ray practice what he preached? It seems he did. For all of his theatrical temperament, he remained faithful to the demands of the cinema for cinematic dialogue, dialogue he can film. This often leads to fights, Ray observed (though he never seemed to have such fights with his screenwriters).

"The director has to fight against this [tendency of the screenwriter to want to keep everything in] and the result is often to make the writer accuse him of being illiterate. There may be a scene in which a writer is especially proud of his dialogue; it may be good dialogue; but what is really needed for the scene is . . . a visual conception. And the dialogue has to go. What replaces it may seem, to the writer, banal—and here another misunderstanding can arise. Someone remarked that a fundamental tenet of Stanislavsky's system is to help an actor say 'What time is it' and mean one of maybe twenty different things—'I want to leave' or 'I want to stay,' 'I love you' or 'I hate you,' 'I'm worried' or 'I don't care' and so on. In that sense the most apparently banal line of dialogue can achieve dramatic meaning. Out of the inner moment, the state of being and the urgent need, comes the whole accent of what is said or done. Only the director is in a position to help the actor create this effect."[11]

5. and 6. Jim's mother completes her entrance/intrusion into Jim's confrontation with his father and interposes herself between them.

7. In the middle of the six minute confrontation, Jim is still trapped by his parents' refusal to get involved in his problem. He tries to go *upstairs*, a Ray index for successful family integration, but is stopped (in a shot after the one shown) by his mother. Jim is completely entrapped; Ray tells us this by surrounding him with a trapezoidal composition designed to give us the "trapped rat" feeling characteristic of similar compositions in German Expressionist art. Although this shot appears for only two seconds, it forever belies the accusation that Ray was a hack or was anything other than a consummate artist.

8. Driven to exasperation by his uncommitted parents Jim counter-attacks and challenges them. These last two minutes in the sequence seems to have given susceptible teenagers in the late 1950s audience the feeling that one could rebel, and thus the superb acting in these scenes somewhat undercut *Rebel's* overall message that a teenager should have a cause. Dean, himself, hated gratuitous violence in films and, after seeing *Blackboard Jungle* remarked, "Why don't they just pass out syringes to the audience?"

If Ray, in effect, structured everything this way, there would be no truth to the claim made by Jim Backus, that James Dean co-directed *Rebel*.

The answer to this contradiction lies in between the two poles. Ray had a total visual concept of the film, which he imposed. But he realized that the authenticity of certain sequences, notably the father-son confrontation sequence, would largely depend on belief in the character of Jim Stark as played by James Dean. Dean, for his part, brought, I believe, a unique form of Method acting geared to cinema, to his three films, and where he had freedom to express it, he could impart superbly authentic dialogue. I believe that Dean did structure the dialogue of the father-son confrontation sequence—in conjunction with Ray—during rehearsals. Ray, for his part, wanted it that way. Ray described how he wanted Dean to tell him how and where, in the Stark house, the confrontation was to take place. Ray originally intended it to take place *upstairs*. But he asked Dean to run through the motions as to what he would do after he came home from the chickie run. Dean, in the dry run at Ray's bungalow in Hollywood's residential hotel, the Chateau Marmont, went up to the refrigerator, got a bottle of milk, and, instead of going upstairs, flopped down on the sofa. Ray then said he got a brainstorm. The father would be asleep in a living room chair and the *mother* would come down the stairs, upon hearing Jim. Yet, this "stage business" alone would not have given the sequence its authenticity. The next step was to set up a complex alternation where the camera would cue the dialogue and the dialogue would then cue the camera. Dialogue was semantically integrated with camera movement and cutting. The result: an extraordinarily tight and economical sequence, even though it lasts for six and one-half minutes.

The change in dialogue, from final script form, to what was used, is worth briefly outlining, along with the main intentions of the camera.

The sequence opens with a fade from the compact Judy has been playing with in her bedroom, a sign of her newfound involvement with Jim, to the door of the Stark living room. Jim Stark is returning from the chickie run, where Buzz has been killed, his car going over a cliff. Jim (Dean) takes a bottle of milk from the refrigerator (a glass bottle), drinks from it, rubs it on his forehead, carries it with him to the living room where he finds his father, sleeping in a chair. He wants to speak to his father, but before this happens, we see a 180

degree vertical downward pan in which the mother starts down
from the top of the stairs, seen upside down by Jim (this is not Jim's
point-of-view shot but the director's). As she descends the stairs,
she gradually emerges right side up, as the pan completes its 180
degrees. When she reaches the living room floor, she is right side
up. This informs us how the mother thrusts herself between Jim and
his father, and the mise-en-scène for the rest of the sequence is like
a football game, where the mother is constantly moving, maneuver-
ing, while Jim is posturing, gesticulating, reacting, and the father is
shrugging.

At the key moment of ominousness in the sequence, Ray un-
leashes his second unusual shot. After the confrontation with the
mother reaches its apex, we see Jim (Dean) feeling trapped, in a
trapezoidal composition on the stairs. After a cut, Dean begs his
father for help and the world goes tilt on him, but partially because
in the middle of the shot, Ray has tilted the camera. This serves as a
jolt to the viewer. Later, Dean, in a less stylized shot, begs his
father (who is sitting) to "stand up for me." When he fails, Jim jumps
on him and begins to choke him. The sequence ends with Jim
running out of the house, after stopping at the french doors to kick
his mother's portrait.

It is clear, with such tight mise-en-scène and cutting, that the
dialogue must conform to the rhythm of pacing. And yet it must also
inform. Despite the clarity and obviousness of the mise-en-scène,
this sequence could, by no means, be a silent film sequence. Why?
Because the pathos of the sequence is entirely in the words of James
Dean.

How the revision of the script works to fit the cutting and mise-
en-scène can be simply illustrated by comparing script and the
dialogue we hear in the film. On a Warner Brothers script, dated
May 2, 1955, there is the notation: "dialogue changes" before all the
dialogue in the father-Jim confrontation sequence.

Since the film started shooting on March 28 and ended the last
week in May, we can assume that the script dialogue here is at least
the *second* version of it (an earlier version would have existed, dated
before March 28). Also, not only did Dean change the dialogue, but
Ray changed the shots and mise-en-scène along with the changes.

As the mother (Ann Doran) enters the room, hurries to Jim, holds
him, inspects him, kisses him . . .

(Script): Mother: What happened, darling. We were so worried. I was going to take a sleeping pill, but I wouldn't till I knew you were home.

(Film): Mother: (screen voice, during shot of Jim on sofa) He's home. You're home. (180 degree vertical pan starts with mother upside down, and follows her as she, in counterclockwise fashion, appears right side up at the foot of the stairs and advances on Jim, who sits up.) You're home. Are you all right? I was going to take a sleeping pill but I wouldn't till I knew you were home . . .

(Script): Jim: I have to talk to someone, Mom. I have to talk to you both. And Dad, this time you got to give me an answer.

(Film): Jim: Can I talk to you, Dad? . . . I have to talk to somebody. *Dad?*

[Dean seems to have changed the entire point of the sequence here. He only wants to talk to his father. His mother is in the way of this. He further emphasizes this by looking through her toward where (as shown in a previous shot) his father sits.]

(Script): Dad: Go ahead.
(Film): Dad: What?

(Script): Jim: I'm in terrible trouble. You know that big high bluff near Millertown Junction?

(Film): Jim: [repeating his earlier line for dramatic emphasis, and establishing his father's cop-out character a bit more for the audience] You got to give me an answer this time.

(Script): Dad: [His line's been expanded, so he's already said this.]
(Film): Dad: Go ahead.

(Script): Jim: [He's already said: "I'm in terrible trouble. You know that big high bluff near Millertown Junction?]

(Film): Jim: I want a *direct* answer. [Dean keeps harping on the fact that he probably won't get a direct answer. As we will see, he *doesn't!*] I'm in trouble. [Almost spoken as an afterthought here] You know that big high bluff in Millertown? [He eliminated "Junction," something he wouldn't say, especially if he were agitated.]

(Script): Dad: Sure—there was a bad accident there. They showed the pictures on T.V.

(Film): Dad: (trying to prove to him, but clumsily, that he's listening) Oh yes, yes . . . There was a bad accident . . . they showed the pictures—on Television, Jim. [Showing parents see the world from a safe distance]

(Script): Jim: I was in it.
(Film): Jim: I was in it.

(Script): Mother: How?
(Film): Mother: How?

(Script): Jim: It doesn't matter how. I was driving a stolen car—
(Film): Jim: I was driving a stolen car. [Makes it more terse, this way.]

(Script): Mother: Do you *enjoy* doing this to me or what—
(Film): Mother: Do you enjoy doing this to me or what . . .

(Script): Jim: Mom—I'm not—
(Film): Jim: Let me explain. [Now appeals not to one parent or the other, but more to the world at large. Again, Dean changes the emphasis.]

We could go on and on here, citing sequences where Ray converted banal lines into Romeo and Juliet-like soliloquies. What remains is a semantic trademark. Dean—like Brando—was not fond of lines over five words in length. "You know/that big high bluff/in Millertown" becomes three sentences, as spoken by Dean. "Moh–ohm" sometimes becomes a two-syllable word. Always maintaining tension, Dean could be electric in interrupting noisily, or poignant in stretching a sentence, filling it with active silences. The Ray-Dean coordination of mise-en-scène is superb. During his slowest line in the sequence, Ray lets him have most of a 24½ foot shot to say just, "Dad. (pause) Answer her. (pause). Dad?"

9

Rebel's Impact in the United States and Europe

RAY'S *JOHNNY GUITAR* (1954) brought him to widescreen, color, and world attention, and gave him, he states, the money to make *Rebel Without a Cause*. (Ray had the ability to do *Rebel* as a cheap, independent production, if he had so desired.) As it was, Warner Brothers consented to make a youth film and did permit *Rebel Without a Cause* to be made, though Ray and the studio clearly had different fantasies as to how it would come out.

Rebel was a triumph for Ray because he made it on his own terms. Those terms, as near as we can guess, were that film is "an eclectic and collective art."[1] *Rebel* was made by five men, really, working in unusually close collaboration during the heady, spring months of 1955. The result was as eclectic as it was collective.

Ray's collective approach was unfortunately violated by the audience's response to the film. His collaboration with James Dean in the creation of the character of Jim Stark was successful, but it is important to point out that the audience excerpted Dean from the film's context. In Europe, as in America, *Rebel*'s success was directly a result of the audience's perception of the film as a statement made by James Dean who was seen, not only as the spokesman for the film, but for his entire generation. Reviewers never referred to "Jim Stark"; it was always James Dean who said this or did that. Ray was not mentioned either, except in rare instances such as Eric Rohmer's review. Imitatory films on the "youth point of view" proliferated, especially in Europe where it was even more exciting to do. Ray had done his work—of having his ideas spoken by Dean's persona—more forcefully than he knew. It now seems that the audience's misapprehension of *Rebel* was a function of the times. Historically speaking it is unfortunate that so much attention was paid to the mythic and James Dean aspects of the film. All this obscured

149

Production still from *Die Halbstarken*, a West German variant on the *Rebel* theme produced in 1956.
credit: Bavaria Films

the value of *Rebel* as a clear cinematic statement by Nick Ray.

As a mark of Nick Ray's *cinematic* style, one can consider *Rebel* an *auteur* film without the usual self-doubt as to whether there really is such a thing as an *auteur* film. Even if one *rejects* the myth of *Rebel*, one finds it stands the classic test of time well and is still quite effective today. For its filmic values alone, it is well worth learning about, and it could easily be the subject of a film course. As for students of art, nowhere can one find a better eclectic work to study than this film, which is really an overlay of *two* projected films: "Heroic Love" and "The Blind Run."

In fact, in a pragmatic sense the film represented a triumph of Ray's Group Theater approach. It was a very American film and it became an American icon, an American "institution" of sorts—and not a "square" one—at a time when America was branded a conformistic country—an icon of what teen-age honesty can do and an index of what it could mean to the nation. As a film, it seemed to be Ray's goal as an *auteur*. (It shows, in fairness to Ray, that the conditions for his filmmaking were rarely right, but this once, they were.)

After *Rebel* came a loosening of sexual standards in youth-exploitation films and many other genres that lured people away from real youth themes. Unfortunately for Ray's talent, he was increasingly used as a workhorse in the Hollywood big-budget area to produce epic, widescreen films—like the generally unappreciated remake of Cecil B. DeMille's *King of Kings*. Much of his talent was wasted after 1955; yet we can enjoy much about any Ray film, and especially—with the power of hindsight—*Party Girl, Bigger Than Life*, and *Bitter Victory*.

But *Rebel* remains the key film in Ray's career for many reasons. Those interested in evaluating him can find out more about how "good" a director he was from *Rebel* than from any of his other films, simply because he was less hampered in exposing himself in this film. Second, *Rebel* is the film that tells you whether you appreciate Ray, or even have a tolerance for him. Third, *Rebel* is both his easiest and his most complex film. It is, therefore, the film with which to begin any serious cinematic study of Ray (as well as the film—on a more popular level—to see before delving into Ray's other films), for *Rebel* contains all of Ray's shot vocabulary. Even though modern audiences react differently to *Rebel* than those two decades ago, taking it less seriously, its best sequences still win approval from highly diverse audiences. Ray's talent in *Rebel* is definitively unveiled.

In Hollywood, Ray's talent at the time he made *Rebel* was seen as that of a distinguished specialist. He was regarded as a moderately radical director even for Hollywood, but also as a sure-fire hand who could produce something that was generally commercial and always original. (One feels that, after 1954 and *Johnny Guitar*, Ray was regarded by the Hollywood studios very much as the talented hippies were who were tolerated by corporations in the late 1960s.) Nineteen fifty-five was the end of Ray's Hollywood honeymoon. *Rebel* was made just in time—before it ended. Ray's despising of Hollywood seems to have come about slowly and steadily after *Rebel*'s release—and significantly—after the death of James Dean. Though he never made a big deal of it, Ray must have appreciated the Hollywood presence of Kazan and other *avante-gardistes*. They helped him dare. Ray was never one to flourish in a cultural vacuum. As long as they were there, he seems to have "handled" Hollywood well. "Kazan and I matriculated about the same time," says Ray, and with Kazan at Warners, Ray had, for once, a brief sense of being among colleagues, a situation he would never find again. He would never again work so comfortably both in an establishmentarian and in an avante-garde world.

Though made in a cosmopolitan atmosphere, *Rebel* owes little to any other *director*. The Kazan influence on Ray in *Rebel* is minor: it is to be seen in the film's professionalism, not in its artistic style. Ray's cutting avoids Kazan's shot-countershot approach; the pacing is different from *East of Eden*, and the film avoids the arty look and moments of *Eden* while it lacks *Eden*'s "A" picture look. *Rebel*, in its own way, maximized CinemaScope and Warnercolor (an ungodly combination) more than *Eden*. Yet despite the occasional moments of flashing "B" movie locales, Ray's professionalism is seen in the swift and sure pace, the lack of eccentricity for eccentricity's sake, the psychologically worked out motivations of the secondary characters, and in the mastery of CinemaScope and color. For all its overdependence on a mythological acceptance of its plot, *Rebel* remains an unusual, compelling example of a highly eclectic and original second-generation Hollywood sound feature film, with hidden previews in it, of the third-generation ontological cinema that was to develop after 1959. This, at least, is its legacy to *American* cinema.

On a personal note, *Rebel* may have been Ray's last particularly inspired film, because, four days before its premier, on September 30, 1955, James Dean was killed. "We all took Jimmy's death pretty hard, but Nick was particularly affected by it," said Natalie Wood years later. And in the grim aftermath year, Ray was to rhapsodize Dean constantly, refer to him, invoke him, mention future projects he wanted to do with him. "The last time I saw James Dean," Ray was to write, "was when he arrived without warning at my Hollywood home, about 3 o'clock in the morning. That evening, we had met for dinner. We talked for several hours of many things, of future plans, including a story called 'Heroic Love' that we were going to do. When he appeared later, he had been given a Siamese cat by Elizabeth Taylor, and he wanted to borrow a book of mine on cats before driving home."[2]

"Heroic Love" was never filmed. The scenario, which seems to derive from the emotionally complex relationship that Ray and Dean shared, was described by Ray[3] and can be summarized as follows:

A boy returns from the war. [World War II?] He's standing on the train platform in a small Western town, and there to meet him is his hero, a distinguished attorney. The boy's father and mother have died during the war, leaving him a ranch in which he has no interest; he wants to become a lawyer and study under this man. The attorney is moved by this and invites the boy to stay at his home. The attorney is married to a much younger wife, who tries to seduce the young man who rejects her. She becomes revengeful, and one day, on a visit to the attorney's law office, the young man finds her and the junior partner making love. But he never says a word about it. Instead, he begins a rampage of seducing every young girl in town. (All the mothers are up in arms but they're secretly jealous if their daughters have been passed over.) A Chinese cook goes berserk, kills three men, but is saved from lynching by the young man and the attorney.

Subsequently, the wife accuses the young man of trying to seduce her. The husband—knowing instinctively that she's been having an affair with someone—assumes that she's right. He calls the boy to the public square and horsewhips him out of town. The boy says nothing.[3]

The book Ray planned to write, "Rebel: The Life Story of a Film," was never completed either though two articles appeared, both excerpts from it.

Natalie Wood has recounted how Nick read the cast a certain chapter from Thomas Wolfe's *You Can't Go Home Again* during the *Rebel* rehearsals.[4] This was prophetic. Surely, it was after Dean's death, that Nick began to contemplate his European exile.

Imitations of *Rebel Without a Cause*

Every film like *Rebel* inspires imitations. Why? Because a sincere yet mythic film benefits from the principle of double-compounded attraction. It works like a magnet in focusing attention. *Rebel* focused attention on the young rebel, his specific origin, and his quest and also on the mythic origin, the sincere quest as a universal phenomenon. Regardless of the sincerity the film undoubtedly possessed, it did lay itself open by its very nature to present a new formula to those who believe that, in the popular arts, the cliché is all there is. In addition, hack and copycat producer/directors had, in 1955, not only the support of Hollywood tradition in copying any hit picture, but also the tacit support of many a distinguished name in the arts for the idea of invoking a basic formula by executing its cliché form over and over again. As T. S. Eliot, for example, claimed:

No poet, no artist of any art has his complete meaning alone. . . . You must set him, for contrast and comparison, among the dead. I mean this as a principle of aesthetic, not merely historical criticism. . . . What happens when a new work of art is created is something that happens simultaneously to all the works of art which preceded it. The existing monuments form an ideal order among themselves, which is modified by the introduction of the new (the really new) work of art among them. Whoever has approved this idea of order . . . will not find it preposterous that the past should be altered by the present as much as the present is directed by the past.[5]

Rebel, for its part, only *seemed* to be a highly original film. Its mythic side, its *aesthetic* realism, rendered it a very formulaic film. As a result, *Rebel* was not only easy pickings for those who wanted to imitate it and to cash in on the American youth market, but its very success helped breed two whole sub-genres of imitation films: the wild youth film and the crazy mixed-up youth film, which, along with *Rebel* itself (which reached Europe in early 1956) would have a strong influence on the young of Western Europe.

Wild youth films were *Crime In The Streets* (1956) in which *Rebel* veteran Sal Mineo starred, playing more of a Buzz than a Plato; *Untamed Youth* (1957) starring Eddie Cochrane, whose blond good looks made him to rock and roll what James Dean was to film— Eddie looked more like Jimmy than any other rock star did, even though, there, the real resemblance ended; and *Juvenile Jungle*

(1958) with Corey Allen, *Rebel*'s Buzz, again playing Buzz. In this way, Hollywood "recycled" the original cast of *Rebel Without a Cause*.

The crazy mixed-up youth films included the four car films: *Hot Rod Girl* (1956), *Dragstrip Girl* (1957), *Hot Car Girl* (1958), and *Dragstrip Riot* (1958)—almost all the permutations on the words *girl, hot rod,* and *drag strip* that Hollywood could dredge up. These films were reuses of Judy (Natalie Wood), the girl from *Rebel* who sat in Buzz's car, etc.

Sal Mineo not only played the heavy in *Crime In The Streets* (despite his light body) but also a drummer in the prototype of a third kind of youth film of that day, a genre that owed all to rock and roll and nothing to the *Rebel Without a Cause* theme. This was *Rock, Pretty Baby,* (1956) which had an amazing cast: Sal on drums, John Saxon on lead sax, and Rod McKuen, the poet, on stand-up acoustic bass. We mention it here for the sake of completeness in listing all the various sub-genres of youth film, but the *Rock, Pretty Baby* sub-genre can be ignored in our study of the mutant formation of youth cult in Europe, for this genre stayed in America and went surfwards.

What now concerns us are the details of the European mutation of the American youth cult fabrication as typified by *Rebel,* through the wild-youth film, the crazy mixed-up youth film, and the emergence of British youth-film stars who looked like copies of American rock and roll stars. Through England, France, and West Germany, these films distributed image, legend, even myth; and Young Europe was never again the same. How did the European imitations of the American films differ from the originals and to what extent were they misreadings of the originals? Answers to these questions will tell us how universal films like *Rebel* were and whether they were authentic or merely seemed authentic.

In Europe, I doubt whether anyone really understood Nick Ray's *Rebel,* especially what it signified to Nick Ray: "A boy wants to be a man, quick." While admiring the tough Hollywood "B" picture and idolizing Ray, Samuel Fuller, and Howard Hawks, the French critics played some dandified games with the American sensibility that arose as a tough-bitter shell against the system in America where hustlers win and sensitive people lose. The successful "American of the 'B' pictures" was only a movie winner: Phillip Marlowe was a winner but Raymond Chandler was attrited to death; Ray was a winner in that he made cinema, but he was made into a nervous wreck by the Hollywood system; Samuel Fuller, whom Godard rhapsodized about in *Pierrot le fou*, sums up the word *cinema* this way: "Film is like a battleground: love, hate, action, death . . ." What Fuller omitted, but Godard should have picked up is: not only is film a battleground; so is life.

The French critics partial to Ray and other "lost" directors probably did not, realize how depressed he was, for they also converted Ray's and others anarchic Americanisms into Continental clichés. Truffaut's review of *East of Eden* (in *Cahiers*) becomes "The beans of evil," a paraphrase of Baudelaire, but a distortion of the significa-tion of the nice, neutral beans in *East of Eden*. While "rescuing" Nick Ray's reputation, and elevating him to *auteur* status, some of the French critics overintellectualized him, and, even more dangerously, tore him loose from his real context.

Rebel, then, was seen, especially in France, as an artistic film *and* as a generational conflict film. As it was an artistic film about the generational conflict, it automatically told some kind of truth. Hence, Eric Rohmer's biggest tribute to the film was that it was so authentic one "marched right along with it." Attention was also focused on the star personality of James Dean, as there was no such French equivalent yet! To be perfectly fair, the French critics at least spoke of *Rebel* as Ray's film, whereas Anglo-Saxon critics were spellbound by Dean. But this gave the French critics a special license to invent Ray. In England, in France, and in West Ger-many, the reaction to *Rebel* differed. In general, it seemed that British kids, West German kids, and French adult critics were the most enthusiastic about the film.

Rebel in England

Rebel arrived in England in February, 1956, a good quarter year before *Blackboard Jungle* brought rock 'n roll there ("Rock Around the Clock" was on its soundtrack). *Rebel* was censored in Britain, most of the knife fight being cut out and not returned to the screen until 1967. Even then, the film was given an X-certificate (for adults only) under the newly introduced British rating system. As a result, more British teen-agers have seen the film since 1967 than during its first run in 1956.

The film was, however, enthusiastically received: "The central triumph of *Rebel Without a Cause* is the character study of Jim; Nicholas Ray and the late James Dean have created a powerful and moving portrait of a tormented adolescent, and the analysis of tensions which beset him has an insight, an understanding rare in this kind of film."[6]

Gavin Lambert, writing this review for *Film Quarterly* (Summer 1956), does not isolate James Dean from the context of the film, as some British critics did in earlier reviews of *East of Eden*. Lambert shows a clear understanding of the directorial input into the film and the creation of its character. But *Sight and Sound*, at the time, would have represented the most detached form of appraisal of a popular film.

Lambert discusses the most effective sequences in *Rebel* from his viewpoint:

> Particularly moving is the scene where Jim tries to explain his feeling after the 'chicken run' accident, and in his parents' reaction the whole gulf between them is exposed." [This is the sequence that best holds up after twenty years. Lambert also seems to like the parallel sequence with Judy:] "Equally intuitive is the handling of Judy's strong emotional attachment to her father, and her rage at his sudden, nervous rejection of it. The rhythm, the tone, of disturbed youth is remarkably conveyed in all these scenes, and the ironic, tender sequence in the deserted house, when the three youngsters suddenly express all their feelings of uncertainty and isolation in a wild night game, is another triumph.

Three elements were most commonly singled out in European reactions to the film: (1) isolating Dean's persona from the context of the film, (2) sociological reacting to it as a gang picture, and (3) seeing the lyricism of Nick Ray. In fact, the film is an eclectic melange of all three. Lambert, on his part, has recognized Ray's lyricism and has "read" *Rebel* in the one of the three ways that is most complimentary to Nick Ray, and he comes closest of any European reviewer I've read to appreciating Ray's input and intention properly. But Lambert's was an adult response to the film.

In England, the adult critics of *Rebel* saw the film in the same way as adult critics (though not adults) did in the United States—as a contrived film that told a story; they did not excerpt, lionize, and mythologize James Dean from the film and make it into "their story." Why didn't most adult critics sense the special impact the film would have on teen-agers?

Due to an odd fluke, the French lionized the image of James Dean right away. François Truffaut was exactly the same age as James Dean, and Truffaut's review of *East of Eden* in *Cahiers du Cinema* was probably a highly personal reaction to Dean as well as to the film, describing it as the first film to give us "a Baudelarian hero." "James Dean has succeeded in making this film commercial . . .," declared Truffaut, with further astuteness. The scene he most praises is the thirty shots covering the episode where Dean tries to get Raymond Massey to take the money he has made speculating on beans. A year later, when *Rebel* reached England and France, and the death of James Dean had occurred, Truffaut joined the English youth generation and some of his own in the cult of Dean, whereas other French critics gave more space to Nick Ray's *Rebel*.

I don't want just to accuse Truffaut of the mythomania he continued to display toward a certain kind of cinema (*East of Eden*, *Rebel*, the Japanese *Rebel*, *Pale Flower* (1958)), for he was loyal to his own generational myth, but to cite the strange dichotomy *Rebel* created between those who swallowed its myths and took it as "their story" and those who just saw it as a narrative film, with some good acting and some exciting events—as an entertaining "B" picture, "made for the matinee crowd," as director George Stevens put it.

Writing in the middle of it all in 1956, in *Sight and Sound*, the prestigious British film quarterly, critic Penelope Houston felt that the basic reason behind the production of films such as *Blackboard Jungle* and *Rebel Without a Cause* was that after being

". . . severely hit by the tornado of McCarthyism, Hollywood, that vulnerable and cautious community, has been some time in recovering its nerve, *in regaining the degree of social awareness* that characterized the American cinema of a few years ago. Predictably, the route back to controversy was clearly suggested at the box office: whatever Terry Malloy's pain-wracked walk in the last sequence of *On The Waterfront* proved, it forcefully indicated that *social comment sufficiently laced with violence, had drawing power*."[7] (italics mine)

Note that Houston puts the blame on *Waterfront's* director, Elia Kazan, for starting the trend. This is significant, if it is true, for Kazan helped train *Rebel's* director, Nick Ray, and simultaneously launched Dean and Brando: James Dean in *East of Eden* in 1954–

55, and the sensitive Brando through the Oscar-winning *On The Waterfront,* in early 1954.

More significant is that Houston's two comments show that the 1940s and middle 1950s were clearly different. Fine, that Hollywood wanted to begin again *"regaining the degree of social awareness that characterized the American cinema of a few years ago."* But *the audiences,* she says, "predictably" wanted "the route back to controversy" to follow the path of giving it "social comment sufficiently laced with violence."

The mainspring of *Blackboard Jungle,* a considerably more expert and shrewd production [than *Phoenix City*] is also violence: it is by disarming a young hooligan in his own formroom that the schoolmaster [Glenn Ford] eventually wins the respect of his recalcitrant pupils.

One could observe that in *Blackboard Jungle,* it is Glenn Ford, the older man and teacher, who is picked on, who plays the same role as James Dean in *Rebel* of the kid who turns the tables on his persecutors. Both men, Ford and Dean, are picked on by a punk— played by Vic Morrow in *Blackboard Jungle* and Corey Allen in *Rebel.* The caption under the photo of Vic Morrow in *Sight and Sound* calls *him* the rebel, but it is Glenn Ford who is really the rebel in that instance, as Houston herself demonstrates in her next sentence.

Isolated between his tired and dejected colleagues [in the *Rebel* analogy, Jim's *parents*] and his classroom of potential delinquents, [Glenn Ford] the idealist is bound, by the happy convention of the problem picture, to convert both parties. Having overstated its case at the outset, the film has to use the utmost contrivance to bring about this triumph; and if the conclusion is invalid, the earlier sequences, for all their parade of angry conviction, are made suspect by their machine-made sensationalism. After launching, by implication, a formidable attack on a section of the American educational system, the film slides off into some facile melodramatics. It is the hit and run technique, guaranteed to leave the audience with little conception of where the truth lies.

Houston then asks some penetrating questions on the subject of "the Movie Without a Cause." About *Rebel,* she asks:

Are we to assume that Buzz and his friends, whose equipment for the first day of term includes switchblades and lengths of bicycle chain, also come from the wrong side (i.e., like the kids in *BJ*) of the tracks and therefore (following the argument of *BJ*) predisposed to violence? And when a large part of the school turns out to watch the "chicken run," is the fact that no one attempts to call a halt to this frightening exploit to be taken as evidence of mass maladjustment? Clearly to push the point is to be unfair to the film. *But the effect is incongruously to suggest not only that unhappy adolescents gravitate towards violence but that only the occasionally lucky avoid it.* In other words, the film takes us only a little farther than *BJ* towards the social problem which is the reason for this instinctive distrust of the adult world of parents and schoolmasters, and of the discipline it attempts to impose (italics mine).[8]

The period after *Blackboard Jungle* and *Rebel* reached England was characterized by a peculiar British resistance to Elvis Presley and a mania for Bill Haley and the Comets. *Rock Around the Clock* was the third American youth movie to hit England and it caused dancing riots and was banned by local watch committees in several towns. Yet the film was widely seen—probably by more people than saw *Blackboard Jungle* or *Rebel*. By the spring of 1957, however, the public had been saturated with Haley, and his popularity in England dwindled.

The fact is that the American youth culture ran rampant over England between 1956 and 1958. The year 1957 was one of reaction when new British pop-teen forms appeared, some of which would surface powerfully in 1958. With the exception of the short-lived (some say it lasted only three weeks) Tommy Steele rock-star explosion in 1956, Britain did not produce its own youth cult forms until 1958, and then in watered-down, mutated form. That year witnessed the rise of the "Holy Trinity" of British pop: Cliff Richard, Adam Faith, and Billy Fury. These were the successful pop singers who would be drafted into "Movies Without a Cause" to exploit their first successful records. What did *Rebel Without a Cause* contribute to this movement?

It helped, principally through James Dean's visual beauty, to encourage the British to favor the visual as well as aural power of the new pop singers and to idolize physically beautiful pop stars. Each one of the "Holy Trinity" was handsomer than his American counterpart.

Cliff Richard looked like a civilized Elvis but sang like Buddy Holly, a double plus for him in England. He ground out so many hits in early-to-middle 1958 that a movie was created as a vehicle for twelve Cliff Richard songs. The movie was called *Serious Charge* (1958) and features Cliff as a kid who reforms in the last reel. Paul Flattery, in *The Illustrated History of British Pop* calls it a "weak imitation of *Blackboard Jungle*." Like *Rebel* and *Blackboard Jungle* the British "honored" the film with an X-rating (for age 16 and over only). In 1959, the British film industry launched a second Cliff Richard film, *Expresso Bongo* in which the late Laurence Harvey plays an evil promoter and tries to tempt Cliff Richard, who, of course, is too "hip" and sophisticated to get lured. In 1959, also, the success of the movie fed back to Cliff's record output. Though there never was a Cliff Richard song by that name, "Serious Charge" became the name of a Cliff Richard extended-play record that same year.

The second of the "Holy Trinity" of pre-Beatle British pop was Adam Faith (real name: Terry Nelhams). As Paul Flattery describes him, his James Dean image was developed through a part in the top TV police series of the time (where he played the head of a motorcycle gang) and by his playing a similar character in *Beat Girl* (1959). "His James Dean image,"—Flattery continues—"was helped by his very high cheekbones and good looks, but he always appeared mean and moody, the whole upturned collar syndrome." Flattery's comments are instructive. Though this was written in 1973, this continual and strange reference to the mean image of the James Dean character by many British writers persisted. In the October, 1975, issue of *Films Illustrated* in a twentieth anniversary overview of Dean's career the same points are made as in several reviews of *That'll Be the Day* (1973), a British sociologically-oriented youth movie; its scriptwriter is quoted as saying essentially the same thing as Flattery—"When we picked our archetypal character to play Jim [note the character's name], we thought of James Dean as the quintessential fifties character, who typified the aggressiveness of the teenagers we were talking about."[9] It is very strange to me, not that teen-agers of the late 1950s were seen as aggressive, but that Dean would be picked as that type! This, of course, I feel, is entirely due to his *image* in *Rebel* and supports the view that screenwriter Stewart Stern put much mythic violence into the film. As the British saw him, James Dean was as much Buzz Gunderson as he was James Stark.

After *Serious Charge* (1958) and *Expresso Bongo* came the turn of the third of the British "Holy Trinity," Billy Fury, to make his appearance in a teen film. Fury—tall and sullenly stately—looked as if he could have been one of the prettier members of Buzz's gang; and he had, in fact, once been wounded by a switchblade in his native Liverpool. Though Fury's success as a singer came from 1958 to 1961, he appeared as Billy Universe of Billy Universe and the Universals—a pop star based on himself—in *Play It Cool* in 1962.

Though Adam Faith was more influenced by James Dean than Billy Fury, Fury *incarnated* Dean better. (Keith Richards of the Rolling Stones even mentions liking Fury, and owning a 1958 Fury LP, and thus the Dean vibration went about as far into British pop as it could go.)

In Britain, *Rebel*, was soberly seen and liked by the British adult critics. Young people, by contrast, idolized Dean. And this made Dean an honorary rock 'n' roller. The film can't be said to have made originally as much impact in London as in Paris or Hamburg (one must remember the British saw the 106-minute cut version of *Rebel*, minus five minutes of the switchblade sequence), but *Rebel*, ever since 1968 (and not, coincidentally, since the removal of the X-certificate) has found a whole new generation of younger, appreciative Dean fans, most of whom were not yet born when the film was made.

Rebel in France

After creating interest in Dean in both British critics and youth, *Rebel Without a Cause* next appeared in France. Eric Rohmer, later famous for his *Claire's Knee*, was then a critic writing for *Cahiers du Cinema*. Rohmer, in a little-known review in *Cahiers*, started off by saying he hated the French title to *Rebel*, *La Furore de vivre* (The Fury of Life). Then he proceeded to praise the film, ending his clever and psychological review with a real fan statement: "By this time you have lost the distance between spectator and the screen." Rohmer wrote about *Rebel*'s climactic ending, "you go along with it, you march along, and their problems are your problems." Rohmer here, in 1956, sounds like a San Franciscan in 1967, saying "We are all one." For a Catholic moralist like Rohmer to believe, the impact must be pretty strong, and the suspension of disbelief well done cinematically. All in all, the reaction to the film in France was very favorable. The Rayophiles, the *Cahiers* critics who loved director

Nick Ray, naturally raved, but the Dean myth was really passed into
French pop culture through two pop singers, Sylvie Vartan and
Johnny Halliday, who are still very popular in France, though both
are now over thirty. Johnny Halliday even wrote a touching
obituary for James Dean.

Rohmer also officially began the *Cahiers* critics' campaign to make
Ray known. Writing in *Cahiers*, Rohmer opened his review of
Rebel:

We deplore that the French distributors have believed to have done well
by way of the title of Nick Ray's latest, with this nonsense, [Rohmer wrote it
"non-sens" in the original French, a pun on the English word "nonsense,"
as *non-sens* means "no feeling" in French.] this grammatical monstrosity,
which is the amalgamation (I don't dare say expression) *The Furor of Life*. It
is an ugly one, it is vulgar, and not something one could strictly correctly
say. The American title is sober, right; [the French title] does not deliver
the essence of the meaning, [the English title] proclaims as it conveys, the
design of its *auteur*: *Rebel Without a Cause*, rebel without cause, the cause
for which one fights.

The readers of *Cahiers* [*du Cinema*] know that we hold Nick Ray to be
one of the greats—the greatest, says Rivette and I agree with him
wholeheartedly—of the new generation of American cinéastes who appeared after the war. Despite the apparent modesty of his discourse, he is
one of those rare ones who possesses his own style, a vision of the world, a
poetic nature about him; he is an *auteur*, a great *auteur*. To discover a
constant all through a work of art is a double-edged thing; it is a proof of
personality, but it is also in certain cases, of barrenness. Such always are the
conditions presented by companies to the *cinéaste*, that however numerous
are the makers, the directors of fabrication, the good foremen, that the
presence of a lietmotif is, *a priori*, a favorable sign. The diversity of subjects
treated by Nicholas Ray, the richness of variation with which he augments
his three or four big themes, comments most favorably on his originality
and shows up his rivals.[10]

The next step in the process of lionizing Ray occurred when the
French critics "sold" the British on the idea that Nick Ray was an
auteur. By 1962, Victor Perkins had written the best essay on Ray
yet for *Movie*, a legendary British "little magazine" devoted to
cinema. After 1962, Ray buffs existed equally on both sides of the
Channel.

The International *Rebel* Tradition

It would be interesting to catalogue who in Western Europe was influenced by the first wave of American youth movies such as *Rebel*. Probably the most important point to be made is that members of the British rock generation, born between 1938 and 1944, were between ages thirteen and nineteen in 1957. They could hardly have missed seeing one or another of these films.

As British pop star Adam Faith said, after he saw *Rebel*, "I just felt I wanted to be James Dean. He made a cock up of it all, but somehow he seemed to say it all."[11] The next point is that European teen-agers took these films differently from U.S. teen-agers. The West Germans, for example, produced a film and a rock star most similar to ones in the United States, namely: *Die Halbstarken*, and blond, handsome rock star, Peter Krause, who made a career converting Elvis Presley to German context. (Krause, for example, made "You're Nothin' But A Hound Dog" into "Haffen Rock." Krause later appeared in a German rock youth "Movie Without a Cause" around 1959, and then disappeared.) England, by contrast, was the most "gung ho" about the authentic U.S. records and films, but never seemed to take its own imitations as seriously as the U.S. import. Yet we took the Beatles seriously. There was always some detachment in British pop from itself; it is as if even the British teen-ager was mature enough to know it was all contrived.

In France, the teen reaction did not come until the early 1960s. But note, France had the most powerful avant-garde tradition in the world, the least opposition to new trends *per se* of any country. What France lacked was a rock 'n' roll tradition in addition to its pop tradition. This had to be invented. In fact, only the self-invented Johnny Halliday, who patterned himself after Dean/Elvis, and the even more self-invented Sylvie Vartan, a female Johnny Halliday, appeared at all to represent rock 'n' roll in France. No "Movies Without a Cause" emanated from French film studios. There was enough positive vigor in French film that France could do without any "Movie Without a Cause" tradition, for the high-water mark of those films coincided with the exciting emergence of the French New Wave, which dominated and subsumed all the new energies and youth audiences in France. The closest thing in France, then, to a "Movie Without a Cause" was not Godard's *Breathless* (1959), but all the earlier Truffaut films, like *The 400 Blows* and *Shoot the Piano Player*. In its absorption of the American romantic gangster tradition, in its self-conscious self-reference to Bogart, American pop, etc., in its obvious statement, through Michel Poiccard, of the director, Godard's, lack of love, *Breathless* is a *candidate* for being a "Movie Without a Cause." Yet, it isn't. It is much too serious, much too controlled, and its director much too certain of what he wanted to do. Its mythic nature autodestructs and its Bogart myth dies with its character, Michel Poiccard's death. *Breathless'* legacy is its jump-cut-oriented cinematic style and not its content; it was not taken as an existential text.

Third, the legacy of the first wave of the "Movies Without a Cause" was that the European imitations and reactions to them was an amalgam of both the serious and the trivial aspects of these films, thus giving the European mutation of U.S. pop culture a double-edged power beyond that of pure caricature. This came out later, for few people shared my initial impression of the Beatles as a carica-ture of the Marx Brothers. Most took them very seriously.

Finally, of the sub-genres of the "Movie Without a Cause" to influence Europe, the youth rock films were the most influential, followed by *Rebel Without a Cause*; the wild youth films were less influential. The crazy mixed-up youth films had no influence in Europe: the *intensity* from the other two types was what was ab-sorbed. But what, in general, the Europeans did to the image of the young protagonist was a real mutation. They could not instinctively absorb Elvis as well as they could James Dean so they com-promised. They made the juvenile delinquent into a rock star, steal-ing his intensity but robbing him of the capacity to do harm. In short, they picked up the mythic contradiction of the Jim Stark character played by James Dean in *Rebel* and formalized this con-tradiction into a type. When the myth was returned to American youth culture via the rock groups, the myth was so entrenched that it remained powerful for many years. Even as late as 1973, when J. Marks [Jamake Mamake Highwater] suggested Mick Jagger was such a contrived self-synthesis, the average Mick Jagger fan turned his or her battle back on Marks' *Mick Jagger* book and, instead, embraced Antony Scaduto's mythological "biography" of Jagger and they buried themselves in the mythic cover-ups of that semificti-tious book.

What we then have seen is how the "Movies Without a Cause"

landed on fertile ground, both in the United States and abroad, because their timing was right, and how the first wave of them (*Blackboard Jungle, Rebel Without a Cause,* and *Rock Around the Clock*) was particularly important during the two years when there was a vacuum in West European teen culture. When Western Europe awoke, embraced, and imitated, it also unwittingly mutated what it had absorbed from the "Movies Without a Cause." This undoubtedly was due to the fact that, by their own susceptibility to myth, the internal mythmakers of these films had created the strangest form of presenting a youth myth: the half real and half fictitious, and surrounded it with reasonably good, professional filmmaking. When these films, with their Trojan horse aspects, hit susceptible minds, it was no wonder that they succeeded in making inroads, despite the fact that—sociologically speaking—these three films were, in the worst way, mythic "Movies Without a Cause." As James Dean said to Leonard Rosenman after the two of them had seen *Blackboard Jungle,* "Why don't they just pass a syringe out to the audience?" Though *Rebel* was, undoubtedly the finest of the American youth films of the mid-1950s, and it remains so, I believe, more for its mythos than for its message, its power in the 1950s was through the iconography of Dean.

Yet, there exist film directors who were personally influenced by *Rebel,* and many actors as well. Most notable among the latter are Bruce Dern, Bob Dylan, perhaps Jack Nicholson in America, the late "James Dean of Poland," Zbigniew Cibulski; Horst Bucholtz, and David Essex in Western Europe. Among the directors, many have expressed an instinctive liking for the film: Chabrol, Truffaut, Rohmer, Godard; but none approaches the current fanaticism for the message and style of *Rebel* and "what it stood for," more than West German "hippie" director, Wim Wenders. Overtly in Wajda's *Ashes and Diamonds* (1958), covertly in Wender's *Alice in the Cities* (1974), we see the unique balance of myth and tension that can still be appreciated in *Rebel Without a Cause.* Wender's film, *King of the Road,* is myth, tension, plus confession, and updates *Rebel's* concerns for audiences in the rootless 1970s.

Rebel in West Germany

In West Germany, *Rebel* was released as . . . *Denn Sie Wissen Nicht Was Sie Tun* (For They Know Not What They Do), an almost biblical translation of the title, and a reflection of the prevailing German pedagogic notion that juvenile delinquency in part was caused by juveniles, who were not violent because they were evil but because they were immature, unable to understand what they were doing, a literal expression of James Dean's line in *Rebel:* "If I could just get through one day without being confused."

By late 1956, the German reaction film to *Rebel* appeared. It was called *Die Halbstarken* (The JD's, or literally, The Half-Strong), the contemptuous German word for juvenile delinquents. Starring Horst Bucholtz as the James Dean character, *Die Halbstarken* was a relatively popular film, and did deceptively well in a year when relatively few films were released by the still-struggling West German film industry. In East Germany, Marxist critics not unexpectedly dismissed the film, calling it "unrealistic."

Moving westward, *Die Halbstarken* played in England early in 1957—when there was no British product in the youth genre to compete with it. Britain had only *Teen Age Bad Girls* coming out that year. Britain could absorb these films (those from the United States and *Die Halbstarken*) perhaps because the youth there were ready, but her filmmakers did not yet have the wild youth film touch.

Ironically, but not surprisingly, *Die Halbstarken* was enough of a success in England that it was soon after introduced into the United States, though with such a mutated title that it takes you a minute to recognize that *Teenage Wolfpack,* starring Henry Bookholt, is in fact the same film.

I have never seen *Teenage Wolfpack,* with Henry Bookholt, but I have seen *Die Halbstarken,* with Horst Bucholtz, and it had its tense moments. It was also a good vehicle for Horst Bucholtz, who, in the fashion of James Dean, became a star overnight. One contrast with *Rebel* was that in *Die Halbstarken,* its delinquents rode bicycles instead of cars, affluence in West Germany at that time not being what it was in California. Also its "hero" (or, properly, its anti-hero) was the head of the gang and not "a good guy." Bucholtz played the Jim Stark and the Buzz Gunderson characters combined into one character. Karen Baal, however, played the familiar Judy character, and Christian Metz, (no relation to the semiologist) the other guy; while not quite a "heavy" Buzz character, Metz was convincing enough as a menace.

Did anyone, I wonder, ever make a study of how many imitations of the same American films were made elsewhere in the world in 1957? If they had, they would have encountered the international high-water mark of the "Movie Without a Cause." *Rebel* had a large role in inspiring these imitations and in passing the iconography of American youth into European culture, largely, because its language was uniquely international; it was the only U.S. film I've ever heard dubbed in German which was convincing.

10

Ray's Post-*Rebel* Hollywood Epics

AFTER HIS 1955 COMMERCIAL SUCCESS with *Rebel*, Ray remained in Hollywood for seven more years, during which he became a pioneer in demonstrating how to film well in CinemaScope and color. He continued to show talent in casting and getting "omnipotent" performances from his actors and actresses. His themes still dealt with outsiders, minorities. He directed James Cagney, James Mason, Richard Burton, Curt Jurgens, Christopher Plummer, Jeffrey Hunter, and never failed to use them as well as he had Dean, Bogart, Crawford, Hayden, Grahame, Derek, and Farley Granger.

Bigger Than Life (1956)

Bigger Than Life was Ray's second independent production. James Mason produced it and also played the leading role of Avery, a schoolteacher who takes cortisone, and not surprisingly becomes "bigger than life." The idea came from a *New Yorker* article, "Ten Feet Tall," that was critical of miracle drugs.

Cinematically speaking, Eric Rohmer's review of *Bigger Than Life*, in *Cahiers du Cinema*, directs our attention to three points about the film that are immediately worth noting: (1) to "reading" the text of the film as not a melodrama about cortisone addiction, but as about the private world of Avery, the schoolteacher, a world with its own interior logic; (2) to seeing the film as a masterpiece of mise-en-scène, action within the shot, and (3), to appreciating that it is a painterly film. (He cites particular instances where Ray has handled Deluxe color well.)

Rohmer's points are all well taken. *Bigger Than Life* is not a melodrama, like Otto Preminger's contemporaneous *The Man with*

169

the Golden Arm, a film about drug addiction, but one with a happy ending. Rather, *Bigger Than Life* is about the interior world of poor Avery, which is very much an alternative world inside America from which he looks out at his environment. I would only disagree with Rohmer when he says that the film is "abstract." It is another example of Ray's aesthetic realism, an allegory, an invented story that could have happened exactly the way it does. Rohmer is right, though, in seeing it as "a mixing of genres" and also in saying that it is neither a philosophical tale (a moral tale, like Rohmer's own *Contes Morales*) nor a popular story. In short, its allegorical moments rise out of a popular story like that of Jim Stark, but the film comes closer to being told through, or via, the kind of inside-out interiority of Marcello Mastroianni in Fellini's *La Dolce Vita.* But unlike *that* specific interiority, which is already a full-fledged interior monologue, Ray's technique is more like Fritz Lang's Expressionism of the 1920s, where the "author" creates a *Filmwelt* in which the characters operate with complete impunity from reality, as long as they are consistent to that *Welt.* Ray's Avery is such a character. He is an *authentic* character as well as Everyman. Rohmer is thus correct, again, when he calls *Bigger Than Life* "psychological realism, theatrical solemnity."

In terms of its chronology, Ray's *Bigger Than Life* was made at the same time, in the same American environment and amid the same initial ripplings of major change in sex attitudes and politics, as Kazan's *Baby Doll* (1956). But one would not think, if one saw them back to back, that they were produced at the same time. Both films were made after Kazan's Brando/Dean period and after Ray's Dean period, but, now, Kazan is unmasking sex, a very popular American film theme of the late 1950s, while Ray is still somewhere in a linear lock step, not having moved on. What was Ray doing? Ray was *still* trying to tell the story of a protagonist "down here below" in America. Avery is rightly seen in Rohmer's words as a kind of witness to something going on in America: "He is literally possessed by a sort of demon of lucidity."[1]

Needless to say, that demon is still not, and never will be, exorcised from Ray's cinema.

To sum up, *Bigger Than Life* is more personal, more obscure, more dependent on the viewer's understanding and agreeing with the idea that much is wrong in the United States (that is, a

Zeitgeist–dependent work of art) than most other Ray films. While similar to *Rebel* in many ways, it is diametrically different in one: *Rebel* is a mythic film; *Bigger Than Life* is not trying to suspend the viewer in a myth, but to hit out at something by a more realistic technique. Its mise-en-scène was very well thought out: the two floors of the house and the staircase aid the viewer to see the *Welt* of the protagonist. The casting is fine. Barbara Rush plays Avery's wife convincingly. But the public didn't pay much attention to the film.

Bigger Than Life is incomprehensible as a genre film, whereas Otto Preminger's *The Man with the Golden Arm* was easy to explain to the public because it fitted every cliché. *Bigger Than Life* was, like *Baby Doll*, about American folkways; but *Baby Doll* succeeded as a sex film *célèbre*, even though the fine points of *Baby Doll's* true nature were missed by a public which saw oral sex going on after every fade. *Bigger Than Life* is not really analogous to these two contemporaneous films, but to two future films that would be made in the United States in late 1956/early 1957: Alexander Mackendrick's *The Sweet Smell of Success* and Kazan's *A Face In The Crowd*. Neither of these two films did well at the box office either, despite the formidable Mackendrick/Clifford Odets and Kazan/Max Schulberg combinations.

It is then curious to see that the American films that succeeded during 1956–1963 were those which pushed against sex taboos, whereas those successful films which conveyed interiority were imported from Europe. Would American audiences have liked and better appreciated Ray's *Bigger Than Life, Bitter Victory*, and *Party Girl* had they been made by Fellini, Godard, Antonioni or Resnais? Is *Party Girl* inferior to *La Notte, Bitter Victory* to *Les Carabiniers*, or *Bigger Than Life* to *La Dolce Vita?* At any rate, *Bigger Than Life* today suffers from an obscurity it hardly deserves.

The True Story of Jesse James (1957)

The True Story of Jesse James is one of a trio of very special Westerns that are genre films but also more than genre films by virtue of what one suspects the director additionally tried to incorporate into the Western form. *Jesse James*, a Ray film in Cinema-Scope, *The Searchers* (1956), John Ford's VistaVision disguised examination of his attitude toward racism in America, and Anthony Mann's *Man of the West* (1958), an erotic Gary Cooper Western which yet enables Mann to play with CinemaScope outdoors, are all highly imaginative films, boot-anchored by popular horse opera narratives. Of the three films, Ray's is, naturally, the most original, as it tries to be just what its title suggests, *the true story* of James à la Ray. To set up his film, Ray did extensive ethno-sociological research on the James Brothers, through the newspaper clipping and folkloric research route. The final script was then given typically Ray cinematic touches during the shooting. Various authorities cite Ray as having a squabble with the producer at the end of the shooting and refusing to edit his film but it seems that he was in the hospital during the editing period with an injured foot. The result was ominous for Ray. The film somehow got lost in the shuffle in America, yet surfaced in France, where Jean-Luc Godard called it a masterpiece.

While not exactly an avant-garde Western, *Jesse James* does call for a revaluation of the James brothers and specifically examines the violence within them. To some extent, they are portrayed as rebels without causes, their violence and their good reasons to be violent are posed against each other in a tense way. There is no comparison whatsoever possible with the earlier versions of the Jesse James story; Fritz Lang's *The Return of Frank James* (1940) with Henry Fonda is maudlin and sentimental. Ray's *Jesse* is kinetic, swift, and murderous and shows Ray's increasing frustration with his own position vis-à-vis Hollywood. It is quite easy in 1977 to see why *The True Story of Jesse James* has not attracted the cult and academic following of a film like *The Searchers*, as its attitudinal stance on the Western antimonies of garden and desert and its stand on whether the West should be civilized or not are ambiguous and not clearly signified for those who like to decode codes. The literalness of the treatment is also a problem. Perhaps Ray should have made a Western based on his own created characters instead of trying once more to film in 1956 a tired subject such as the James gang.

As it stands, the film is best seen as an exercise in CinemaScope, which Ray handles beautifully, and as a film which was grounded in a genre that was beginning to become a dinosaur unless one introduced enough modernistic elements to upgrade it into an avant-garde Western. As Westerns go, the majority of the Ray-viewing public prefers *Johnny Guitar*, whereas those who like their Westerns tried and true have *She Wore a Yellow Ribbon*, *The Searchers*, and the pseudo-Western, *Giant*, to look at again and again.

It was as if the undercurrents of new themes, new forms, were making demands on filmmakers during this era, and sometimes a film would be made which would be a move forward; other films seemed regressive. Compared with *Bigger Than Life*, *Bitter Victory*, and *Party Girl*, which Ray was still to make, *The True Story of Jesse James* seems anachronistic, even for Nick Ray.

One minor note pertaining to the casting. Ray, for the only time in any of his films, cast his son, Tony Ray, in a minor part. (Unlike the Fonda family, this is as far as nepotism went with the Rays.)

Comparison of Ray's Westerns and the "SuperWestern"

Although Nick Ray did not make classical Westerns, he did make two neurotic ones, and because many "SuperWesterns" are synonymous with the word neurotic, his *Johnny Guitar* and *The True Story of Jesse James* should be put into genre perspective by comparing them to some of the "SuperWesterns" produced at the same time. These two films can be compared with analogous films by Anthony Mann (Emil Bundsmann), Samuel Fuller, and John Ford, though it would be rather pointless to go further and contrast Ray's *opus* with normal Westerns such as Howard Hawks' *Rio Bravo* (1959) or George Steven's *Shane* (1953). As scholarly interest in the films of Mann, Fuller, and Ford remains high, the inclusion of Ray in a comparative study of Westerns by these four directors will shed a little more light on all of them.

There is a general theory that the "SuperWestern" of the late 1950s came about as the result of widescreen and the urgent desire to update the Western in more than a visual way, by treating contemporary themes such as the cold war, male-female relationships, the eternal triangle, and so forth within the grand scope of the classic Western form known as "the horse opera." The "SuperWestern" in short, was created when an American 1950s problematic was imposed on a Western genre film structure, which was then filmed in widescreen or CinemaScope, thus making the neurotic content even more obvious through the vastness of the wide aspect ratio.

The following table should show how the "SuperWestern" ever-relentlessly moved itself toward wider screens.

Film	Director		Aspect Ratio
Fort Apache (1948)	John Ford	black & white	1:1.33
She Wore A Yellow Ribbon (1949)	John Ford	Technicolor	1:1.33
Johnny Guitar (1954)	Nicholas Ray	Trucolor	1:1.85
The Searchers (1956)	John Ford	Panavision	1:1.85
The True Story of Jesse James (1957)	Nicholas Ray	CinemaScope	1:2.35
Forty Guns (1957)	Samuel Fuller	black & white CinemaScope	1:2.35
Man of the West (1958)	Anthony Mann	CinemaScope	1:2.35
The Man Who Shot Liberty Valance(1962)	John Ford	black & white	1:1.33

Of these eight films, the four by Ford have already gotten an inordinate amount of attention in studies of his work. *The Searchers*, in particular, has been analyzed in dozens of articles in the United States and, especially, in England. But a cross-directorial analysis of *Jesse James* (1957), *Forty Guns* (1957) and *Man Of The West* (1958) has never, to my knowledge, been done, and perhaps this would not only illuminate the problematic of Ray's disguised Westerns (as well as give a hint as to why they haven't held up) but would also elucidate the flaring up and death of the "SuperWestern" during this period.

Let us briefly look at the problematic of the SuperWestern and see how it relates to the career of Nick Ray, and the lack of critical and commercial success of his *Jesse James*.

To begin with, all the films in our table can be enjoyed by people who don't particularly like Westerns. This was the unique quality of the SuperWestern; in one respect, its narratives weren't those of Westerns at all. This suggests that none of these films have to be experienced as Westerns and thus they don't function as coded films. This is obvious. Not so obvious is the non-Western quality of the SuperWestern "hero"; all of the cited contain a problematic on the thematic level of the hero: either the "hero" is an anti-hero or there co-exist in the same film heros who contain a touch of anti-hero and vice versa. Thus the caring person and the nihilist are often not too far apart in this special genre of cinema, and somehow embrace each other by the end of the film. This is exemplified by the two main characters in John Ford's *Liberty Valance*, Tom Doniphan and Ransom Stoddard, who, in the "surprise" ending to the film, turn out to be much more alike than one at first suspected.

The SuperWestern problematic, furthermore, is rarely anchored on other than male characters. In its use of female characters, the SuperWestern is conservative. Ray, in *Jesse James*, breaks no new ground with female characters. Here, as always, he is closer to Ford (in the quartet under discussion) than to Mann or Fuller. His post-1955 female characters are really of the helpmate type: Vienna in *Johnny Guitar* (1954) is an exceptional *Ray woman character*, and perhaps overmuch has been made of her. Post-1955 Ray women hang back or give lines stronger than their characterizations taken as a whole. By contrast, Fuller's Jessica Drummond (Barbara Stanwyck) in *Forty Guns* (1957) stands out in proverbial left field compared with even Ray's Joan Crawford as Vienna. (And Barbara Stanwyck continued as a strong champion of the independent female role as "Victoria Berkeley" in the TV series, "The Big Valley.")

Ray's women throughout the 1950s have always had temperament, but, with the exception of Vienna, some of the time, they have been there to help men, specifically to help men learn love. The Julie London character, Billie Ellis, in Mann's *Man of the West* (1958), functions more autonomously than any Ray woman and only fellow-travels with Link (Gary Cooper) while they're going in the same direction. Barbara Stanwyck's Jessica Drummond in *Forty Guns* goes a step further on the freedom axis, and is the most independent feminine character of the lot; she fights hard as well as is fought over. The Hope Lange character we see in Ray's *Jesse James*, after these comparisons, seems rather like the Connecticut blond she is, stuck in a Western. Her bright-eyed looks are instantly reminiscent of Hallie Ericson and Laurie Jorgensen (both played by blond Vera Miles) in Ford's *Liberty Valance* and *The Searchers* respectively. (Note Ford's contrivance of making a WASP character out of the pioneer woman; Hallie and Laurie really fit their future husbands' last names better than their parents', reversing the real order of things, i.e., Hallie Stoddard and Laurie Paley. Ray, by contrast, was more inclined to leave his women on earth with first names only: Vienna, Judy; and Vickie Gaye sounds less a first and last name than a chorus girl's double name.) All the Ford and Ray women mentioned here suggest: "I'll help you and then I'll be the mother of your children." (Not uncoincidentally, these films were made at the height of the baby boom.) All this is to say that the Ray and Ford women in their post-1955 Westerns were more like icons of contemporary 1950s women than the "men folk" were, and those who are seriously interested in Western women would do well to find out about the real Calamity Jane and should read Frederick Jackson Turner. Finally, these women characters are, amazingly, not neurotic and never carry the problematic of the film, which is usually a neurotic one, in their characterizations. It is here that the off-beat SuperWesterns, *Man of the West* and *Forty Guns*, depart most dramatically from the Western-genre-woman formula and possibly, for this reason, hold up better, still making excellent viewing today.

The inescapable conclusion is that Ray did not create a body of good unconventional Westerns (*Johnny Guitar* seems to have been a fluke) on a level comparable to those of Fuller and Mann, both less talented than he in many ways. His interests seemed to have been more in contemporary man versus the pack, than in the Western genre.

There are still other cross-directorial points of comparison that can be made. One could, for example, compare and contrast the use of Lee J. Cobb, in virtually the same role three times, in Kazan's *On The Waterfront* (1954), Mann's *Man of the West* (1958) and Ray's *Party Girl* (1958). It is Mann who iconographizes Cobb as Cobb best and not Ray (or Kazan), both of whom use him theatrically. In this vein, we can generalize that Ray's Western characters are never as *indexical* in the semiological sense, as Fords' or Manns' or Fullers'. Ray usually made his characters up eclectically with a dash of the iconic and a dash of the symbolic. This sign dualism often led to two interpretations of the same character not only being possible but being necessary; one interpretation, iconic, easy to perceive (an oversimplification for some) the other, symbolic, with far-reaching import. For this reason alone, perhaps no one warmed up to the title character in *Jesse James* for Ray neither indexically invested him with known Western dimensions, nor did his usual trick of composing the character by splicing together two dashes from either end of the arbitrary sign spectrum, Ray thus arguably failed to give Jesse a brand new symbolism.

It was thus possible to see Ray semiotically as a hack and as an artist at the same time and argue both cases, a view of Ray which grew in the late 1950s. Ray's failure to create a lasting "masterpiece"

Ray's failure to create a lasting "masterpiece" in the SuperWestern sub-genre, can be still best explained by his attitude. His lack of interest in creating indexical characters, the in-betweens in degree of certitude given by the signifier/signified relationship of the arbitrary sign in film, is to blame and denied his talent the option to create a great Western. Thus Ray never made a lasting contribution to this genre, and *Jesse James* remains—despite its beautiful photography and cinematography—one of Ray's weaker narratives.

Summary

Like Fuller, Ray only toyed with the SuperWestern; with *Johnny Guitar,* he got away with it, though the film's reputation will, in all likelihood, soon fade. Unlike Fuller, he never seemed to even believe in the genre. Like Ford, he wanted to show a *Welt,* and this is what is always interesting in any Ray or Ford film. Like Anthony Mann, Ray did care about the CinemaScope craftsmanship of *Jesse James,* his one 1:2.35 SuperWestern: Ford, through dramatization, Fuller through manipulation, Mann through an unhurried, open, laconic style, and Ray through aesthetic realism and through CinemaScope technique all contributed in varying degrees and with varying results to the SuperWestern, a sub-genre whose rise and fall coincided precisely with the span of Ray's career. Because of disinterest Nick Ray did not add his own *classic* Western to that rich genre of films that seem never to die, and, today, *The True Story of Jesse James* (1957) does not, on its narrative level, seem to function as a completely satisfactory SuperWestern. Ray himself appears to have realized this, and took no part in its editing.[2]

Bitter Victory (1957–58)

Bitter Victory (Amère Victoire) was released in France in 1957 and not in the United States until 1958. It was Nick Ray's overt anti-war film, but, under the surface, the story, based on a French novel, continued his exploration of the dark humanism in every hero and every villain. In terms of conventional cinematic narrative popular around 1957, the film's two leading characters did not supply the clichéd types. Major Brand (Curt Jurgens) and Captain Leith (Richard Burton) were neither villain nor hero; nor was Brand a villain and Leith an anti-hero; nor was Leith a fashionable Existential hero, or a classic heroic villain. At best, we can say Brand was a poison and Leith an anti-hero, with circumstances always threatening to make them into each other. This facet of the characterizations both made the plot interesting and simultaneously made the film a bit unfathomable to the contemporary audience and critics.

Critical reaction to *Bitter Victory* was mixed and contradictory as it always was on a Ray film. Jean-Luc Godard ranked it as the best American film of 1957, Eric Rohmer also rated it highly, as fifth best film, but only two out of the other twenty-two *Cahiers* critics even mentioned it in their 1957 U.S. films round-up. In England, a cut version was seen, which left off the end. In the United States, the film passed largely unnoticed.

Bitter Victory boasts two Ray touches: a conscious choice to shoot in black-and-white CinemaScope, and the "blocking" of the film into "acts." Ray divided the film, essentially, into a prologue, two acts, and an epilogue:

Prologue: World War II: in an English officer's club, with Major Brand, a WREN-uniformed Mrs. Brand (Ruth Roman), and Captain Leith. Brand beings to suspect, just before he and Leith are sent off on a mission behind the German lines that Leith has had an affair with his wife (and rightfully so. Leith did, but *he* backed out).

Act I: The Raid. Brand shows cowardice under fire, cruelty during the retreat, and tries to cover this up through disposing of Leith by leaving him behind to guard a wounded man; Leith rightly suspects that Brand wants to get rid of him, *both* because he witnessed Brand's cowardice and to revenge himself on Leith for the affair with Jane Brand.

Act II: While still in the desert, Leith returns safely, confronts Brand, and has the "bitter victory" conversation. Leith is then fatally bitten by a desert scorpion and again left to die. In a final conversation Brand asks whether Leith has any message for this wife. Leith tells Brand to tell her she was right, *he, Leith,* should have gone further in his love for her. Brand abandons the dying

Leith and soon sees a British truck convoy that rescues him and the surviving party of soldiers.

Epilogue. Brand returns, gives Jane Brand Leith's message, is awarded a medal, realizes that he's lost "the war"—lost his wife, his honor—and, in the final shot, abjectly, disgustedly pins the medal futilely on a rifle practice dummy hanging in a shed.

The *British Film Institute Bulletin* gave *Bitter Victory* a particularly nasty review:

> Made for a French production company, Nick Ray's film, like Aldrich's *Attack!*, strives to make some pertinent comments on the effect of war on the minds of men, and paints a reasonably unromantic picture of combat. Regrettably, the director's temperament is such that these comments are obscured by a heavy coating of violent, melodramatic incident. . . . Forced to express Leith's intellectual disgust in literary, prosy dialogue, it is no wonder that Richard Burton's sober performance fails to convince: also Curt Jurgens' glum, inflexible playing is unable to invest Brand's moral dilemma with real psychological depth or meaning. (The initial triangle situation involving a poorly directed Ruth Roman, is, in any case, very clumsily expounded.) In fairness to the film, it should be noted that the French original is some ten minutes longer and includes a final episode that is totally missing from the British version.[3]

But Jean-Luc Godard, who had not yet made a feature film of his own, was wildly enthusiastic about what he called the best American film of 1957. He also described the power/success/cinematic *schwehrpunkt* of the film in cryptic terms, calling it "an abnormal film." In it, "one is no longer interested in objects and which becomes an object in turn. Nicholas Ray forces us to consider as real something one did not consider at all." What does Godard mean? "*Bitter Victory* is like a drawing in which children are asked to find the hunter and which at first seems to be a mass of lines," he concludes.[4] Is he saying: "*Bitter Victory* has a hidden text?" That the first text obscures the second text? That the film is not about what it seems to be about? That the film is supposedly about war and possession of a woman but really about love? Perhaps what Godard meant is that the film does talk about winners (and losers). A loser, who is treated like an "object," becomes a "subject" and thereby emerges as a *winner* at the end, and makes one consider that war is hell and love is love. In the end we see that Brand, Jane

Brand, and Leith do have something in common after all: their humanity.

Gavin Lambert (British critic and scriptwriter) described how the film came about. If we see the obstacle course Ray had to run to get the film made, we can better understand *Bitter Victory*, for the making of the film was, as much as for Captain Leith, a bitter victory for Nick Ray. Gavin Lambert, writing in *Film Quarterly* (the account was translated for *Cahiers*) told the story of his working with Ray and all the trouble Ray had, as follows:

Producer Paul Graetz sent Nick Ray a synopsis of the translation of a French novel by Rene Hardy, *Amère Victoire (Bitter Victory)*, which was soon to be published. Contracts were signed and while Ray was preparing to shoot *The True Story of Jesse James* (early 1957) Hardy came to California for a few weeks, and spoke with us about the final treatment. . . . When we went to Paris, Graetz, in effect, allowed us to change the script, despite objections by Hardy. Then, two blows hit one after the other. First, Graetz hired Curt Jurgens, a German actor (some kind of contractual obligation) to play a *British* officer, and, secondly, we didn't know that Graetz had a contract with Hardy, where he had given him complete control over the script. The rest of the story (it dragged on nearly a year before the film was finished) is nothing but lost hopes, threats of lawsuits, incessant fights, and the "free" film with an American director made in Europe became a pillory, a situation similar to the most severely controlled Hollywood production.[5]

Party Girl (1958)

Party Girl marked Nick Ray's tenth year as a filmmaker. Considered successful in Hollywood, an *auteur* in France, Ray had yet to make a second film which would become as much of a household word as *Rebel. Party Girl* should have been that film, but it wasn't. Yet *Party Girl* deserves to be looked at as carefully as if it were an instant classic because it represents the mature yet untired Ray before Hollywood's depredations on him made themselves finally felt. And of course, because *Party Girl* is an optimistic extension beyond all his other films, an ever-so-slight but noticeable change away from the bitterness of Ray's never-so-happy endings. After the rebellion of *Rebel*, the desperation of *Bigger Than Life*, the hatred in *Bitter Victory*, and the revenge of *The True Story of Jesse James*, we see fused in *Party Girl* a simultaneous mastery of the color and widescreen form and an ever so slight hope for middle-aged America.

Set in Chicago in 1933, the film rapidly informs that it is not an authentic period piece or gangster film. F. Hoyveda wrote in 1960 that Ray evidently did not think it important in *Party Girl* to re-create the Chicago of the past, because Ray merely indicated with a title that the setting was "Chicago in the early 30's."[6] The film opens with a localizing shot without bothering with any skyline-establishing shot. We see a neon light, screen left, and the camera moves in and pans toward the light, like a firefly seeking entrance to a brighter spot. A long travelling shot soon takes us inside the club, "The Golden Rooster." The shot vocabulary of a film (the type of shot, montage of shots, whom the shot favors, the length of shot, the length of the first few sequences, the way the sequences are connected) establishes how a film will inform, by what rhythm it will inform, and how it will not inform. The vocabulary established in roughly the first fifteen minutes of this film soon informs us that

---

The following eight illustrations are 16mm frame enlargements from the first encounter between Vickie Gay, played by Cyd Charisse, and Tommy Farrell, played by Robert Taylor, from *Party Girl* (1958).

1. Louis Cannetto played by John Ireland, wants to take Vickie home and looks toward where she is standing off screen.

2. Ray cuts to a moderate telephoto shot which gives Vickie an apparition-like look. She is seen from the point of view of Tommy who is sitting in a chair facing her. This remarkable sequence shows how Ray informs a female-male encounter entirely through mise-en-scène motion and cutting with lens changes. The cuts are set up so we always see, via sight-lines, the characters not shown in the frame. We now *anticipate* seeing Tommy.

3. Unexpected cut to a medium shot as Vickie eyes Tommy, whom she has never met but whom she wants to escort her out of the club so she can excape Cannetto.

4. Same shot. The mise-en-scène reveals itself through the micromimetics of her face, as she speaks to him.

1

2

3

4

5
6

7

8

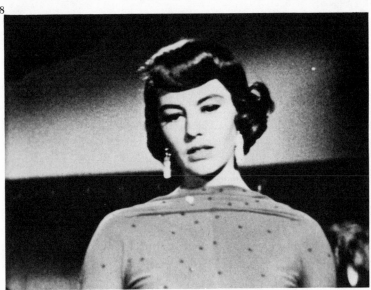

Party Girl is only (or primarily) interested in underscoring—in a non-sociological way—what Hoyveda quite rightly called "the melody of the look." (The critic is here quoting Ray's response to an earlier review in *Cahiers du Cinema* No. 27.)

Specifically, *Party Girl* is about a man and a party girl. It is a five-character film, about *the* intimate group as well as *an* intimate group, about an "artificial family," a nocturnal, nightclub *Welt*. Farrell, a gangland lawyer played by Robert Taylor; his boss, Rico Angelo (Lee J. Cobb); Canetto, another gangster (John Ireland); Cookie LaMotte, a petty gangster (Corey Allen); and Vickie Gaye, a dancer, but more than a dancer (Cyd Charisse). Note not only the types, but the previous history of the actors. We know how important casting was to Ray, as casting presupposed some skill related to certain kinds of mise-en-scène the director wished to construct. The casting always related to an internal logic in Ray's mind. Then there was playing with or against Hollywood type casting. Cyd Charisse,

5. Vickie asks Tommy if he wants to dance.

6. He says, "no"; she does not know he is crippled. Note the reverse cut to him is back to a normal lens; the telephoto effect is reserved by Ray only for his view of her.

7. Cut to a medium-close, moderate telephoto shot. Vickie is one of Ray's foreward-thinking women; she does not let the rejection destroy her honest interest in him. She looks at Tommy sympathetically . . .

8. . . . and then, sexily . . . and, as the shot ends, we see what Ray wanted to have revealed on her face: her candid desire. This theme of the healthy woman "curing" the neurotic man ran through many 1950s and most Ray films, but *Party Girl* transcends the banality of the convention through Ray's fine cinematic rendering.

one recalls, did not, as the public knew her, belong in the gangster film genre. *Singing in the Rain* and *Silk Stockings* were what the public equated with Cyd Charisse. Ray, by taking a musical star, and putting her in a gangster film, played Charisse against type. Or did he? Isn't *Party Girl* as much a musical as a "gangster film"? It is obvious here that Ray did not pay any attention to genre convention. All he tries to do with Charisse is to *authenticate* her as a singer/dancer (yes, Cyd dances) named Vicki Gaye in the film, someone who dances and sings like Cyd Charisse but is romantic like a Ray woman. Robert Taylor, more leading man than villain, near the time this film was set, looked like a gigolo and had starred in *Camille* with Garbo. Taylor was not an illogical choice, for Ray sensed a tentative screen quality in Taylor that we can see if we carefully scrutinize his early films: he was not too sure of himself. And Corey Allen, after teen roles on TV and hot rod films is restored to the role of an intense, interesting villain simply because he looked well in a black pin-striped suit. John Ireland, like Arthur Kennedy, could play weak men well, and Lee J. Cobb had heavy experience as a gangster heavy. The least congruous factor in the casting was the couple: Taylor and Charisse. But they work well together visually (both dark, the same height) and are a convincing couple.

There are very few close-ups in *Party Girl*. Most of the film is shot in Hollywood shot (medium shot) with the characters shown from their heads to their knees. (Ray continued to favor this kind of shot when using CinemaScope; starting in *Rebel Without a Cause*, when groups of people are shown and intercut—unless there is a *reaction* shot to emphasize something—they are predominantly in Hollywood shot. Kazan's *East of Eden*, by contrast, did not maintain a predominantly medium-shot scale.) There is also, as Hoyveda points out in Bazinian fashion, "nearly a total absence of montage." The film is "told" in shot sequences ("scenes") rather than through a complex rhythm of editing. *Party Girl*, in rhythm, is more placid than *Rebel*. But this is good, because the tempo of the story is not as frenetic as *Rebel* et al. It shows Ray's ability to modify the pace to suit the theme. But within the shot, there is still the Nick Ray variance of tempo, which is his signature, the mark by which we recognize *Party Girl* as a Ray film.

The greatest attention is paid to mise-en-scène. This is the heart of most Ray films, but in *Party Girl* it goes beyond being part of the narrative component of the film: it informs this film, for, as Hoyveda notes, "decor, color, and framing, constitute the most important elements of mise-en-scène, where the actors live."

From the mise-en-scène more than the merely reinforcing dialogue, we learn who Farrell and Vickie Gaye are. Yet Ray is too commercial to dispense with dialogue's use to rally audience sympathy, to do what Antonioni was soon to do in his *L'Avventura* trilogy. *Party Girl* has no omissions of story line.

In the sense that the film is about Farrell's distrust of Vickie Gaye and his growing attraction to her, we would expect a series of scenes when their relationship develops, where they put each other to the test, and where Farrell's growl grows to a smile. If we are to believe Farrell's loss of self-doubt, an important Ray theme, the formal elements of the film must work to this end. They do. (See frame enlargements.)

As is usual in a Ray film, there is a father figure. This is the gangster, Rico. If the overall narratology strives to underscore Farrell's ongoing relationship with Vickie (whose red dresses show her to be the rebel demanding attention), the plain theme or plot of the film is that Farrell must detach from Rico to attach to Vickie. In the closing shot, we have long ago left the plot behind, and the ending uses purely cinematic means to tell us that Farrell's and Vickie's themes are resolved together. A final shot shows a compact being made between Farrell and his new self-confidence—like the "compact" (cosmetic container with mirror) that passed from Judy to Jim and back in the middle of *Rebel Without a Cause*—in the form of Farrell giving the trick watchband he used to tell sob stories to the jury with to his new friend and former antagonist, the prosecutor, a gesture far more subtle than the hero laying down his gun at the end of a Western.

The only point I disagree with in Hoyveda's brilliant essay on *Party Girl* is his statement that the French title for the film, *Traquenard* (The Tracked Down One) is nonsense. On the contrary, it says perfectly what the film is about. Farrell is tracking down his past while he is tracking down Vickie—who is at the same time tracking him down. The tracking ends when they find themselves and each other and the tentative becomes the possible for both of them.

Does *Party Girl* differ from, improve upon, or show a pulling away from Ray's previous films? *Party Girl*, after all, was made the year the "New Wave" began.

Hoyveda is right again, I feel, in calling *Party Girl* "pushing aesthetic inquiry and contempt for the exaggeration of technique." Like *Johnny Guitar*, it is an "anti-technique" film. *Party Girl* inspires, says Hoyveda; and to its critics he says, "Long live the kind of idiocy that dazzles my eyes, fascinates my heart, and lets me find myself in the skies." On viewing *Party Girl*, one feels the kind of triumph felt at the end of a successful romantic comedy; only here the subject matter has been updated from Howard Hawks—the theme is no longer the attraction of romantic comedy, but the aversion of romantic tragedy. The step from *Party Girl* to *Jules et Jim* is a tiny one.

Epic Years in Hollywood

After *Party Girl*, Ray remained in Hollywood four more years. His projects became larger and larger epics. Why? What were Ray's reasons for making *King of Kings* and *55 Days at Peking*. Money? Unlike *Wind in the Everglades* and *The Savage Innocents*, obvious "outsider" films, which he also made during this period, the former two films were out-and-out Hollywood production numbers: the former, once having been made by Cecil B. DeMille, the latter, also a very DeMillean concept, similar to the Settlers-and-Indians epic DeMille produced, called *Unconquered* (1946).

Ray suggested that he had hoped to make money, save it, and then become independent of Hollywood. He later called this strategy "a mistake."[7]

When asked, years later, why he made *King of Kings* (1961), Ray answered that he was in Europe at the time and was approached by a friend of producer Sam Bronston, to help Sam out with the film, which was to be made in Spain. Ray said he recruited the "toughest Jew screenwriter in the States, top Hebrew musicologists, people from the Vatican, a Dean from Christ Church College (Oxford), and met with the hierarchy of the Spanish Orthodox Church. They asked me how I was going to show Jesus, and I answered: 'Well, if he is walking down a dirt road with his disciples, and he has to take a piss, dust will rise from the road.' Then I showed them the first shot in the film, which was a tilt from the gentiles to the money lenders in the temple, and asked them if it should be in the film. They said no. Then, *Newsweek* had a spy in the Vatican, a Jesuit priest, who made available the 774 reforms of the Vatican against anti-Semitism. If anyone goes in to see this film, at least they will not walk out being anti-Semitic."[8]

Ray's Unrealized European Projects (1962–1968)

In 1962 Ray was engaged to direct 55 *Days at Peking*, a Hollywood epic, at one of the highest salaries then paid. (He later felt it had been a mistake to take the offer.) For obvious reasons—this film was not his metier, he was overworked—he couldn't finish the film, and Andrew Marston, the second unit director, was called in to co-direct and finish up. At this point, Ray left Hollywood for good and, shortly thereafter, he went to Europe, remaining there for most of six years.

According to his own account, Ray was not happy with the way he was lionized in Paris. At any rate, none of his many European projects were ever realized. The nearest he came to completing any of them was in 1966, when he was engaged to direct a film based on Dylan Thomas's story, "The Doctors and the Devil." The film was to be shot on location, partly in Zagreb, Yugoslavia, where a set was even built to make a local street look like one in nineteenth-century Edinburgh, Scotland.[9] Ray's film would have included the epic line uttered by the graverobber doctor: "What's the matter with what I do; some people have green thumbs. I have a black thumb." Again Ray failed to finish this film—he had become something of an alcoholic; and Italian director Baldi completed it.

Finally, Margarethe von Trotta, wife of director Volker Schlondorf, reports that while Ray was with Chabrol, one time, in Paris, a producer wanted to see him about a project he had for him, but Ray, again due to being drunk, passed out just at the moment the producer wanted to speak to him.

Ray's frustrations during these six years are most satisfactorily outlined in a chronological table, and can be found as an Appendix in the filmography.

In 1968, Ray went to Chicago and was active during the Democratic Convention, trying to shoot and edit a film on the youth turmoil there. Ten minutes of footage are devoted to him and the Chicago house he rented as a studio, in Marcel Ophuls' documentary, *America Revisited* (1971). But, again, Ray never finished this film. Instead, he turned up at Harpur College (S.U.N.Y.) at Binghamton, New York, as a teacher-filmmaker-in-residence, in 1971, where he began yet another film he never completed, variously titled *Gun Under My Pillow* and *You Can't Go Home Again*.

11

Nick Ray's Legacy

DESPITE ROLAND BARTHES' CAUTION that the film critic should never abandon the question of theme in trying to analyze a film, Nick Ray's themes do not do more than give one the feeling that they are not intended to stand up to scrutiny shorn of their context in being but working drafts for a *motion* picture film. His themes are, if subjected to Proppian morphological analysis, all about the hurt male and the redemption of that hurt.

It is how he filmed these themes that counts. It is how Nick Ray's cinema works that is worth recounting. Though a born raconteur, Ray's neurotic themes are a bit too much when posited before their cinematic rendering. Thus I have made a painstaking effort to show the development of one Ray film, *Rebel Without a Cause*, through its historic stages. This book, then, has not focused on theme, but on theme before the camera.

The information system of a film functions only through living language. Ray is one director who gave each and every one of his films *all* of the *Zeitgeist* of the year in which it was made. Rays' films are an outsiders' iconography of the American 1950s, as presented by a director with a didactic point of view. Each of his films is an attempt to authenticate a point of view as to some historic situation in the United States: *Johnny Guitar* attempted to "save" the Western and blast Joe McCarthy; *Rebel* attempted to announce the rise of the upper-middle class delinquent and to give him a historic resolution and mission.

"The one essential requirement for a historical film is that it should have authenticity on a grand scale," wrote Dr. Fritz Hippler, Third Reich script advisor, in his book *Reflections on Filmmaking*. Most of Nick Ray's films, if not all of them, aim at grand scale authenticity. Most of Ray's films, in their own special way, were historical films, films which would be set in their time period, and

193

then be given Ray's personal stamp. *King of Kings*, for example, featured *Nick Ray's* Jesus Christ. As the 1950s progressed, and themes changed, so did Ray's cinema. Slowly. Even though many of his films have a murky reputation, simply because most people have not seen them, each one has a historic, defining characteristic.

It is as if Ray were protesting false history and trying to rewrite it as true history. *Rebel Without a Cause* is an attempt to sum up not only the causes of a certain era of juvenile delinquency but also the emotional turmoil behind causelessness. In retrospect, the film defined 1955 far better than it did delinquency. *The True Story of Jesse James* purports to tell just what its title says. Making this film presupposed, for Ray, that all the other Hollywood versions of this legend were false, which they were. This film was designed to authenticate that outlaw, something none of the previous James brothers films even tried to do. *King of Kings* is Ray's personal version of Jesus Christ. The tracking shot of the Sermon on the Mount in the film is Ray's version—based on historical research—of how he supposed Jesus constantly moved around and engaged small groups of ever-different people in Socratic dialogue about Christianity, and thus, that Jesus never stood still on the top of the mount, as icons picture him, talking to the multitude of ten thousand.

Party Girl is Ray's historic version of Chicago in 1933, and not a remake of *Scarface*. Ray's comment on this film is revealing: "I only regret the film doesn't have more of the great jazz music of the time in it." (Ray had lived in Chicago during that period.) *Bigger Than Life* is a historical case study of a particularly dated 1950s phenomenon: the miracle drug craze; and *Johnny Guitar* is a history of the McCarthyized American landscape, set—like such a post-Civil War Western epic as John Ford's *The Searchers*—in a peculiar American time period and context and in such a way that the film demands (and takes advantage of) the viewer's familiarity with the America of 1953.

The popularity versus failure of a Ray film depended, almost totally, not on the cinematic side of the effort, but on whether he authenticated his film on a grand enough scale. Like a neorealist film, each of his films was set up so that there could be no halfway success; they either had to succeed grandly, or fall. It seems that only in *Rebel Without a Cause* did the public say that he succeeded grandly. With his other films, after 1955, the endings often mar the films. Given some corrections, Ray's final films might have communicated better. His interest, however, seemed to have been to continue to try to film banal narratives with good acting and camera movements rendering them into *cinema*.

Ray's Critical Reputation as of the Mid-1970s

To many of his contemporaries, Elia Kazan and not Nicholas Ray was "the" avant-garde director of the 1950s. Yet, after 1970, the pantheon of who was who in the 1950s (and 1960s) in American cinema looks quite different than in those years when Ray was turning out films. Another generation of cinema-goers exists; entire new directions in cult propaganda for certain directors have been established; the advantage of hindsight, perspective, re-runs, retrospectives exists. And Nick Ray has fortunately gained a wider audience if not wider respect.

I don't propose to go into any detail on who supported Ray on paper and who didn't after his active career ended in 1963. But it is important to note in passing that it was after 1970 that Ray's reputation jumped upward, for many subjective reasons. First of these was a sense that much of the Hollywood cinema of the 1970s was going nowhere. It takes a Peter Bogdanovich to make one appreciate a Nick Ray. And this aimlessness went beyond individual directors. Many of us felt that the Hollywood cinema of the 1970s was unrepentantly Hollywoodian (the "New Hollywood" is not a bad title) and that it would perpetuate its products in a less personal way than ever. It was going to be computerized by accountants, based on box-office receipts, and what would emerge was going to be a "rationalized" cinema. At the same time, a new generation had tasted a bit of fresh cinema, especially those who began to embrace cinema, first as buffs, and then as connoisseurs in its essence as metaphor. That very generation that was now the median age cinema-goer had grown up on personal art: rock albums, their own fantasies, antisystem thoughts, etc., and they were only too glad to look backward at the masterpieces (some overlooked) of the American cinema, made by Howard Hawks, and others, including the ever-popular Hitchcock. And when they did that, it is obvious that some of them would discover, find, stumble upon Nicholas Ray.

Second, the media glut of the late 1960s produced a curious situation. Some younger people, writing books, articles, appreciative essays, went toward more personal and more obscure subjects.

Ray was one of them. You could discover him through Kazan, through James Dean, through the French New Wave references to him, through Marcel Ophuls' documentary, *America Revisited,* through the history of CinemaScope. Ray was cross-indexed in a lot of places. For some people, Ray emerged in the 1970s. He was literally dug out of the past.

Third, after 1971 the articulate and crankily attractive, wildly visual Ray became increasingly visible. He taught filmmaking at Harpur College, State University of New York, at Binghamton, starting in the fall of 1971. There he and his students were to make a joint film. He became available for interviews and spoke intelligently, sometimes soberly, and at great length about his films and how they were made, theatrically, cinematically, in a way that people under thirty, especially, could practically grasp.

Finally, the documentary on Ray, the hour-long *I'm A Stranger Here Myself,* directed by David Helpern, Jr., produced Ray on Ray on film, and again made him better known. In 1974, the film began making the rounds; by January, 1975, it was reviewed in the *New York Times* by Vincent Canby. This film served as the most valuable post-1963 Ray interview. (No pre-1963 American interview with Ray is as revealing as his own writings and his two *Cahiers* interviews described in the bibliography.) In short, the best source on Ray has always been Ray; and now he was speaking out again, reminding people what he stood for, what he had once been. His answers, his volunteered statements in *I'm A Stranger Here Myself* stand as some of the most lucid presentations of what filmcraft is about. And through Ray's persona, one could be immediately drawn toward seeing his films. And these, after 1971, became slowly available on the screens and quite readily available through television.

Ray's reputation is still in a state of flux (and will probably stay so in the next twenty years). However, his legacy is far greater than his reputation. Those few people in filmmaking who were fortunate enough to have met him in person or were familiar enough with how and why he worked found him valuable far beyond his minimal public reputation, and thought of him as a colleague, as a symbol of the director who can produce poetry on the screen, as an index of "not failure but low aim, is crime," as an icon of a man who is not embarrassed to show grasping for emotion in a way most cold intellectuals would find "adolescent." With the notable exception of the *Cahiers du Cinema* directors (Truffaut, Godard, Rivette, Chabrol)

Ray's influence on *specific* post-1955 films is hardly to be found. It was not, then, through "selling" other directors on using his trademarks or signatures, that Ray left his legacy to American and world cinema.

What then is Ray's legacy? What is it to the development of cinema, American cinema specifically, to Hollywood's future and to the younger Hollywood directors?

Ray's best work was done during the second generation of sound cinema. Simply stated, he helped pave the way from directorially guided genre cinema (second generation) to ontological cinema (third generation) by making *his* directorial films into ontological experiences. This is what Godard meant when he said "And the cinema is Nick Ray."[1]

Ray's Cinematic Legacy: His Use of Color

Color is not new to American cinema. Two-color technicolor films were made as early as 1928. But color films were not made as quickly as the existence of the technology would have indicated. But, after *Gone With The Wind* (1940) clearly showed Hollywood had mastered the technology of the three-color Technicolor process, the only criterion for whether to film in color was whether the project was grand enough to deserve it. During the heyday of one-a-week movie-going in the early 1940s, the black-and-white film dominated. (Wartime shortages and priorities also reduced the supply of color stock.) After World War II, black and white continued to dominate, but by 1949 Warner Brothers had developed their own ideas about use of color. Using a three-color Eastmancolor stock, and renaming it Warnercolor, the studio allied it with CinemaScope in 1954 to produce *East of Eden*. The formula worked, and thus Nick Ray's third color film was *Rebel Without a Cause*, which followed *East of Eden* in the Warner's chronology by six months. The idea of doing *Rebel* by the same process was spurred by a three-week period of box-office success for *East of Eden* just before *Rebel* starting shooting. (Besides, it was found that the early CinemaScope contract required that films shooting in Scope also had to be shot in color.)

Ray first worked with color in *The Flying Leathernecks* (1951), but he had no particular interest in this conventional 1:1.66 ratio film and did not develop his theory on how to use color until before his second color film, *Johnny Guitar* (1954). *Johnny* was shot in three-color Trucolor and wide screen (but not CinemaScope). In filming *Johnny Guitar*, Ray stated that "it was the first film to use color properly" and that it obeyed a color strategy he invented.[2]

Each of Ray's color films has a color trademark, something that occurs specifically in that film: reserving James Dean's putting on Jim's red jacket until the most frenetic point in the plot in *Rebel*, the color dissolve to the yellow sea of taxis in *Bigger Than Life*, the purples and golds of *Party Girl* shifting the palette away from the browns and greens and reds and occasional pastels of Ray's earlier color films and informing the "false" Roman splendor of 1930s Chicago. But it is his use of color counterpoint throughout all the color films that forms a more interesting clue as to how and why Ray used color cinematically. As in *Party Girl*, Ray often used color as psychological counterpoint: to show where the characters are live.

Take the color red, for example. He does not use it in opposition to blue in *Rebel*, (as has been suggested by David Dalton in *James Dean: The Mutant King*). Nor did he create a horde of red-jacketed, blue-jeaned young men. Dean "graduated" from brown to red as his personality and awareness changed. Natalie Wood likewise graduated from green to pink, after having gotten off to a red start by wearing the color along with red lipstick to furnish the motivation for her father's driving her out of the house because she looked like a prostitute to him. Buzz wears black leather; Plato stays in dark clothes. These are the characters who "do not progress."

But color counterpoint is more Ray's forte. He uses color aesthetically rather than filmically. Dean lies in a red jacket on a maroon sofa in *Rebel* in the same color fashion as Vickie Gaye (Cyd Charisse) wears a red dress to the trial of Canetto in *Party Girl* and also sleeps on a maroon bed. The world of Dawson High School that James Dean goes to in *Rebel* is brown, as is the school where Avery (James Mason) goes to teach in *Bigger Than Life*. One character in all the Ray color films wears some form of red: Johnny in the love sequence in *Johnny Guitar*, Jim in the father confrontation sequence in *Rebel*, the son of the schoolteacher in *Bigger Than Life*, Vickie Gaye at the trial in *Party Girl*, Natalie Wood in the opening sequence of *Rebel Without a Cause*. Red suggests that the character has passion, but the interpretation should go no further because we must know what the background of the character is to see the metaphor of the color.

Ray often uses color not so much decoratively, but as a grace note for a character (the reds above mentioned, the pink for Natalie Wood's love sequence in *Rebel*, orange for Barbara Rush in Avery's over-colorful world in *Bigger Than Life*—as well as violet for the cortisone bottle and yellow for the taxis that Avery has to drive in his night job to help support his wife and child. The color is loosely integrated with what the character is representing or how he or she is behaving, and, on occasion, aesthetically, such as the purples and golds of *Party Girl*, and, on occasion, as a filmic component of a tightly structured shot, such as the eerie blue-green backlighting of the alien living room Jim Stark finds himself in which he comes home from the "chickie run" and expects no communication. Ray does not, in other words, use color coding or color decoration as a formal attempt to define for us the unreal ontology or point of view of a character, as Antonioni did in *Red Desert*, but he uses colors in an informative, psychological manner and so as to contribute to the overall aesthetics of the film. Colors are thus loosely integrated into the structure of the film (instinctively) but integrated nonetheless. They do not "inform" on their own: It is a mistake to call Dean's red jacket "a flag of rage" or some such term, but it is correct to say Dean is in a rage when he puts on the red jacket. His line: "Ten years . . ." he won't wait that long, is the final line before he puts on the jacket. This non-filmic information informs what the red jacket is. Of course, it is a subject for further debate, whether the jacket is then an icon of Dean, or a symbol he wears. But the salient point here is that Ray thought up most of the above-mentioned color devices and integrated them non-gratuously into the narrative.

The cinematographers on Ray's films were all competent men; some, like Ernest Haller, brilliant cameramen. But they all are pushed into the background by Ray's color *auteurism*, and are left to do the field work rather than make the prime choice of color effects. In his personal use of color, Ray worked very differently from— totally in contradiction to—the Hollywood system, wherein color was almost in the province of special effects. We do not find, then, as we do in the 1960s, the name of Nick Ray linked with one cinematographer he favored throughout his films, as in relationships like Antonioni and Carlo di Palma, or Bergman and Sven Nykvist. Ray's study of architecture made him his own expert. The rest was intuition, a feeling that color was the director's ultimate responsibility anyway, and a strong desire not to let any of the vocabulary of the cinema go unused. In view of the fact that Ray never specifically *elected* to make any of his post-*Rebel* films in color, but merely received the instructions to film *Bigger Than Life* in DeLuxe color, or *Party Girl* in Metro Color, he did a great job of combining necessity with wisdom and perhaps producing the most striking aspect of his films, his directorial signature, through his color coding and color counterpoint.

Ray's Cinema Legacy: Use of Wide Screen

There are two aspects of CinemaScope most worth discussing from the viewpoint of a film director. They are framing and cutting. Since CinemaScope is no longer extensively used, but has become but a mutant stage in the evolution of cinema from 1:1.35 to 1:1.85, it is not worthwhile making a CinemaScopic analysis of Ray's 1:2.35 Scope films—something best left to theoretical cinema magazines—but we want to make two general comments on Ray's aesthetic ideas on framing and cutting when the film medium is CinemaScope.

We have already mentioned in Chapter 1 how Ray felt that "the horizontal" interested him. Scope is a very horizontal medium. Thus, if the subject warranted it, Ray said, he would use Cinema-Scope. If it didn't, he wouldn't. In his CinemaScope films, Ray avoided extreme close-ups, concentrated on medium shots with interesting groupings and mise-en-scène. Using it to advantage, he never was bothered by its "excessive space on either side."

As for cutting, Ray had a theory as to how cutting in CinemaScope could produce more kinesthetic effects than with non-anamorphic projected images. "I've felt for a long time and I still think [as of January 1962] that the effect of cutting in CinemaScope, when one goes from a wide angle, from a 40 mm to a 75 mm, is that one increases the dynamic forcefulness [kinesthesia] of a scene."

Ray's own words as to why he favored CinemaScope are revealing. "I will say that the most drastic effect [Frank Lloyd] Wright had on me, by the way, was a sort of philosophic attitude . . . not, not a philosophic attitude, but a particular way to look at things, so that I like CinemaScope because I like the horizontal line: and the horizontal is essentially Wright's thing. . . . I am very fond of the Cinemascope format, and when I have the liberty to use it the way I please, as was the case with *Rebel*, I shot with it well, in a way that satisfied me."[3]

One of the great appreciators and defenders of CinemaScope (and Ray's use of it, among others) was Charles Barr, who began one of his pro-Scope articles by attacking some misconceptions about it and citing positive examples of when directors used it well. His examples were often drawn from Ray's films.

Barr quoted Claude Chabrol and Erich Rohmer in their book on Alfred Hitchcock as saying that "the extreme edges of the [CinemaScope] screen are virtually unusable," apparently because they can not be used for the placing of details meaningful for their own sake. On the other hand, the French writer/directors claim that the biggest advantage of CinemaScope is its opening up of the frame, the greater sense it gives us of a continuous space—as illustrated by the film that they are discussing, Hitchcock's *Rope* (an experiment in filming a continuous action limited to one interior setting).

Other theorists like Bazin and Lenhardt have imagined that CinemaScope would come to eliminate cutting in the sequence, and others have thought it would kill the close-up; but Barr argued effectively that it is wrong to assume that the close-up and montage would become impossible in CinemaScope—"Montage is at once less necessary and more acceptable."

Barr's biggest concern was to argue that in CinemaScope one can use the edges of the screen to locate *en passant* characters and naturalistically create a grade of emphasis between central character and incidental character. He cites a shot from Ray's *The True Story of Jesse James:* "Jesse decides to retire; he goes out into the garden to play with his children; a green and white image, Jesse on the right: a man walks past, glimpsed on the extreme left of the frame, and calls out a greeting: the strong horizontal effect here reinforces the feeling of a new freedom."[4]

Barr then also argues that in Scope, because of "its more vivid sense of space, the impact is direct, and there is no need to emphasize it by putting it into literal slow motion . . ." He cites another shot from *Jesse James,* in a sequence showing Jesse's revenge killing of a farmer.

The crucial shot here has the farmer ploughing his land. Jesse rides up to him, stops, and lifts his rifle. The man starts to run but Jesse keeps with him. The camera tracks back with them, holding this composition—the farmer in the foreground, running into the camera, Jesse inexorably behind, aiming—until finally Jesse shoots him dead. This is over in a moment but has a hypnotic, almost a slow motion impact, which again is the result of the greater physical involvement (kinesthesia) achieved by Scope, its more vivid sense of space. The impact is direct, and there is no need to emphasize it by putting it into literal slow motion, or making a significant pattern.[5]

In addition to the first example from Ray, which relates to *Composition*, and the second example, which relates to *tracking* to achieve apparent retardation of motion, Barr cites a third example from a Ray film, *Rebel*, to illustrate how a cut from a cramped inside-outside shot to a horizontal Close-Up, following by lateral tracking, creates—by suddenly opening the frame—an impression of depth.

In *Rebel*, a shot of extraordinary beauty comes after the first 20 minutes of the film, during which the surroundings have been uniformly cramped and depressing, the images physically cluttered up and dominated by blacks and browns. Now, James Dean is about to set out for school; he looks out the window. He recognizes a girl (Natalie Wood) walking past in the distance. Cut to the first day/exterior shot, the first bright one, the first "horizontal" one. A close shot of Natalie Wood, in a light green cardigan, against a background of green bushes. As she walks the camera moves laterally with her. This makes a direct, sensual impression which gives us an insight into Dean's experience, while at the same time remaining completely natural and unforced. On the small screen, such an image could not conceivably have had a comparable weight.[6]

Nick Ray's Legacy to The French New Wave

The main thing François Truffaut seems to have wanted from the American world of cinema, from Hollywood, from its directors—besides using them as a glove in the face of the French producers and directors he wishes to oppose for polemical purposes—was to use them as a base and basis for his own strategy. As a basis, he wanted the style, polish, and form of Hollywood-produced film (the expensive look, perhaps, more than the matched cut) but the content of an interiorized, personal, and quirky-idiosyncratic novel. To that end, he cultivated the *politique* of the director, not the film: "I'll never like a film by Delannoy; I'll always like a film by Renoir."[7] This is not the *"auteur* theory," fabricated by some New York critics, who took an unallowed semantic liberty to invent something different, and made out of *cherchez l'auteur* a mania for classification. Truffaut was looking at those directors who represented to him the basis for the *future* of film. As Alexandre Astruc said in his seminal article, "The Camera-Pen": "What I am trying to say is that the cinema is now moving towards a form which is making it possible to write ideas directly on film . . .[8] a kind of film even more personal than a novel, more individual and autobiographical than a confession or a private diary."

At the same time that he was attracted to Nick Ray and to Howard Hawks, Truffaut was attracted to the cinema of Hitchcock. If translated to the screen, this attraction meant Truffaut stood for a unique combination of form *and* content. Truffaut belonged to the school of thought about cinema of André Bazin but by no means was identical with him; this school rationalized that form over content meant freedom for film language to express itself uniquely. By adhering to certain self-imposed organizing devices, one could be more subjective in other areas. In practice, the form/content idea is very difficult to apply, and, in these days of semiotics, seems very arbitrary and subjective. One could, for example, say that William Wyler practiced form over content in *The Best Years of Our Lives*, and Ray did in *Johnny Guitar* and *Rebel*. Yet all three of these films seem quite different in respect to how realistic as against how melodramatic they seem. What these films have in common is that they express something personal without formally "falling apart" structurally, in order to do so. Yet Truffaut was on the right track. This combination of rigid formalism and subjective content is what gave Hitchcock a personal license to kill without killing, and this combination was obviously not to be found in the films of many Hollywood directors. Nick Ray, then, was one of those directors, who, while he was based in Hollywood, seemed, in French eyes, too good to be true. It was not long before the American-oriented Truffaut and the "European sensibility of Nick Ray"[9] (Truffaut's words) met half way in Truffaut's mind, and led to a further justification of Truffaut's polemic position toward cinema.

The requirement Ray filled for Truffaut was that Ray used Hollywood production values (big stars: Bogart-1950, Wayne-1951, Mitchum-1952, Cagney-1955, color, wide screen, CinemaScope). One has to recall that Truffaut wanted to and did use a form of

CinemaScope (Dyaliscope, with an aspect ratio of 1:2.17) in *Le Quatre cent coups*, even the title of which has a Ray-like ring. ("All Hell Breaking Loose" would be a better translation of the title than the customary Anglicization, *The Four Hundred Blows*) There is no doubt that, as Truffaut scanned the horizon with his precocious radar, the "European sensibility" of Nick Ray, mixed with Ray's obvious command of the Hollywood production tools and skills, made him *uniquely* interesting to Truffaut and the others of the "Inner Four" of the *Cahiers* clique—Rohmer, Godard, Rivette.

From 1953 to 1962, Ray is mentioned dozens of times in *Cahiers du Cinema*, the monthly French magazine devoted exclusively to film, and *Arts*, the weekly magazine in which the *Cahiers* critics wrote many of the film reviews. One can see, at a glance, the favorites of the Inner Four; Elia Kazan, for example, who was a major director in the United States and *the* 1950s avante-garde director to some, never rated an article or interview until 1962. His possible influence on Ray was never mentioned. His *East of Eden* was suspected of being arty. Bazin begrudgingly gave it a second chance, Truffaut excerpted Dean out of it. Yet, Nick Ray is already praised for *The Lusty Men* in 1953! Here, at once, we see a significant result of the *politique d'auteurs*: who gets exposure.

Ray is first mentioned in the pages of *Cahiers* when he is praised by Jacques Rivette, for *Run For Cover* in October, 1953. Truffaut discovers James Dean—and he is one year older than Truffaut, totally empathized with him. When reviewing Kazan's *East of Eden*, Truffaut, though he by no means pans the film, puts an emphasis on Dean as a kind of actor-*auteur*, rather than on Kazan's *auteur* direction. This *politique* enables Truffaut to praise Dean while panning *East of Eden*. Truffaut next sees *Johnny Guitar* and finds it an important film. It makes him personally aware of Ray. His predisposed liking of James Dean, and his admiration of Ray make it almost inevitable he will like *Rebel Without a Cause*. He gives it three stars. Then Eric Rohmer praises *Rebel* to the skies in his essay-like "review":"Ajax or Le Cid." Rivette and Jean-Luc Godard join in the chorus and both give *Rebel* three stars. (Meanwhile, back in the United States, Bowsley Crowther praises Dean but is highly suspicious of the film, and gives it a reluctant two-star qualified review.) *Tambourine* ("Hot Blood"), Ray's gypsy film, is not liked, Truffaut and Rivette giving it two polite stars, Rohmer a thumbs-down one star, and Godard ignoring it. *Bigger Than Life* seems to have escaped their notice (though Godard commented on it a few years later), but *The True Story of Jesse James* is hailed as a four-star masterpiece by Rivette (he likes Westerns) with two stars from Rohmer and Godard. Godard then calls *Bitter Victory* the best American film of 1957. So far, each of the Inner Four has found his favorite Ray film: Truffaut—*Johnny Guitar*, Godard—*Bitter Victory*, Rivette—*The True Story of Jesse James*, Rohmer—*Rebel Without a Cause*. (Truffaut's favorite theme is love, Godard's the dialectic of war, Rivette's crazed love, Rohmer's the moral tale of a boy.)

Next, a major interview with Nick Ray by Charles Bitsch appeared in *Cahiers* in 1958; in 1960, a major essay by Hoyveda on Ray's *Party Girl*; in 1962, a second major Ray interview.

The *Cahiers* Inner Four could not pay more than this homage to Ray, for, as of late 1958, they were busy making the New Wave. From here on, to trace the relationship between these men and Nicholas Ray, we must look at the other side of the coin: not what they say about him, but what of Nick Ray's cinema is in their films.

As for Ray's personal reaction to the *laudateurs*, it made him uncomfortable, he said.[10] Upon leaving Hollywood in 1962 and going to Paris, he found himself not able to connect up with what had been said about him. And no wonder! For as much as they were sincere reviews of his work, these reviews also contained propaganda and departure points for what the *Cahiers* people liked. Their reviews were subjective, allusive, literary, emotional, philosophical, psychological, occasionally metaphysically correct in their understanding of Ray, but they were not very cinematic (with the exception of Rivette's famous comment that Ray cuts at the height of tension, at the "*paroxysme*," the moment of outburst in a shot). And they were almost totally out of context with Ray's career and how he was critically perceived in the United States. If the truth be told, the *Cahiers*' appreciations are certainly closer to comprehending Ray's value as a director than American ones, but these men in Paris did not seem to know how tough it was for Ray to fight Hollywood, to deal with the black and gray lists, and how much each film cost him in psychic effort. But they were young and they didn't care. He was their hero much as heroes appeared on the American screen. To the *enfant terrible*, Truffaut and to the didactic Godard, Ray was polemically useful as a springboard to "making tomorrow's film . . . more personal than a novel."

Ray's Reputation: Still in Flux

Ray was rediscovered in the United States by the youth culture around 1971—largely, perhaps, as movies replaced rock music as the most "in" thing for young people to concentrate on.

Ray has since then received nothing but praise from writers thirty years younger than himself; and, instead of retreating to Tahiti, he seems to have thrived on this adulation. In 1973 he became increasingly visible, appeared for three days at the Orson Welles Cinema in Cambridge, Massachusetts, at a retrospective of his films and allowed a documentary about him to be filmed, which included interviews with John Houseman, Natalie Wood, and François Truffaut. In January, 1975 this documentary, *I'm a Stranger Here Myself*, was screened in New York City, bringing together Elia Kazan, John Houseman, and Ray, in a last hurrah for the man from La-Crosse, Wisconsin, who did more for the American political conscience by the use of a nervous camera rhythm, by his narrative style of always having a main character confront what antagonized him, and by an eloquent verbal statement somewhere in each of his films that acted as a synopsis of what he was willing to say. Unlike the *auteurs* who "wrote" films, Nick Ray filmed screenplays and performed his "magic" in rehearsals and with the camera on location. But what raised Ray to the pantheon of directors of films of lasting value was in his ability to give a sense of omnipotence to his cast. In the way he did this he was unique. His casts loved it and rarely can one notice a lame performance in a Ray film. Film critic and semiologist Peter Wollen rightfully ranks Ray a notch above Elia Kazan and everyone ranks him well above average. For a man who never had the inclination to join a bandwagon, who had to work with very well-known as well as very unknown actors, and who had neuroses and personal visions constantly dancing in front of him, this is a fine track record.

On that account, Ray's neurotic temperament perhaps kept him out of the mainstream more than his ideas. The paradox is that some critics think Ray is not so radical a filmmaker while Ray himself probably thinks he is more radical than he is. As John Houseman astutely observed in *I'm A Stranger Here Myself*, Ray was thwarted often enough that he built up a "perverse" guard, to try to "avoid getting screwed," and thus increasingly fled the mainstream areas of the pragmatic Hollywood groups who often decided the making of the next big film.

Interestingly, a man like Ray not only loved, but bore (quite rightfully) grudges (à la Jules Pffeifer's "Hostileman") against those who were neither genteel nor politically honest. Those performers who darkened his memory with the darker side of the American dream—with negative, willful political activity; those involved in helping to blacklist, or even those who gave money to blacklisting organizations, he would never work with. The only filmmaker of high reputation in the world today similar to him is Marcel Ophuls, son of the great Max and maker of *The Sorrow and the Pity*. Ophuls, like Ray, makes films that are genuinely controversial in content.

As a result, we can see Ray best by the company he kept. Among those he liked: Humphrey Bogart, James Dean, and Tuesday Weld. Among those he disliked were Ginger Rogers and her mother. Among those he admired and belonged to—living or dead—were John Garfield and Clifford Odets. The obituary words Odets wrote about Garfield would also serve as Nick Ray's epitaph: "he was proud to be an American, even rudely so."

Ray, an elitist despite himself, never exposed himself to ridicule as such, because he was always respected as "The Great Thespian" and never seen as "The Great Pretender." What people saw in his films (at least two million people saw "Rebel" even before it reached TV) was the sincerity of effort and the love of his craft that made him a film artisan. Jean-Luc Godard noted this, even five thousand miles away. Ray, Godard felt, could never have been anything other than a filmmaker.

Thus Nick Ray's servitude to film is unveiled. He combined within himself the elegance of Hollywood in the 1940s mixed with a neurotic, "I-can't-be-anything-else" of the James Dean–John Lennon–Brian Jones types of the 1950s and 1960s to produce a powerful and viable drive responsible for some of the finest films of individualism of the 1950s. I hope he makes it to Valhalla . . . America was none too kind to him, but he respected America.

Epilogue

In this book, I have avoided psychoanalyzing Ray. It would have been tempting to do so; there is a strong relationship between quests delineated in his films and his private wish to stage a revolt against a society that did not permit him to express himself in his chosen medium, but doing this would reduce his cinema only to its neurotic content and overlook Ray's cinematic achievements. It has been said that Ray is neither the best nor the worst of directors. I take issue with this bland pronouncement. Ray's work is uneven; admittedly, his best sequences surpass his weakest by far. However this makes him the best *and* the worst of directors. My approach has been to compare his best sequences cinematically with the bulk of 1950s American feature films and to arrive at an evaluation of his overall place in cinema in that way.

It has also been said that Ray limited himself in that he created only films showing a man's world. This is true to some extent but Ray was not a misogynist; his specialization in largely male worlds on film came about because he understood and instinctively specialized in male and in father-son neuroses. Yet he also worked intensely and productively with actresses; his name must be linked with the successes of Natalie Wood, Tuesday Weld, and Gloria Grahame. As Natalie Wood said, "He was able as Kazan is able to do, to kind of judge people almost like a psychologist/psychiatrist, and say those things to that person [actor or actress] which were meaningful to them. Nick gave me a career, in a sense, with *Rebel*, because up to that time, although I'd worked a lot, I was just a child actress really. And I think by giving me that chance in *Rebel*, he also gave me a kind of insight and a point of view of my work. Because he regarded me as an actress with a meaningful contribution to make, I felt better of myself and better of my work, and I didn't do whatever the studios said. So, in a way, I guess he taught me to be more of a rebel—which benefited me personally greatly, for which I'll always be grateful to Nick. And I think he did that for a lot of people because of his humanity and sensitivity towards people." "The charge of misogyny or, at the very least, a strictly male point of view is also belied by Ray's use of the Romeo and Juliet theme in *Rebel Without a Cause*. He captures the essence of the drama perfectly: two innocents teach each other to love. The point is not dominance but sympathy. (Ray, it is also worth pointing out, had undoubtedly seen Castellani's Technicolor film version of *Romeo and Juliet* the year before he directed *Rebel*.)

I have also avoided typing or psychoanalyzing Ray's characters, except for a brief comparison of Vienna with other women of 1950s Westerns, because, unlike the case with Howard Hawks' characters, we always know why Ray's exist. Ray's characters are Zeitgeist characters—if one understands the year of the film—one understands them. That is why I've placed special emphasis on the context of the 1950s.

It is Ray's transformation of characters into fodder for cinematography that has interested me and I have concentrated on a few key sequences to show his rigor, imagination, and sense of beauty in dealing with images in *Rebel* and *Party Girl*. Ray, under constant pressure after *Rebel* (1955) never had equally good circumstances under which to make an equivalent film, so this book concentrates most of its detail on what he did well; his later films, those after *Party Girl* such as *55 Days at Peking*, just do not deserve close analysis.

Of his twenty feature films only two, *They Live by Night* and *Rebel*, were made under favorable circumstances and these are two of his best. Did Ray's talent have an upper limit? If it did, we never saw it. I've seen Kazan's limit: *On the Waterfront*; Kubrick's limit: *2001*; Truffaut's limit: *The 400 Blows*; Godard's limit: *Two or Three Things I Know About Her*; Hitchcock's limit: *Vertigo*; Coppola's limit: *The Conversation*; Wyler's limit: *The Best Years of Our Lives*; Welles's limit: *Citizen Kane*. Ray never made his peak film. The only other directors I can think of that haven't either are Resnais, Antonioni, and, unless he finally makes *The Big Red One*, Samuel Fuller.

I have unqualified admiration for Ray's decision in 1963 to stop making films; I interpret this not as a failure of nerve but as his own decision to avoid the strain involved. He is the only American Rimbaud—he quit while he was ahead. (This is a marvelous thing today when we are looking forward to concerts by rock groups of 80 year-old super stars.) I have thus not taken (perhaps wrongly) his post-1963 efforts as seriously as they may deserve.

Finally, I place Ray among the most significant film directors because of his best work: most of *Rebel*; sequences from *Bigger Than Life, Bitter Victory*, and *Party Girl*; and his development of screen actors and actresses.

I personally rank Ray above Kubrick, Bogdanovich, Frankenheimer and Coppola of our younger American directors. None of them are film poets and never will be; none of them seem to have a sense of the authority of their imaginations as Ray did. Cinematic consciousness appears to have passed out of Hollywood at the time Ray left.

I give Ray credit for being the magnet which attracted to *Rebel* one of the strongest casts in what was then the rising generation of young actors. The saddest part of this Epilogue is the Fate of some of that cast: James Dean, Sal Mineo, and Nick Adams, three of the finest actors of their generation, are dead, all prematurely and violently removed. However, Natalie Wood is still acting and, in her own words, "owes a lot to Nick Ray; Tuesday Weld whom Nick helped coach as a fledgling actress returned the favor with her performance in *Pretty Poison* (1962) an acting job not one of the younger Hollywood women can match. It is to Ray's credit that he'd rather now direct Marilyn Chambers (in *City Blues* Ray's current project) than any of Hollywood's TV trained blandnesses.

Due to the general reader's unfamiliarity with Ray, I decided to leave out several themes I would have liked to have developed, particularly a comparison between the way Ray and Kazan handled actors, shot and cut in CinemaScope, and how they regarded each other's films. I also left out a detailed description of the events of Ray's screening of *You Can't Go Home Again*, January 17, 1975, as it would have been anticlimactic and would seem out of place a few years from the time of this writing.

The Ray legacy is thus alive, both in the form of an alumni club as well as in the films. One can learn as much about the craft of film acting from a Ray film as from a drama school course because, more than most directors, Ray realized that cinema could transmit a dramatic/cinematic message only if it remained a living language. During Ray's active career, he *totally* identified with a generation younger than himself. Thus the eclectic legacy of Ray: the craft of Hollywood filmmaking machinery put to use to exemplify the ideas of the young. (It is worth noting that he started to make films at 36, a time when many directors today have already made ten films, and he "retired" at 52. *Rebel Without A Cause* can be seen as *Romeo and Juliet* not for adults but for teenagers. Though not all of his films are structured equally well, their communication systems are never there as the result of dumb accident. Ray's films are, to me, a semiologist's dream, icons, indexes, symbols are all there with the *full* knowledge of the director.

Notes and References

Chapter One

1. As quoted by Nicholas Ray, speaking at a retrospective showing of his films at the Orson Welles Cinema, Cambridge, Massachusetts, October 23, 1973.
2. All quotations from Michel Ciment, *Kazan on Kazan* (New York, 1974), pp. 49–50.

Chapter Two

1. Michel Ciment, *Kazan on Kazan* (New York, 1974), pp. 49–50.
2. Ray's comment in the documentary film, *I'm a Stranger Here Myself* (1974).
3. Charles Bitsch, "Entretien avec Nick Ray," *Cahiers du Cinema*, No. 89 (November, 1958), p. 4.
4. Ibid.
5. *From Reverence to Rape* (New York, 1974), p. 248.
6. Roger Tailleur, "La Fureur de vivre: les causes et les effets," *Positif*, No. 17 (June–July, 1956), p. 40 (translation by J. F. Kreidl).
7. John Belton, *Robert Mitchum* (New York, 1976), pp. 66–68.
8. Ray's speech at the Orson Welles Cinema, October 23, 1973.

Chapter Three

1. Quoted in Lawrence J. Quirk, *The Films of Joan Crawford* (New York, 1968), in the section on *Johnny Guitar*.
2. Phillip French, *Westerns* (New York, 1974), p. 35.
3. Bernard Tavernier, "Interview with Phillip Yordan," *Cahiers du Cinema*, No. 128 (February, 1962), p. 18.
4. Ray's speech at the Orson Welles Cinema, October 23, 1973.
5. Tavernier, p. 18.
6. The Russian artist Wassily Kandinsky defined "lyric" to mean expressing one theme only, structurally simplistic, and "symphonic" to mean mul-

tilayered, dense, structurally complex. The lyric and symphonic styles have, according to Kandinsky, totally different functions. "Symphonic" works are *deeper*, and it is not fair to compare them to lyric works. In music, one cannot compare George Gershwin's lyric "An American in Paris" with Beethoven's "Pastorale" Symphony. Applying this distinction to film, one finds that Ray's *Johnny Guitar* is lyric, whereas *Rebel Without a Cause* is symphonic. All of François Truffaut's films are lyric; whereas all of Jean-Luc Godard's films, even *Breathless*, are symphonic.

Chapter Four

1. Leonard Rosenman in a telephone interview with the author, October, 1975.

2. The opinion expressed by Dr. Norbert J. Kreidl, then director of chemical research for Bausch and Lomb Optical Company, which developed the first CinemaScope lens.

3. Rosenman telephone interview, October, 1975.

4. *Cahiers du Cinema*, No. 45 (March, 1955), p. 40 (translated by J. F. Kreidl).

5. Ray seems to be the prophet of disorder leading to re-order; Brooks seems to insist order should win. These cinema viewpoints anticipated the polarization of the Nixon era.

6. David Manning White and Richard Averson, *The Celluloid Weapon* (Boston, 1972), p. 162–63.

7. Ibid.

8. Eugene Archer, "Rebel Without a Cause" *Film Comment*, 2 (No. 1, 1956), pp. 18–21.

9. Ibid.

10. Ibid.

Chapter Five

1. Nick Ray, "Portrait de l'Acteur en Jeune Homme." *Cahiers du Cinema*, No. 66, pp. 4–12.

2. All quotations above are from Jean Douchet and Jacques Joly, "Entretien avec Nick Ray," *Cahiers du Cinema*, No. 127 (January, 1962), pp. 1–17. (All translations by J. F. Kreidl).

3. Ibid.

4. Ibid.

5. "Story into Script," *Sight and Sound*, 26 (Autumn, 1956), p. 72.

6. John Houseman speaking in the documentary film, *I'm a Stranger Here Myself.*

7. Remarks at the Orson Welles Cinema, October 23, 1973.

8. Unpublished interview with Natalie Wood by James Gutman.

9. "La Fureur de vivre," *Arts et Spectacles*, No. 619 (May 15–21, 1967), p. 6. (Translated from the French of Charles Bitsch by J. F. Kreidl).

10. Andrew Kopkind in *The Real Paper* (Cambridge, Massachusetts), January 10, 1975, p. 230.

11. Telephone interview with J. F. Kreidl, October, 1975.

12. Remarks at the Orson Welles Cinema, October 23, 1973. Ray, however, has repeated this remark many times.

13. Nick Ray, *op. cit* pp. 4–12.

Chapter Six

1. Quoted by David Dalton in *James Dean: The Mutant King* (New York, 1973), p. 263.

2. Wolf Rilla, *The Writer and The Screen; On Writing For Film And Television* (New York, 1974), introduction.

3. All quotations concerning Ray's relationship with Dr. Lindner from Ray's article "Story into Script," *Sight and Sound*, 26 (Autumn, 1956), pp. 70–74.

4. Ibid.

5. Ibid.

6. Ibid.

Chapter Seven

1. Natalie Wood's real-life experience furnished the raw material for this scene.

2. Telephone interview with Rosenman, October, 1975.

3. Quoted in English in Peter Graham, *The New Wave* (New York, 1968); p. 102 from *Cahiers du Cinema*, No. 138 (1962).

4. Eric Rohmer, "Ajax ou le Cid," *Cahiers du Cinema*, No. 59 (May, 1956), p. 36.

5. Ibid. pp. 34–35.

6. Peter Biskind, "Rebel Without a Cause: Nicholas Ray in the Fifties," *Film Quarterly* Fall, 1974, p. 36.

7. David Dalton, *James Dean: The Mutant King* (New York, 1974), p. 263.

8. Eric Rohmer, "Ajax ou le Cid," p. 36.

Chapter Eight

1. "Ajax ou le Cid," *Cahiers du Cinema*, No. 59 (May, 1956), p. 35.

2. All dialogue is taken from the shooting script dated May 2, 1955. As

the sequence quoted here was probably shot no later than the third week in May, it is probably the final version of the script for the sequence.

3. Douchet and Joly, "Entretien avec Nick Ray," *Cahiers du Cinema*, No. 127 (January, 1962), pp. 1–17 (translations by J. F. Kreidl).

4. Michel Ciment, *Kazan on Kazan* (New York, 1974), pp. 122–23.

5. (New York, 1974), p. 48.

6. (New York, 1969), p. 183.

7. Dalton, *James Dean*, p. 248.

8. Robert Setlik, "Truffaut: On Vacation," Quincy *Patriot-Ledger*, October 13, 1973.

9. Quoted in Bernard Rosenberg and Harry Silverstein, *The Real Tinsel* (New York, 1970), p. 345.

10. "Story into Script," *Sight and Sound*, 26 (Autumn, 1956), Ray repeated these remarks at the Orson Welles Cinema, October 23, 1973.

11. Response to question at Orson Welles Cinema, October 23, 1973.

Chapter Nine

1. Ray speaking in the film *I'm a Stranger Here Myself*.

2. *Cahiers du Cinema*, No. 66 (End of 1956 Special Issue), p. 12.

3. Interview with Nick Ray by Mike Goodwin and Naomi Wise, "Nick Ray: Rebel!" *Take One*, Vol. 5, No. 6 (January, 1977), pp. 13–14.

4. Unpublished interview with James Gutman.

5. T. S. Eliot, as quoted in Marsha Kinder and Beverle Houston, *Close-Up*, (New York: 1972), p. 9.

6. Quotations are translated from a reprinting of Lambert's article, "Tournons la Page," *Cahiers du Cinema*, No. 89 (November, 1958), pp. 19–23

7. All quotations from "Rebels Without Causes," *Sight and Sound*, 25 (Spring, 1956), pp. 178–83.

8. Ibid.

9. Ray Connelly, mini-article on his film, *That'll Be the Day*, *Films Illustrated*, November, 1975, p. 28.

10. "Ajax ou le Cid," *Cahiers du Cinema*, No. 59 (May, 1956), pp. 32–36.

11. Communicated to the author by David Essex as appearing in several sources in the Ray Connelly archives.

Chapter Ten

1. [Review of *Bigger than Life*], *Cahiers du Cinema*, No. 69 (March, 1957), p. 41.

2. Ray shares a further, interesting link with Mann. Mann's *Man of the*

West and Ray's *Rebel*, both used ace Hollywood epic cinematographer, Erny Haller (who had worked on *Gone With The Wind*). Thus, though the two films are not of the same genre, in a few significant places, they look more alike than do *Man of the West* and *The True Story of Jesse James*. As *Man of the West* and *Rebel* are considered exceptional films, some of their success can be attributed to Haller.

3. *British Film Institute Bulletin* No. 290 (March, 1958), p. 30 (Review signed only J. G.)

4. Tom Milne, *Godard on Godard* (Garden City, N.Y., 1967) p. 65.

5. Translated by J. F. Kreidl from *Cahiers du Cinema*, No. 89 (November, 1958), pp. 21–22.

6. All quotations from "La Reponse de Nick Ray," *Cahiers du Cinema*, No. 107 (May, 1960), pp. 13–23.

7. Remarks at Orson Welles Cinema, October 23, 1973.

8. Remarks at First Avenue Screening Room, New York City, January, 1975.

9. Thanks for information to Dr. Ante Peterlic, who interviewed Ray in Zagreb.

Chapter Eleven

1. Tom Milne, *Godard on Godard*, p. 64. Godard's remark was evoked by *Bitter Victory*.

2. Remarks at the Orson Welles Cinema, October 23, 1973.

3. Charles Bitsch, "Entretien avec Nick Ray," *Cahiers du Cinema*, No. 89 (November, 1958). pp. 1–17.

4. Charles Barr, "CinemaScope Before and After," in Gerald Mast and Marshall Cohen, eds., *Film Theory and Criticism* (London, 1974), pp. 128–29.

5. Ibid.

6. Ibid.

7. Quoted in C. G. Crisp, *François Truffaut* (New York, 1972), p. 15.

8. Alexandre Astruc, "The Birth Of A New Avantgarde: La Caméra-Stylo," as quoted in Graham Petrie, *The New Wave* (London, 1968), p. 19.

9. François Truffaut in *I'm A Stranger Here Myself*.

10. Remarks at Orson Welles Cinema, October 23, 1973.

11. Natalie Wood in an unpublished interview with James Gutman.

Selected Bibliography

The best source is Nicholas Ray himself. He is highly articulate about his work, both in regard to strategy and results. He also has a colorful and anecdotal style, which is most revealing. It is a pity he has not written an autobiography. Ray comments on his own work on the soundtrack of David Helpern, Jr.'s documentary film about Ray's career, *I'm a Stranger Here Myself* (1974). A 16mm. print is available from Films, Inc., Wilmette, Illinois. As it stands, the two best articles are autobiographical, both seemingly intended as parts of a book he was preparing, but has never finished, called "Rebel: Life Story of a Film":

"Portrait de l'Acteur en Jeune Homme." *Cahiers du Cinema*, No. 66 (End of 1956 Special Issue), pp. 4–12 [in French].
"Story into Script." *Sight and Sound*, 26 (Autumn, 1956), pp. 70–74.

There is another article written by Ray in English, but never printed in this language:

"La Fureur de vivre" ["Rebel Without a Cause"]. *Arts et Spectacles*, No. 619 (May 15–21, 1967), pp. 6–8. Translated into French by Charles Bitsch.

Equally valuable are two interviews with Ray, also published only in French:

Bitsch, Charles. "Entretien avec Nick Ray." *Cahiers du Cinema*, No. 89 (November, 1958), pp. 1–17.
Douchet, Jean, and Jacques Joly. "Entretien avec Nick Ray." *Cahiers du Cinema*, No. 127 (January, 1962), pp. 1–17.

As this book goes to press, a third interview, in English, has been published: Goodwin, Mike, and Naomi Wise. "Nick Ray: Rebel!" *Take One*, Vol. 5, No. 6 (January 1977), pp. 7–16.

Secondary Sources

Articles on Ray in English are limited, but some have appeared since 1970. Some of these are of questionable value; others are interesting if one already knows enough about Ray's cinema to regard thematic and "message" interpretations with a grain of salt.

BARR, CHARLES. "CinemaScope Before and After." In Gerald Mast and Mark Cohen, *Film Theory and Criticism*, pp. 120–46. London: Oxford University Press, 1974. Reprinting of an article from *Film Quarterly* (1963) that gives superb description of how Ray used CinemaScope in at least two of his films—*Rebel Without a Cause* and *The True Story of Jesse James*.

BELTON, JOHN. *Robert Mitchum*. New York: Pyramid, 1975. Briefly discusses the "triangle" in *The Lusty Men*.

BISKIND, PETER. "Rebel Without a Cause: Nicholas Ray in the Fifties," *Film Quarterly*, Fall 1974 pp. 32–38.

HOYVEDA, FEREYDOUN. "La Reponse de Nick Ray." *Cahiers du Cinema*, No. 107 (May, 1960), pp. 13–23. An article on *Party Girl*, which Hoyveda treats as Ray's "reply" to critics of his cinema.

LEDERER, JOSEPH. "Film as Experience: Nicholas Ray—the Director Turns Teacher." *American Film*, 1,ii (November, 1975), pp. 60–64. A soap-opera-like account of Ray's tribulations while trying to shoot the never-completed "You Can't Go Home Again" at Harpur College (State University of New York at Binghamton) with inadequate campus resources.

McCARTHY, TOD, and CHARLES FLYNN. *King of the B's*. New York: Dutton, 1975. Contains a brief chapter on *They Live by Night*.

PERKINS, VICTOR. "The Cinema of Nicholas Ray." In *Movie Reader*, edited by Ian Cameron. New York: Praeger, 1972.
Reprints from *Movie 1* (1962) an indispensable introduction to Perkins' idea of the importance of "upstairs" and "downstairs," as concepts, as *more* than just geographic loci in the cinema of Nicholas Ray.

———. *Film as Film: Understanding and Judging Movies*. Harmondsworth (England): Penguin Books, 1972. Contains some valuable interpretive comments on *Rebel Without a Cause*.

TAILLEUR, ROGER. "*La Fureur de vivre*: les causes et les effets." *Positif*, No. 17 (June–July, 1956), pp. 38–40. This obscure, but well-argued review is the first assessment of Ray's cinema that was not entirely favorable.

WOOD, ROBIN. "On *Bigger Than Life*." *Film Comment*. September–October, 1972, pp. 56–61. Describes the film as one of cinema's most intelligent and searching statements about man in society. Wood says Ray says the only real failure is to give up, in the sense of Henry Miller's first line from *Tropic of Capricorn*, "Once you've given up the ghost everything follows even in the midst of chaos." In his sociological article Wood doesn't show that not giving up in America made a sad neurotic out of Ray.

Filmography

THEY LIVE BY NIGHT. RKO-Radio (1947–49) Filmed in 1947 and re-
leased in Great Britain in 1948 as *The Twisted Road,* but not released
in U. S. A. until 1949 after *A Woman's Secret* and *Knock On Any Door*
Producer: John Houseman, under Dore Schary
Screenplay: Charles Schnee, based on an adaptation by Ray of Edward
Anderson's novel *Thieves Like Us* (1937).
Cinematographer: George D. Diskant
Set: Darrell Silvera, Michael Yates
Music: Leigh Harline
Editor: Sherman Todd
Cast: Farley Granger (Bowie), Cathy O'Donnell (Keechie), Howard daSilva
(Chicamaw), Jay C. Flippen (T-Dub)
Running Time: 95 minutes
New York premiere: November 4, 1949
16mm rental: Films, Inc.

A WOMAN'S SECRET. RKO-Radio (1948)
Producer: Herman J. Mankiewicz
Screenplay: Herman J. Mankiewicz, based on Vicki Baum's novel *Mortgage
on Life* (1946).
Cinematographer: George E. Diskant
Set decoration: Darrell Silvera, Harley Miller
Music: Frederik Hollander
Editor: Sherman Todd
Cast: Maureen O'Hara, Melvyn Douglas, Gloria Grahame
Running time: 85 minutes
Released in 1948, but not shown in New York City
16mm rental: Films, Inc.

KNOCK ON ANY DOOR. Columbia (1949). Released in France as *Les
Ruelles du malheur (The Little Byways of Misfortune)*
Producer: Robert Lord
Assistant Directors: Daniel Taradash and John Monks, Jr.

Screenplay: Daniel Taradash, adapted from Willard Motley's novel of the
   same title
Cinematographer: Burnett Guffey
Set decoration: William Kreinem
Music: Georges Antheil
Editor: Viola Lawrence
Cast: John Derek (Nick Romano), Humphrey Bogart (Andrew Morton),
   Allene Roberts (Emma), George Macready (District Attorney)
Running time: 100 minutes
New York premiere: February 23, 1949
16mm lease: Columbia Cinematograph, 562 W. 113th. St., New York, N.Y.
   16 mm rental: MacMillan Films and others.

IN A LONELY PLACE. Santaro Productions- Columbia (1950) Released in
   France as *Le Violent (The Violent Ones)*.
Producer: Robert Lord
Screenplay: Andrew Solt, based on Edmund H. North's adaptation of
   Dorothy S. Hughes' novel (1947).
Cinematographer: Burnett Guffey
Set decoration: William Kreinem
Music: Georges Antheil
Editor: Boris Stoloff
Cast: Humphrey Bogart (Dixon Steele), Gloria Grahame (Laurel Gray),
   Frank Lovejoy (Brub Nicola), Carl Benton Reid (Capt. Lochner)
Running time: 94 minutes
New York premiere: May 17, 1950
16 mm rental: MacMillan Films and others.

BORN TO BE BAD. RKO-Radio (1950)
Producer: Robert Sparks
Screenplay: Edith Sommer, based on Charles Schnee's adaptation of Ann
   Parish's novel *All Kneeling*, with additional dialogue by Robert Sorlen-
   berg and George Oppenheimer.
Cinematographer: Nicholas Musuraca
Set decoration: Harvey Miller, Darrell Silvera
Music: Frederik Hollander
Editor: Frederic Knudtson
Cast: Joan Fontaine (Christabel Caine), Robert Ryan (Nick Bradley),
   Zachary Scott (Curtis Carey), Mel Ferrer (Gobby), Joan Leslie (Donna
   Fortes)
Running time: 94 minutes
New York premiere: September 28, 1950
16mm rental: Films, Inc.

ON DANGEROUS GROUND. RKO-Radio (1951) Released in France as *La Maison dans l'ombre (The House in the Shadow)*.
Producer: John Houseman
Screenplay: A. I. Bezzerides, based on his adaptation (with Nicholas Ray) of Gerald Butler's novel *Mad with Much Heart* (1945).
Cinematographer: George E. Diskant
Set decoration: Harvey Miller, Darrell Silvera
Music: Bernard Herrmann
Editor: Roland Gross
Cast: Ida Lupino (Mary Madden), Robert Ryan (Jim Wilson), Ward Bond (Walter Brent), Ed Begley (Captain Brawley)
Running time: 81 minutes
New York premiere: February 12, 1952
16mm rental: Films, Inc.

THE FLYING LEATHERNECKS. Howard Hughes for RKO-Radio (1951)
Producer: Edmund Grainger
Screenplay: James Edward Grant, from a story by Kenneth Gamet.
Cinematographer: William E. Snyder (in Technicolor)
Set decoration: John Strutevant, Darrell Silvera
Music: Roy Webb
Editor: Sherman Todd
Cast: John Wayne (Don), Robert Ryan (Griff), Don Taylor (Cowboy), Jane Carter (Joan Kirby), Jay C. Flippen (Clancy), William Harrigan (Dr. Curran)
Running time: 102 minutes
New York premiere: September 19, 1951
16mm rental: MacMillan

THE LUSTY MEN. RKO-Radio (1952) Released in France as *Les Indomptables (The Indestructible Ones.)*
Producers: Jerry Wald and Norman Krasna
Screenplay: Horace McCoy and David Dortort from the novel by Claude Standish
Cinematographer: Lee Garmes
Set decoration: Darrell Silvera, John Mills
Music: Roy Webb
Editor: Ralph Dawson
Cast: Susan Hayward (Louise), Robert Mitchum (Jeb), Arthur Kennedy (Wes)
Running time: 122 minutes
New York premiere: October 24, 1952
16mm rental: Films, Inc.

JOHNNY GUITAR Republic (1954)
Producer: Herbert M. Yates
Screenplay: Phillip Yordan, based on Roy Chanslor's novel
Cinematographer: Harry Stradling (Widescreen and Trucolor)
Set decoration: Edward G. Boyle, John McCarthy, Jr., with uncredited
    additions by Nicholas Ray
Music: Victor Young; "Johnny Guitar," sung by Peggy Lee
Editor: Richard L. Van Enger
Cast: John Crawford (Vienna), Sterling Hayden (Johnny), Ernest Borgnine
    (Bart), Mercedes McCambridge (Emma), Ben Cooper (Turkey), Ward
    Bond (John McIvers, Head of Posse), Scott Brady (Dancin' Kid), John
    Carradine (Old Tom)
Running time: 110 minutes
New York/World premiere: May 27, 1954
16mm rental: Ivy Films/16, 165 West 46th. St., New York, NY 10036

RUN FOR COVER. Paramount (1955) Released in France as *A l'Ombre
    des potences*
Producers: William H. Pine, William C. Thomas
Screenplay: Winston Miller, based on a story by Harriet Frank and Irving
    Ravetch
Cinematographer: Daniel Fapp (VistaVision, Technicolor)
Set decoration: Sam Comer, Frank McKelvy
Music: Howard Jackson
Editor: Howard Smith
Cast: James Cagney (Mat Dow), Viveca Lindfors (Helga Sweson), John
    Derek (Davey Bishop), Jean Hersholt (Mr. Swenson), Grant Withers
    (Gentz), Ernest Borgnine (Moza)
Running time: 92 minutes
New York premiere: April 29, 1955
16mm rental: United Films and others

REBEL WITHOUT A CAUSE. Warner Brothers (1955)
(French title, *La Fureur de vivre*; German title, *Denn Sie Wissen Nicht
    Was Sie Tun*)
Producer: David Weisbart
Screenplay: Stewart Stern, based on an adaptation by Irving Shulman of a
    story idea by Nicholas Ray. Title from a book by Dr. Robert M. Lind-
    ner (1944)
Cinematographer: Ernest Haller (CinemaScope and Warnercolor)
Set decoration: William Wallace
Music: Leonard Rosenman
Editor: William Ziegler

Cast: James Dean (Jim Stark), Natalie Wood (Judy), Sal Mineo (Plato), Jim Backus (Ray Stark), Ann Doran (Mrs. Stark), Corey Allen (Buzz Gunderson), Dennis Hopper (Goon), Frank Mazzola (Crunch), William Hopper (Judy's Father)
Running time: 111 minutes (A British X-rated version, running 105 minutes, was circulated from 1955 to 1968)
World/New York premiere: October 27, 1955
16mm lease: Warner Brothers, Non-Theatrical Division, 4000 Warner Boulevard, Burbank, Cal. 91503; 16mm rental prints available from almost all agencies.

HOT BLOOD. Columbia (1955) Released in France as *L'ardente Gitane (The Passionate Gypsy)*
Producers: Howard Welsch and Harry Tatelman
Screenplay: Jesse L. Lasky, Jr., based on a story by Jean Evans
Cinematographer: Ray June (CinemaScope and Technicolor)
Set decoration: Frank Tuttle
Music: Les Baxter
Editor: Otto Ludwig
Cast: Jane Russell (Annie Caldash), Cornel Wilde (Stephen Torino), Luther Adler (Mario Torino), Joseph Calleia (Papa Theodore), Nina Koshetz (Nita), Helen Wescott (Velma)
Running time: 87 minutes
New York premiere: March 23, 1956
Not currently available for rental.

BIGGER THAN LIFE. 20th Century-Fox (1956) Released in France as *Derrière le miroir*
Producer: James Mason
Screenplay: Richard Maibaum and Cyril Hume, based on article by Berton Roueche in the *New Yorker*, September 19, 1955
Cinematography: Joseph McDonald (CinemaScope, DeLuxe color)
Art Direction: Lyle Wheeler, Jack Martin Smith
Set decoration: Walter M. Scott, Steward A. Reiss
Music: David Raskin
Editor: Louis Loeffler
Cast: James Mason (Ed Avery), Barbara Rush (Mrs. Lou Avery), Walter Mattheu (Wally Gibbs), Christopher Olson (Richie Avery), Robert Simon (Dr. Norton)
Running time: 95 minutes
New York premiere: August 2, 1956
16mm rental: Films, Inc.

THE TRUE STORY OF JESSE JAMES. 20th Century-Fox (1957) Released in France as *Le Brigand bien-aimé (The Well-Loved Bandit)*.
Producer: Herbert Bayard Swope, Jr.
Screenplay: Walter Neuman, based on a script by Nunnally Johnson for an earlier film *The Well-Loved Bandit*, directed by Henry King (1938)
Cinematographer: Joseph McDonald (CinemaScope, DeLuxe color)
Set decoration: Walter M. Scott, Stuart A. Reiss
Music: Leigh Harline
Editor: Robert Simpson
Cast: Robert Wagner (Jesse James), Jeffrey Hunter (Frank James), Hope Lange (Zee), Agnes Moorehead (Mrs. Samuel), Alan Hale (Cole Younger), Alan Baxter (Remington), John Carradine (Rev. Bailey)
Running time: 93 minutes
New York premiere: March 22, 1957
16mm rental: Films, Inc.

BITTER VICTORY. Transcontinental Films S. A.-Columbia (1957)
Producer: Paul Graetz
Screenplay: Rene Hardy, Nicholas Ray, and Gavin Lambert, based on Rene Hardy's novel (1956).
Cinematography: Michel Keller
Set decoration: Jean d'Eaubonne
Music: Maurice LeRoux
Editor: Leonide Azar
Cast: Curt Jurgens (Major Brand), Richard Burton (Captain Leith), Ruth Roman (Jane Brand)
Running time: 97 minutes (British cut version, omitting last sequence, 90 minutes)
Not shown in New York City.
Not available for rental.

WIND ACROSS THE EVERGLADES. Warner Brothers (1958)
Producer: Stuart Schulberg
Screenplay: Budd Schulberg
Cinematographer: Joseph Brun (WarnerColor)
Art Direction: Richard Sylbert
Set decoration: Ernest Zatorsky
Editors: Joseph Zigman, George Klotz
Cast: Christopher Plummer (Walt Murdock), Burl Ives (Cottonmouth), Gypsy Rose Lee (Mrs. Bradford), Tony Galento (Beef), Emmett Kelly (Bigamy Bob), Pat Henning (Sawdust), Peter Falk (Writer), MacKinlay Kantor (Judge Harris)
Running time: 93 minutes

New York premiere: September 11, 1958
16mm rental: Warner Brothers

PARTY GIRL. Enterprise Productions-Metro Goldwyn Mayer (1958) Released in France as *Le Traquenard* in 1959.
Producer: Joe Pasternak
Screenplay: George Wells, based on the unpublished novel by Leo Katcher
Cinematographer: Robert Bronner (CinemaScope and Metrocolor)
Music: Nicholas Brodszky; lyrics to song "Party Girl" by Sammy Cahn
Editor: John M. Sweeney, Jr.
Cast: Robert Taylor (Tommy Farrell), Cyd Charisse (Vickie Gaye), John Ireland (Louis Canetto), Lee J. Cobb (Rico Angelo), Corey Allen (Cookie LaMotte)
Running time: 99 minutes
New York premiere: October 28, 1958
16mm rental: Films, Inc.

THE SAVAGE INNOCENTS. Magic Film/Playart/Gray Fils/S. N. Pathe Cinema/Joseph Ianhi, a French-British-Italian co-production, released by Paramount (1959) (French title, *Les Dents du diable*; Italian title, *Ombre Bianche*)
Producer: Maleno Malenotti
Assistant director: Don Ashton
Screenplay: Nicholas Ray, based on an adaptation by Hans Ruesch and F. Solinas of Ruesch's novel *Top of the World*.
Cinematographer: Aldo Tonti, Peter Hennessy (SuperTechnirama 70, Technicolor)
Set decoration: Wyn Ryder
Music: Angelo Lavagnino
Editor: Ralph Kemplen
Cast: Anthony Quinn (Inuk), Yoko Tani (Asiak), Marie Yang (Powtee), Peter O'Toole, uncredited and dubbed (1st trooper)
Running time: 89 minutes
New York premiere: May 24, 1961, in neighborhood theaters
16mm rental: Films, Inc.

KING OF KINGS. Metro Goldwyn Mayer (1961)
Producer: Samuel Bronston
Associate Producers: Alan Brown, James Prades
Assistant director: Carlo Lastracati
Second unit directors: Noel Howard, Sumner Williams
Screenplay: Phillip Yordan
Cinematographers: Frank F. Planer, Milton Krasner, Manuel Berenguer

Special Effects:
Art direction: Georges Wakhevitch
Set decoration: Enrique Alarcon
Costumes: Georges Wakhevitch
Music: Miklos Rosza
Narration: Orson Welles
Editors: Harold Kress, Renee Lichtig
Cast: Jeffrey Hunter (Jesus Christ), Viveca Lindfors (Claudia), Hurd
    Hatfield (Pontius Pilate), Siobhan McKenna (Mary), Rip Torn (Judas),
    Robert Ryan (John the Baptist), Rita Gam (Herodias), Carmen Seville
    (Mary Magdalene)
Running time: 165 minutes
New York premiere: October 11, 1961
16mm rental: Films, Inc.

55 DAYS AT PEKING. Allied Artists (1962)
Producer: Samuel Bronston
Replacement director: Andrew Marston
Screenplay: Phillip Yordan, Bernard Gordon
Cinematographer: Jack Hilyard (SuperTechnorama 70, Technicolor)
Art direction: Veniero Colusanti, John Moore
Set decoration: David Hildyard
Music: Dimitri Tiomkin
Editor: Robert Lawrence
Cast: Charlton Heston (Major Matt Lewis), David Niven (Sir Arthur Robin-
    son), Ava Gardner (Baroness Natalie Ivanoff), Nicholas Ray (American
    Minister), Flora Robson (Dowager Empress Tsu Hzi), Paul Lukas (Dr.
    Steinfeldt)
Running time: 150 minutes
New York premiere: May 29, 1963
16mm rental: Films, Inc.

Appendix

Nick Ray's Unrealized European Projects (1962–1968)

1962   After *55 Days of Peking*, Sam Bronston, producer of *King of Kings*, asked Yordan to script a circus film and Ray to direct it. Eventually, the film, *Circus World* (1964), was directed by Henry Hathaway.

1963   "Next Stop Paradise." Script by Merek Hlasko. Ray had envisioned Stephen Boyd for the leading role. (Unrealized project)

1963   Ray involved with Simone de Beauvoir script. Ingrid Bergman was to have played one of the roles. (Unrealized project)

1964   Ray and James Jones *(From Here to Eternity)* prepared a script. Ray had envisioned Steve McQueen, Paul Newman, and Alain Delon to be in this Western. (Unrealized project)

1965   *The Doctors and the Devil.* Based on the Dylan Thomas story of the same title which was a fictionalization of a true nineteenth century event about a doctor who was a "misunderstood" grave robber. Ray had built a set and was about to start shooting the film in Zagreb, Yogoslavia when he was taken off the project and the film was finished by Italian director Baldi.

1965– "Only Lovers Left Alive." Ray was considered as the director of this
1966   film about only children surviving a holocaust. The Rolling Stones were also considered for parts in the film. It would have been a strange film. As it was, the story was never filmed by anyone. (Unrealized project)

1966   "Avant l'aube." A Western, with Anthony Quinn. (Unrealized project)

1966– Ray was considering a film on the life of Jean Arthur Rimbaud, but
1967   the project did not get off the ground. A film based on Rimbaud and Verlaine was made in France in the early 1970s, but there is no connection between this and the unrealized Ray project.

Index